WALKING IN TUSCANY

About the Author

Gillian Price was born in England and moved to Australia when young. She took a degree in anthropology and then worked in adult education before moving to Venice, which she had visited as a student and to which she had vowed to return permanently.

Gillian now lives there with her husband, Nicola, a native Venetian, and works as a writer and translator, including stints for the Venice Film Festival.

Venice is only two hours from the Dolomites. Starting there, Gillian has steadily explored the mountain ranges of Italy and brought them to life for visitors in a series of outstanding guides for Cicerone.

Other Cicerone guidebooks by Gillian Price

Walking in the Central Italian Alps
Walking in the Dolomites
Shorter Walks in the Dolomites
Walking in Italy's Gran Paradiso
Walking in Sicily
Trekking in the Dolomites
Walking in Corsica
Trekking in the Apennines
Through the Italian Alps

WALKING IN TUSCANY

by
Gillian Price

2 POLICE SQUARE, MILNTHORPE, CUMBRIA LA7 7PY
www.cicerone.co.uk

© Gillian Price,1998, 2002, 2006
Second edition 2002; ISBN 1-85284-361-6
Third edition 2006
ISBN-10: 1-85284-489-2
ISBN-13: 978-185284-361-8

Maps by Nicola Regine

A catalogue record for this book is available from the British Library.

ACKNOWLEDGEMENTS

To Nicola with all my love, not to mention gratitude for all the maps! A special dedication for Alastair and James – hope it's not too long before they tread these ancient pathways with us. Thanks to Bet and Dave who survived the book's recon-naissance stages bashing through scrub, braving hazardous brambles and wading across streams with us in the search for elusive tombs. Then there were Anna and Henk who provided an unforgettable lunch at Lago di Bolsena, and Colleen her inimitable chauffeur service and unflagging enthusiasm up and down countless 'vie cave'. Piero and Carlo of Venice's historic Marciana Library helped locate George Dennis' masterpiece, and Dorothy's helpful comments enhanced the text.

Advice to Readers

Readers are advised that while every effort is taken by the author to ensure the accuracy of this guidebook, changes can occur which may affect the contents. It is advisable to check locally on transport, accommodation, shops, etc, but even rights of way can be altered.

The publisher would welcome notes of any such changes.

Front cover: Enigmatic Pitigliano, whose houses seem to grow out of the tufa rock base (Walk 30)

CONTENTS

The route passes through the olive groves and wooded hills of the Tuscan countryside (Walk 1)

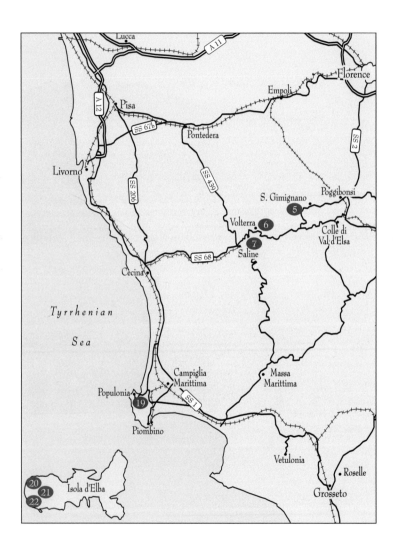

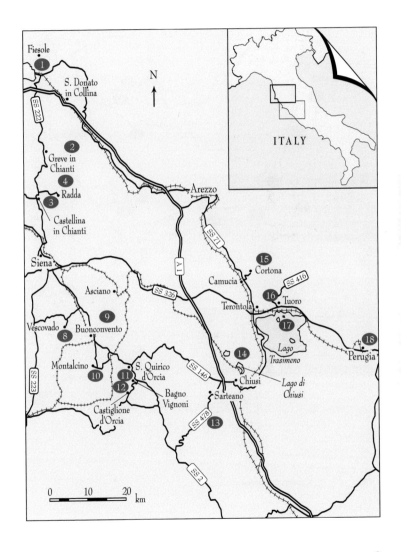

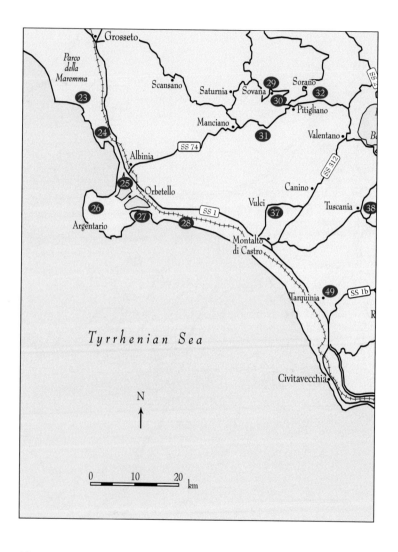

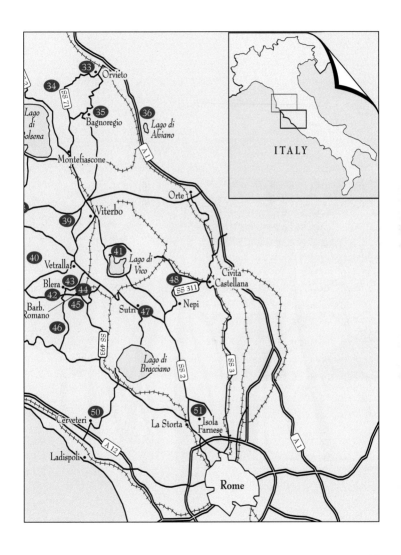

Barratti's stunning 'pineta' (Walk 19)

INTRODUCTION

This guide covers an intriguing part of central Italy that was once known as Etruria, home to the ancient Etruscan people from about 8th until 1st century BC. Roughly speaking it is bounded by the Arno and Tiber Rivers and the Tyrrhenian Sea, straddling present-day Tuscany (Toscana in Italian), Umbria and Latium (Lazio). This encompasses an extraordinary range of landscapes from modest mountains clad with dense conifer forest through to lightly wooded hills where wild boar still roam, rural areas with expanses of waving wheat fields dashed with the red of poppies, and some stunning stretches of coast in the west with pristine beaches backed by typical Mediterranean maquis vegetation. Scattered throughout are great Italian cities of Etruscan, Roman, medieval and Renaissance fame.

The aim of this walking guide is to encourage people to get out of their car and explore the area on foot. A series of walks is presented to take visitors through the maze of age-old tracks and discover the delights of the Tuscan and surrounding countryside, often taking in fascinating little-known Etruscan sites. There are mysterious tombs excavated out of volcanic tufa cliff sides, original sunken roadways, dominating acropolis sites and impressive sanctuaries, all set in inimitable picture postcard countryside. Such forays will hopefully stimulate curiosity in the enigmatic Etruscan civilisation itself. In addition to the archaeological interest is the great attraction of nature reserves and parks, without neglecting the idyllic medieval hamlets and Renaissance townships traversed for the sake of some mythical tale or in search of elusive ancient remains.

ETRUSCAN ITALY

As concerns the Etruscans themselves, new discoveries are still coming to light and theories proposed in an attempt to disperse the shroud of mystery that still envelops many aspects of their life. In the midst of tribal cultures, theirs was highly sophisticated in terms of art, architecture, city life and civil engineering, and the language quite distinct. Scholars have been arguing for ages about where the Etruscan people actually came from. Back in ancient times the prevalent theory, attributed to Greek historian Herodotus, accorded them Lydian origin. The Greeks in fact called them Tyrrenoi after a legendary figure, Tyrrhenus, sent away from his native Lydia in western Asia Minor due to famine conditions. The name lives on in the Tyrrhenian Sea, while the name for Tuscany is derived from the Roman version Tusci. Other experts claim they were but another of the numerous indigenous tribes who peopled the Italian peninsula in the millennium prior to Christ. However, convincing

13

recent work by a Spanish linguist suggests they came from North Africa, some 6000 years ago. The advancing desert forced inhabitants of the vast area between Libya and Morocco to migrate en masse and they headed for the Iberian peninsula, the Canary Islands, the Italian peninsula, Sicily and Sardinia. The theory is based on a series of surprising similarities that have emerged between Etruscan and the Euskara language of the Basque people, the only one in southwestern Europe to have survived the Roman conquest when Latin was imposed.

The language itself was written employing an adaptation of the Greek alphabet passed on by colonisers, but in mirror fashion, from right to left. While some 11,000 inscriptions have been saved, mostly of a religious and funerary nature, nothing in the way of

Painted 2nd century BC terracotta sarcophagus with reclining figure and Etruscan inscription, Chiusi

A stretch of the original Etruscan way between Sovana and Pitigliano (Walk 30)

Etruscan literature has yet been found. To date experts have managed to decipher over 500 words, aided in part by bilingual Etruscan–Latin inscriptions on tombs from the early Roman period. Among the latest vocabulary revelations are *mlach* for 'beautiful' and *ein* – a negative affix.

The earliest expression of Etruscan civilisation is identified in the Iron Age culture of the Villanovans around 9th century BC. Groupings of circular huts on raised sites with natural defences were occupied by tribes who raised crops and livestock and whose craftsmen were highly skilled metal workers. Their trademark was pit burials. Cremated remains were interred in rough earthenware pots, the lid akin to an upside-down dish. From these humble roots, the Etruscans gradually developed their unique style, and

by 6th century BC had become the leading power in central Italy. Rather than a nation as such, they were a loosely grouped confederation of twelve city states based on Phoenician and Greek models, and who met for religious and political reasons. Their modern-day names are Arezzo, Cerveteri, Chiusi, Orvieto, Perugia, Populonia, Roselle, Tarquinia, Veio, Vetulonia, Volterra and Vulci. Each was headed by a *lucumones*, a sort of king or prince whose authority also encompassed religious affairs. With the exception of Populonia, these cities stood some distance back from the coast to facilitate defence in case of pirate attacks. On the other hand the numerous ports, with road links to the relevant city, were often sizeable settlements in their own right, along with a sanctuary. The Etruscans were a

15

seafaring people and their vessels, depicted in tomb paintings, are engaged in naval battles when not busy plying the trade routes around the Mediterranean.

Trade was the main reason behind the expansion southwards out of Etruria proper around 7th century BC. The Tarquin dynasty founded Rome as a city proper when the first of a line of Etruscan kings established themselves in what had thereto been a rough grouping of Latin farming villages. They also left their mark with sizeable cities and trading centres around Naples, thus coming into conflict with the Greeks who also had consolidated footholds in the south of the Italian peninsula. From 550BC they moved north into the Po valley, where a mammoth land reclamation and river diversion scheme was realised near Mantua, resulting in flourishing agriculture. The northern Adriatic city ports of Spina and Adria, which spelt direct access to the peninsula's eastern sea, also date back to this period. Trading contacts were extended north to the mountainous South Tyrol and the resident Rhaetians, who themselves adopted the Etruscan alphabet. Further afield, traces of Etruscan workmanship have also turned up in France, Spain, Switzerland and North Africa.

The turning point in Etruscan power is generally accepted as 535BC, the date of a failed attempt to capture the Greek city of Cumae, near Naples. Soon afterwards the Etruscan kings were expelled from Rome when the republic was proclaimed. Meanwhile

the outer reaches of Etruscan influence were threatened by the advancing Gauls in the north and Italic peoples in the south. In 396BC Veio was the first of the city states to fall to the Romans, who steadily took over the rest by various means including surrender, concluding around 280BC. Many later received Roman citizenship and Etruria itself officially became a region of Roman Italy, a title recycled centuries later when Napoleon called the region Kingdom of Etruria.

Many complain that one of the 'problems' with the Etruscans is the dearth of relevant remains, compared for instance to the Romans and the plethora of their monuments. As has been the norm through the ages, with each new conqueror, cities are destroyed then either abandoned or reconstructed for continuing settlement. This leads to stratification, and one of the lowest levels is naturally Etruscan, but is inaccessible on the whole as excavation is barred by modern buildings. Visible remnants mostly consist of the odd city gateway, fragment of ancient walling or temple altar that emerge from layers of civilisation. However all provide enticing clues. Minor abandoned sites such as San Giovenale even provide the foundations of houses, while beneath Orvieto and Chiusi are extensive networks of tunnel-like drainage channels threading through the volcanic tufa rock. Urban layout can even be seen, at Marzabotto and Roselle.

In contrast to the cities, extensive cemeteries known as *necropolises* or

The winged horses in terracotta from the Ara della Regina sanctuary at Tarquinia

'cities of the dead', located outside the walls, have long been accessible to archaeologists and looters alike. Though the first 'Etruscologist' was probably the Roman Emperor Claudius, the 1600s marked the first serious studies, notably *De Etruria Regali* by the Scot Thomas Dempster, professor at the University of Pisa. Systematic excavations followed on much later, with an outbreak of Etruscan fever and campaigns in the 1800s, when countless sepulchres were emptied under the undiscerning shovel and pick of the likes of Napoleon's brother.

Tomb types were by no means uniform. Some reflected dwelling forms, for instance the artificial hut-shaped mounds or tumuli covering the burial chambers at Cerveteri. False or step vaulting, the precursor to the arch,

is common in many interiors, the Castellina in Chianti chambers for instance. A *hypogeum* or underground premises belonging to several of the monumental tombs is entered by way of a slanting corridor or *dromos*.

Burial methods started with the practice of cremation, the ashes entrusted to urns in terracotta or local rock. Later on, bodies were laid to rest on stone benches carved out of the walls of rock chambers, surrounded by their personal possessions for the after-life. The sarcophagus or stone coffin entered the funeral sphere around 5th century BC. The name comes from the Greek and means flesh devouring, as the stone used was believed to destroy the corpses. There are countless examples of sarcophagi with intricately carved decorations from mythology, the

17

lid often bearing the reclining figure of the aristocratic occupant, youthful for the most part as life expectancy was in the 30–40 year range. More often than not they are depicted in elegant dress, exquisitely coiffured and holding a saucer-like dish or *patera* with a raised knob, with divine symbolism. A funeral for a noble would involve a procession of musicians and relatives, then a series of offerings to the appropriate divinities. If the chamber was to be used for a later burial, a brazier would be left alight inside to lower the oxygen level and hence retard decomposition. Embalming was not practised.

Many sites come complete with roads, which generally followed valleys and watercourses. However in order to reach the townships set atop tufa platforms in southern Etruria, a cutting was made through a cliff. The repeated passage of carts and chariots would leave the surface deeply rutted in a short space of time, necessitating levelling work, thus dropping the level deeper and deeper over time. Many of these ensuing sunken roads have survived to the present, though a good number were extended and paved by the Romans to make them more durable. The prime example is the Via Clodia. Branching off the Via Cassia on the northern outskirts of Rome, it traversed the southern Etrurian heartland through to Saturnia, hence a westward link with the Via Aurelia on the Tyrrhenian coast. It was adapted by the Romans 3rd–2nd century BC, and probably named after the consul in charge.

Artifacts, tomb goods more often than not, indicate very sophisticated craftsmanship as well as providing precious insights into daily life. Along with the plethora of painted Greek and locally made vases, there are braziers, candelabras and curious items such as hinged clogs of wood and metal, safety pins, engraved bronze mirrors, ivory dice and exquisite gold jewellery – brooches, necklaces and earrings painstakingly worked using the 'gold dust' (*pulviscolo*) and granulation techniques. Other objects in metal were strainers for filtering out herbs like rosemary from diluted wine as per Greek usage. At a typical Etruscan banquet, the guests brought food while the host provided the wine. Many cities minted their own currency, while roughly shaped coins were often found in the hands of the deceased to pay Charon the ferryman for the passage over the River Styx to Hades.

Of undeniable Etruscan invention was the famous black *bucchero* ceramic ware, widely exported. The kiln would be sealed off to reduce oxygen levels and thus transform the red ferric oxide in the clay to black ferrous oxide. The highly developed art of sculpture produced works in bronze and stone, and huge statues with the likes of sphinx, lions and hippocampus were put on guard at tomb entrances. Terracotta was the medium for masterpieces the likes of the winged horses from Tarquinia, the Apollo statue from Veio and the Cerveteri sarcophagus which depicts a couple of newlyweds. Curious minor works in terracotta and

Masses of wild flowers overlooking the village of Chiessi on Isola d'Elba (Walk 22)

bronze are the votive objects offered to divinities as a request for healing by the slaves and labouring class to whom good health was essential for survival. Museums carry collections of anatomical objects that verge on the bizarre – heads, hands, feet, noses, knees, babies wrapped in swaddling clothes, a breast or two, male and female sexual organs, intestines, and one piece identified as a uterus with a growth akin to a fibroma! Of a purely decorative nature are the intricately modelled and painted antefixes and pediments that once graced temple roofs as was the case at Veio.

At this point a brief note on the religious practices is in order. The Etruscans were experts in the art of divination, and developed it to great levels of sophistication. Under the guidance of a sort of high priest or soothsayer known as a haruspex, animal organs, earthquakes, thunder and lightning were interpreted for signs of the future. As concerns lightning, one of the most important phenomena, not only did they interpret divine will by observing the exact points of origin and return as well as the trajectory, but reportedly evoked it – as did King Lars Porsenna of Chiusi against a monster on a rampage through the countryside. The Etruscan haruspices were in great demand well into Roman times, and enjoyed great respect. Decisions taken by a group of 60 appointed by Claudius could even override the authority of the Roman magistrates. Even in later years after persecution initiated in 4th century AD, a group offered their services to the Pope to erect a barrier of lightning against threatening hordes of Goths.

Among the galaxy of deities the Etruscans revered and to whom they dedicated their temples and sanctuaries were the supreme being Tinia, akin to the Greek Zeus and his wife Uni (Juno), Menerva and Fufluns, a sort of Bacchus. Each occupied a designated sector of the heavens.

Etruscan achievement is by no means exhausted with this summary. Their heritage and contribution to western civilisation incorporates a number of items generally accepted as quintessential Roman. Many of these were of course learned in turn from the Greeks and Phoenicians and more ancient cultures, though a high percentage were original.

A cloak-like garment thrown over a tunic and known as the *tebenna* was the precursor of the Roman toga, while the short lace-up boots were adopted by the senators. Another classic, the symbol of Rome, namely the Capitoline or she-wolf bronze statue of Romulus and Remus, is in actual fact a 6th century BC Etruscan piece, though the twins were affixed in 1509. To these must be added the fasces, chariots, gladiatorial combat and theatrical performances involving music. The very word *histrio* for an actor is of Etruscan origin, as are triumph, atrium and taberna. An Etruscan king built the Circus Maximus and sent for pugilists and race-horses. One of their most extraordinary achievements was the Cloaca Maxima sewer in Rome.

On the Strada di Mezzo above Lago di Vico (Walk 41)

Constructed to drain the Forum area, it still functions today, and is said to contain Italy's first known instance of the perfect arch.

Much in the field of city planning and layout was introduced, such as the use of two perpendicular main streets oriented north–south and east– west, later the Roman *cardo* and *decumanus*. Greek principles were applied to the all-encompassing Etruscan world view, and the city, like the cosmos, was divided up into organised sections.

The Etruscans were unequalled experts in Europe at the time in hydraulic engineering. They excavated tunnels to divert rivers, carried out vast land reclamation schemes and drained their necropolises scrupulously. In addition to their widespread excavation in the relatively soft tufa rock, the Etruscans are believed to have passed on techniques for hard-rock tunnelling to the Romans. In the so-called 'fire-quenching' method, rock was heated by fire to a high temperature then suddenly cooled by water, causing it to crack and hence facilitate removal.

Many interesting and essential museums are worth a visit in their own right, as well as being good for those rainy days. Most are closed on Mondays, unless this coincides with a public holiday. Key Etruscan sites not covered by the walks are given in the Appendix at the end of the book. State-run sites and museums usually mean free entrance for the under 18s as well as the over 65s. Moreover, for a full week in the month of April, the Italian State Archaeological Authority waives entrance fees at all its sites and offers extended opening hours.

The essential work is the exceptional *Cities and Cemeteries of Etruria* by George Dennis, first published in 1848. The comprehensive two-volume travel-book-cum-guide makes for riveting reading as the author provides enthusiastic and detailed accounts of the sites discovered around the time of writing. Unless a search in a library or second-hand book shop turns up a copy, try the internet. Its precursor, *Tours to the Sepulchres of Etruria* by Elizabeth C. Hamilton Gray (1840), is even rarer.

A very readable account is D.H. Lawrence's 1920s poignant reflections on these long-gone people and their culture in *Etruscan Places* (in *D.H. Lawrence and Italy*, Penguin, 1985). Last but not least, quite a few of the travel essays in Henry James' *Italian Hours* (Penguin, 1992), written 1872–1909, shed further light on these Etruscan places.

A selection of books of a strictly archaeological nature that have appeared in English include:

- Banti, Luisa (1974) *The Etruscan Cities and their Culture,* Batsford
- De Palma, C. (1967) *Etruscan Culture, Land and People*, New York
- Keller, Werner (1974) *The Etruscans*
- Paget, R.F. (1973) *Central Italy – An Archaeological Guide*, London

- Pallottino, Massimo (1975) *The Etruscans,* Penguin
- Potter, T.W. (1979) *The Changing Landscape of Southern Etruria,* London
- Time-Life Books (1975) *The Emergence of Man: The Etruscans*

Similar publications in Italian are:
- Celuzza, M. ed. (1993) *Guida alla Maremma Antica,* Siena
- Cristofani, M. ed. (1985) *Dizionario della Civiltà Etrusca,* Firenze
- Various Authors (1993) *Guida ai luoghi etruschi. Guide Archeologiche De Agostini,* Novara

WHEN TO GO

The beauty of Etruria is that walking is feasible the whole year round. Each season offers its own special delights. Spring is undeniably the most beautiful time for lovers of infinite shades of green along with extraordinary expanses of colourful wild flowers. Apart from the Easter break and the long weekends that coincide with the public holidays April 25th and May 1st, the country areas covered in the walks are unlikely to receive more than a sprinkling of visitors.

Midsummer is not particularly suitable for walking at low altitudes as the heat and mugginess take the pleasure out of it, and haze can spoil visibility. However, higher altitude areas such as Monte Cetona offer pleasant temperatures even in July and August. The cities are best avoided at this time of year due to crowding and the problems involved in finding accommodation.

At the start of a walk in the Parco della Maremma (Walk 24)

Autumn is a very promising season as visitors are few and far between, let alone walkers. Italy stays on daylight savings time until the end of October, meaning good long walking days (it gets dark around 7pm). The vegetation can be simply spectacular with brilliant reds, hues of yellow and orange amidst the grape harvests, and even sporadic colours from a surprising number of flowers in bloom. Leaves scrunch underfoot and in the woods you risk bombardment by falling spiky chestnuts. Good visibility is virtually guaranteed. The sole negative note comes from the Sunday gun shots and yapping dogs who belong to the hunters. As well, November is probably best avoided as it is notoriously foggy.

As far as winter goes, the only itineraries that might be actually snowed under are Monte Cetona and the upper reaches of the Cortona route, though snowfalls in Perugia are not uncommon. However, brisk crisp weather is usually the norm. Conditions are excellent for bird watching at both coastal and inland reserves as huge numbers of migrational species stop over. Furthermore the wilder parts of north Latium, for example, will be easier to visit as the dense summer vegetation that makes some routes impassable will have died off. This also improves the chances of spotting wildlife. Remember though that days are shorter (expect it to get dark around 4.30pm at the worst in midwinter) and there may be restrictions on visiting times of sites and museums.

GETTING THERE & AROUND

The nearest international airports are Pisa and Rome. For train arrivals, any of the major cities such as Florence or Rome make suitable starting points. By car several motorways are useful, either via Genoa then down the Tyrrhenian coast, otherwise via Florence hence southwards. All of Italy's *autostrada* are subject to toll payment. Other main roads are usually denominated SS 123 or the like, meaning *Strada Statale,* namely State Road. Detailed directions with relevant roads are given in each walk's Access section.

Tuscany, Umbria and Latium have a surprising capillary network of trains and buses to remote hamlets. Though it is obviously more time-consuming and less flexible than travel by car, using the local transport gives visitors the chance to enjoy the scenery in relaxation, meet local inhabitants as well as other travellers, and, more importantly, means that you are not bringing another polluting vehicle to this beautiful countryside.

With the rare exception, all the walks are feasible using public transport. In remote country areas a car, on the other hand, can be a great help. In the cities, though, traffic can be chaotic and parking a costly enterprise. A combination of public and private vehicles is probably the best bet.

The majority of bus companies post updated timetables at bus stops. In most cases tickets should be purchased beforehand, usually at a bar or tobacconist, then stamped on board the bus. The bus companies referred to in the individual walks are listed here with the areas they serve (NB numbers beginning '800' mean toll-free calls):

- Arezzo LFI tel.0575/39881 or **www.lfi.it** covers covers Chiusi, Cortona & Sarteano.
- Florence ATAF tel.800/424500 or **www.ataf.net** for Fiesole.
- Florence SITA tel.800/373760 or **www.sita-on-line.it** serves the Chianti region.
- Grosseto RAMA tel.0564/25215 or **www.griforama.it** covers the Maremma, Orbetello, Argentario, Pitigliano & environs, as well as Bagno Vignoni & Castiglione d'Orcia.
- Isola d'Elba ATL tel.0565/914392 or **www.atl.livorno.it** for Chiessi, Marciano & Poggio.
- Orvieto ATC tel.800/431784 or **www.atcterni.it** for Orvieto and Bolsena.
- Perugia APM tel.800/512141 or **www.apmperugia.it** for Lago Trasimeno.
- Perugia FCU tel.800/512141 or **www.fcu.it** for Volumni.
- Piombino ATM tel.0565/260134 or **www.atm.li.it** for Baratti.
- Rome ATAC tel.800/431784 or **www.atac.roma.it** for Isola Farnese & Veio.
- Rome COTRAL tel.800/150008 or **www.cotralspa.it** for Cerveteri.
- Siena TRA-IN IN tel.800/570530 or **www.trainspa.it** (funnily enough, a bus company) does the Crete district, Montalcino, San Gimignano, Vescovado & Volterra.

- Viterbo COTRAL tel.800/150008 or **www.cotralspa.it** serves Blera, Barbarano Romano, Civitella Cesi, Sutri, Tarquinia, Tuscania as well as running the Ferrovia Roma Nord railway line to Rome.
- For the State Railway (FS) the nationwide information service can be reached at tel.892021 or **www.trenitalia.com** nationwide information service can be reached at 848/888088.
- The Treno Natura (Ferrovia Val d'Orcia) programme is available at tel.0577/207413 or **www.ferrovie-turistiche.it**.

Some terminology to help understand timetables:

Cambio a ...	change at ...
Coincidenza	connection
Estivo	summer
Feriale	working days ie. Monday to Saturday
Festivo	holidays ie. Sundays and bank holidays
Giornaliero	daily
Invernale	winter
Lunedì a venerdì	Monday to Friday
Sabato	Saturday
Sciopero	strike
Scolastico	during school term

Lunch under the colossal iron cross on Monte Cetona (Walk 13)

WALKING

Central Italy is crisscrossed by a web of ancient paths and mule tracks trodden, over time, by the likes of traders, shepherds, armies and pilgrims. Many have surprisingly survived intact to this day and age, even with their original flag stones, while others have fallen into disuse or have been obliterated or simply flooded by asphalt. In the walk descriptions 'path' is used to mean just that, whereas a 'track' is wider and may serve jeep-like vehicles. A 'road' is sealed unless specified otherwise.

Difficulty is hardly a relevant term for these walks as for the most part the itineraries described follow clear if unmarked routes with brief and trouble-free climbs and subsequent descents. Any significant height gain and loss are dealt with in the preface to each walk, along with special notes.

Remember that the timing given in the walk heading is for normal-pace walkers not marathon entrants. However it **does not** include rest stops or time for exploring archaeological sites, so always add on extra time when calculating the day's load.

Distances are in kilometres, as is usual in Italy (with miles in brackets). The measurements given in metres (m) during the route description are not distances but altitudes of towns, villages and prominent points en route. In addition to right and left, compass directions are often used (eg. north-west), with longer ones abbreviated, for example to NNW.

Country routes often pass through private property, and walkers should

Descending to the River Orcia, looking over to Vignoni Alto (Walk 12)

stick to the main track so as not to give the omnipresent guard dogs any extra reason to bark. Remember to fasten all gates behind you and do not disturb livestock in any way. It goes without saying that no wild flowers should be picked, no fires lit and rubbish carried out to the nearest village for suitable disposal. As for toilet stops, *please* use your discretion and do your utmost to ensure that no unsightly paper is left lying around.

MAPS

Recommended road maps of the area covered in this guide are the 1:200,000 'Grande carta stradale d'Italia' series put out by the Touring Club Italiano – 'Toscana', 'Lazio' and 'Umbria Marche'. They can be found in bookshops all over Italy. Many tourist offices provide a variety of free road maps for their surrounds, usually on a provincial basis.

As concerns walking maps, only about one-third of the walks in this guide are covered by commercial maps, namely the popular hill areas of the Chianti and some coastal areas, notably the island of Elba. Relevant editors and sheet numbers are listed under each walk heading. Every effort has thus been made to incorporate sufficient detail in the sketch maps in this guide to accompany each walk. The legend for these maps appears below.

The best source of maps are newspaper stands and bookshops, such as the

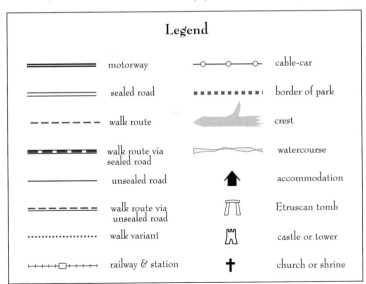

	Legend	
motorway	cable-car	
sealed road	border of park	
walk route	crest	
walk route via sealed road	watercourse	
unsealed road	accommodation	
walk route via unsealed road	Etruscan tomb	
walk variant	castle or tower	
railway & station	church or shrine	

following specialists in walking maps: Libreria Stella Alpina, via Corridoni 14, Florence (**www.stella-alpina.com**) or well-reputed Libreria La Montagna, Via Sacchi 28 bis, 10128 Turin (**www.librerialamontagna.it**). Overseas suppliers include leading outdoor suppliers and bookshops such as the UK's Stanfords which has stores in London, Manchester and Bristol (**www.stanfords.co.uk**).

A range of geographical terminology used on Italian maps can be found at the end of the book in the Glossary.

ACCOMMODATION

Walkers will have the pleasure of staying in a series of lodgings that range from farms, private rooms in historic hamlets, a convent and hostel or two, and a good selection of those typically modest family-run hotels or *pensioni* scattered through the Italian countryside that excel in hospitality. Each walk description is accompanied by convenient listings. Small hotels have been preferred with one- or two-star ratings, and where unavoidable there is an occasional upper range listing, with a note to that effect. There are, however, considerable differences in rates between hotels in the same category, so check recent price lists if possible. Furthermore, most hotels cut room charges drastically during off-peak times, and it's always worth enquiring if they have anything

Old shop front, San Gimignano (Walk 5)

cheaper: *Avete qualcosa di più economico?*

Homely B&Bs or *affittacamere* have been mushrooming of late. Usually in stunning locations and equipped with all mod cons, many of these comfortable establishments even serve walkers'-size breakfasts.

Farm stays, usually called *agriturismo*, can be interesting as they encompass everything from wine and oil properties to honey, spirits and cereal farms, and guests get to sample the produce. For those not included in this guide, check that *pernottamento* (accommodation) is offered, as a good number act purely as restaurants or sales points. Tourist offices can provide exhaustive lists.

Do phone ahead for all accommodation. English and the common European languages are widely understood in the popular areas of Tuscany and Umbria, though an Italian phrase book is warmly recommended. Do try your hand at speaking Italian. All efforts on the part of visitors are unfailingly appreciated and encouraged. A suitable opening phrase on the phone is: *Pronto, cerco una camera doppia (singola) con (senza) bagno per una notte (due notti) da oggi (domani)*, which translates as 'Hello, I'm looking for a double (single) room with (without) bathroom for one night (two nights) as from today (tomorrow)'.

Lastly, should none of the accommodation suggestions listed be available, the local bar or bakery is often a good source of information for a *camera privata* or private room.

In terms of camping, unless you're especially discrete and find secluded spots not on private property, free camping is not a good idea and may not be safe. It is forbidden in parks, reserves and other protected areas. However there is no dearth of well-signed camping grounds, and tourist offices can be contacted for addresses and opening periods.

In general it's advisable to advance book accommodation on the coast late July–August. In spring, on the other hand, bookings are best made a few days ahead for towns and cities on weekends.

In some small hotels you'll have the chance of taking *mezza pensione* – half board, which covers lodging, breakfast and dinner (drinks excluded), often a good deal.

Note: When telephoning, remember that the full area code including the zero must be used, even for local calls and from overseas. The only exceptions are toll-free numbers that begin with '800' and mobiles.

FOOD AND WINE

A guide to Tuscany, Umbria and Latium could hardly be considered complete without at least a passing mention of the vast culinary delights in store for visitors. And walking naturally demands substantial nourishment.

A visit to one of the numerous fresh produce markets held throughout the country is a good introduction to local fare. Stalls are set up at an

At the ruins of Cosa (Walk 27)

ungodly hour and the bustle will only peter out around midday. In addition to the season's fruit and vegetables, which come in colourful photogenic stacks, suggestions for picnics are tangy fresh sheep cheese, *pecorino fresco*. This can be consumed with the typical saltless bread sold in huge floury loaves at the *panificio* (bakery). *Pecorino* is also sold in a slightly drier, stronger, aged form, more suitable for grating over pasta dishes. A request for *un formaggio locale* (a local cheese) will always turn up something interesting. Also, with a bit of luck there'll be an open-sided van selling *porchetta*, luscious roast sucking pig, flavoured with herbs and served in thick slices. In addition to the markets, delicatessens and supermarkets unfailingly have mouth-watering displays,

and many places will make up fresh rolls (*panini*) on the spot with your choice of filling.

In restaurants, a good rule is to be adventurous and enquire what's on that day – *Che cosa avete oggi?* Some staples are *bruschetta* and *crostini*, wonderful *antipasti* or starters. The former are thick toasted slices of bread with a hint of garlic, a dribbling of olive oil and some fresh tomato, while the latter are morsels of toast smothered with home-made paté, sausage, mushroom spread or whatever takes the cook's fancy that day.

One topping might be fragrant nutty *tartufi,* namely truffles or earthnuts, edible tuberous fungi that grow underground. They are also grated and sprinkled over pasta such as *pici*, thick home-made spaghetti. As soups go, you'll come across *acqua cotta*, literally 'cooked water', a simple tasty brew made with a variety of vegetables, while *caciucco* consists mostly of fish. Olive oil, preferably the cold pressed *extra vergine* variety, reigns over the lot.

Game meats such as *cinghiale*, wild boar, are widespread and found in excellent pasta sauces or hearty stews, an alternative to the legendary oversized Florentine steak. Those who make it to dessert may opt for *panna cotta*, literally 'cooked cream', a divine blancmange-type sweet flavoured with a variety of fruit. One worthwhile after-dinner norm is a handful of *cantucci*, crisp almond biscuits more often than not consumed with a glass of sweet, rich, amber-coloured Vin Santo.

The wines of Etruria really deserve a book apart. Following are brief notes on several of the special vintages from areas covered in this guide. The best known, the wines from the Chianti district, come in many recommended varieties, though the 'imitations' served in a straw-covered flask are best avoided. As a general rule, table wines are a fairly good deal, though ordering a bottle means a drastic improvement in quality.

Of the other reds, the dark, full-bodied Brunello di Montalcino must head the list, while those on a budget can enjoy the younger Rosso di Montalcino. A little further south, the Maremma inland produces a robust red, Morellino di Scansano. On the coast, the Argentario promontory is home to Parrina, which comes in both red and white, as does the excellent Elba Rosso or Elba Bianco, which can also be a little fizzy but never sweet.

The southern reaches of Etruria are home to some memorable white wines. San Gimignano's superb dry Vernaccia is one, while Orvieto is renowned for a golden nectar of likely Etruscan origin. The area's volcanic heritage, hence rich soil, is also responsible for the Aleatico dessert wine from nearby Lago Bolsena.

Early morning mist over the Val d'Orcia (Walk 11)

A delicate crisp white from tufa country is the Bianco di Pitigliano, and a final mention goes to the very drinkable red and white wine known as Baccio del Trasimeno.

Visitors travelling by car will be tempted by the countless wineries and village shops where all these and more vintages are on sale at very reasonable prices.

WHAT TO TAKE

Clothing will depend on the season and personal preferences. Winter will mean several layers of woollen garments with the addition of a windproof jacket and hat, while a T-shirt, shorts and sun hat are perfect spring–summer. Long trousers and a longsleeved shirt are strongly recommended for overgrown, thorny stretches.

A comfortable pair of well-cushioned, nonslip gym shoes is sufficient for the majority of the itineraries. However lightweight trekking boots providing ankle support are advisable on the longer routes over rocky terrain, namely those on Elba and in the Maremma Park. Boots are also an advantage in muddy zones, the sunken roadways around Pitigliano for example.

WILDLIFE

Despite the widespread agriculture, sprawling built-up areas around cities and popularity of hunting, a surprising number of wild animals and birds still inhabit the inland hills and coastline of erstwhile Etruria. Majestic lions,

Checklist

- Day pack.
- Rain gear.
- Swimming costume.
- A compass always makes a good companion, and can be used for identifying distant reliefs and towns.
- Water bottle.
- Torch or head-lamp for exploring the interior chambers of minor tombs, as many lack lighting.
- A stick is useful on overgrown stretches for clearing brambles and nettles out of the way, not to mention discouraging over-enthusiastic watch dogs.
- Binoculars.
- Sunglasses, shady hat, protective cream.
- Basic first aid kit, including plasters and insect repellent.

leopards, panthers and acrobatic dolphins adorn Etruscan friezes and ornaments, along with the more common squirrels, ducks, pigeons, dogs and wild boar. Wildlife populations have since undergone radical alterations, and while walkers can no longer expect to encounter animals from the former group, most of the the latter roam freely along with a number of introduced species.

Fallow deer graze freely in the magnificent Feniglia Reserve (Walk 27)

Boar hunting was long a favourite sport with both the Etruscans and Romans and continues to be so with today's inhabitants, though a heftier variety from Eastern Europe has all but taken the place of the indigenous boar. So successfully have they adapted and reproduced that thousands are officially slated for slaughter each year as they wreak immeasurable damage to crops and woodlands. Large-scale hunts are organised in autumn. Despite their fierce reputation, wild boar are extremely timid and the closest a walker will get to one is the stuffed variety on display in the hill towns to advertise their hams! However their telltale hoofprints, slide marks and rootings are clearly identifiable in muddy terrain throughout central Italy.

Another somewhat invisible creature is the protected crested porcupine, whose visiting card is the black and white quills it litters along paths in woodland. It is believed to have been introduced from Africa by the Romans, presumably for its flesh, reputedly a great delicacy. In contrast foxes, fallow deer and the magnificent common ring-necked pheasant are a relatively common sight in dew-soaked fields early morning. The latter were originally brought from southwest Asia by those same hunting enthusiasts.

Otters have been on the endangered list for years now due to the heavy pollution in the watercourses and unjustified slaughter. Of late there has been cause for optimism, and the odd exemplar reported in the Maremma Park as well as the Vulci

Oasi run by the World Wildlife Fund for Nature of Italy. In recent years the organisation has been purchasing terrain as part of its policy to extend protection, and a number of *oasi* or reserves are covered in the walking itineraries, mostly of interest to bird lovers. The coastal reserves around Orbetello make for a fascinating visit, as does Lago di Vico. The bird life is extraordinarily rich and includes such notables as the striking black-winged stilt, hoopoe, ospreys, peregrine falcons, crested grebes and bright kingfishers, to name but a few.

One dog needs a quick mention. A bit like a labrador, the Pastore Maremmano, as they are known locally, are fluffy white-haired creatures with a persistent bark, widely used as watch dogs on country properties. They are not always on a leash and it's a good idea to give them a wide berth where possible or brandish a stick, continuing on your way at a normal pace.

The only other warning regards snakes. The poisonous viper with its characteristic diamond markings inhabits several parts of Etruria (eg. Elba and Populonia), along with a multitude of harmless relations such as the similar smooth snake. Encounters are rare as, given time, it will slither away from the path or clearing where it was taking the sun. The best deterrent is to tread heavily to give warning of your approach, and wear long trousers as protection.

To conclude on a more positive note, a magical pastime for balmy summer evenings is to go spotting fire-flies or glow-worms, alias a type of beetle. Once the sun has gone down, gardens and waysides come alight with flickering pinpoints of greenish-white light which double as their mating calls.

VEGETATION AND FLORA

The marvellous array of unusual flowering plants and trees is reason alone for a visit. A broad range of vegetation zones is encompassed, the highest a little over 1000 metres and verging on subalpine with conifers. Below that are vast expanses of deciduous forest featuring sweet chestnut in hilly country, giving way to the typical evergreens and widespread impenetrable Mediterranean maquis and the drier garigue cover that back the coast.

Stretching from the coast and well up into the hills walkers will encounter glossy-leaved holm oak, lentisc and the unique cork oaks whose thick fissured bark, impervious to fire, is harvested every 7 years or so for bottling purposes. Majestic stands of pines are found along the Tyrrhenian coastline, dominated by the umbrella and maritime varieties often bent into artistic sculptured shapes by the wind. Another notable is the unusual strawberry tree which bears its white bell flowers and trademark fruit at varying stages of maturity at the same time. When ripe they consist of rough red balls that taste like strawberry, despite the lumpy bits. The second part of its Latin name *Arbutus*

The curious blossom and fruit of the strawberry tree

Spring walkers in Etruria will encounter masses of delicate paper-like rock roses

The crocus-like *Sternbergia* bloom in autumn

Wild orchid growing along a Tuscan country lane

unedo means 'eat one', implying that one is enough.

Prolific wild herbs reveal their presence with a pungent aroma or fragrance emanated when inadvertently trampled or even lightly brushed. The long list features oregano, thyme, rosemary, sage and 'stinking everlasting', thus dubbed for its curry smell.

As wild flowers go, the record goes to the ubiquitous yellow broom bushes whose multitude of varieties brightens landscapes, the air heavy with their distinctive perfume. Spring visitors will also be delighted by the precious wild orchids, rainbow masses of paper-like rock roses, not to mention the emerald green wheat

fields streaked with the brilliant blue of cornflowers and the red of poppies. A final spring bloomer is the straggly spiny caper shrub with its pink flowers, to be appreciated in haste as the locals gather them for pickling.

Walkers in late summer/autumn will not be disappointed as a surprising array of plants flower with the rainfall that marks the end of the summer dry period. Coastal areas, for example, will mean sea lavender and rosemary, while woods feature delicate cyclamens, myriad mushrooms and edible berries.

Nor in winter is the ground wholly devoid of flowers. As early as February, wattle trees (of Australian origin) are decorated with dazzling yellow

Olives ripening

Autumn colours in the Chianti vineyards

feathers and fruit trees produce fragile white and pink blossoms. Fields and woods mean black-centred pink-mauve anemones, periwinkle, crocuses, grape hyacinth, intense indigo bugloss, common mallow, white tree heather and the fresh green hellebore.

Flanking the extant 'wild' vegetation bands are the cultivated zones where ridges between fields are punctuated with archetypal cypresses. The other omnipresent essentials are the olive trees of ancient standing and orderly ranks of grape vines.

For more information, wild flower enthusiasts are advised to obtain a field guide such as *Mediterranean Wild Flowers* by M. Blamey and C. Grey-Wilson (Collins), or the classic *Flowers of the Mediterranean* by O. Polunin and A. Huxley (Chatto & Windus).

1: A Stroll in the Hills Around Fiesole

Walking time:	2h + 45min prelude
Distance:	6.1km/3.8 miles
Map:	on p.41, also Kompass 1:50,000 n.660 'Firenze-Chianti' or Multigraphic 1:25,000 'Dintorni di Firenze e Mugello' sheets 26/27

Access: Fiesole can be reached by local ATAF bus n.7 from Florence's main railway station (8km).

Those who drive up will face the fierce competition for the limited parking places in Fiesole's main square or along the narrow side streets. The end point of the walk, Settignano, has buses (ATAF n.10) back to Florence. It is also possible to transfer to the Fiesole line by changing at Piazza di San Marco, should you opt for accommodation there, well away from the chaos of traffic-choked Florence.

After savouring the wealth of Etruscan, Roman, medieval and Renaissance monuments in this delightful hill town on the outskirts of Florence, a wander through the surrounding countryside is in order. History is quickly left behind as nature takes over on this itinerary through woods, olive groves, fields and vineyards. Clearly marked and straightforward on good tracks, the route is suitable for all walkers. There is a steady but trouble-free climb of about 100m to the Monte Ceceri viewing point, then it's mostly smooth descent, terminating in the quiet village of Settignano, itself a treasure trove of artistic memories from Renaissance and later times.

Fiesole's position some 300m above Florence is a guarantee of cooler and cleaner air, however midsummer can mean large crowds and sweltering conditions here as well.

A brief historical overview starts with the evidence of Bronze Age settlements unearthed in Fiesole, though it was the Etruscans who put it on the map around 7th century BC, during their period of expansion towards the Po plain. The site, in a commanding position between the Arno and Mugnone rivers, was probably founded as a military outpost and was the most northerly settlement of Etruria proper. The city came under Roman rule around 3rd century BC, buildings and monuments being incorporated and expanded into Roman models, the usual practice. Much later on in the early 1100s, rivalry with neighbouring Florence was the cause of wide-scale destruction. Of course Fiesole went on to flourish in Renaissance times. A curiosity: *pietra serena*, a blue-grey type of sandstone excavated from Monte Ceceri, was widely used for sculpted fountains as well as door and window frames; it has been estimated that a good half of the mountain was incorporated into Florentine monuments! Some 19 quarries functioned up until the 1960s.

Prelude: 45min

Before embarking on the main walk, the easy climb to the viewing point over the amazing spread of Florence is recommended. Near the cathedral in **Fiesole's** main square, Piazza Mino da Fiesole, take Via San Francesco. The steepish paved lane climbs past craft shops to a famous panoramic terrace where – pollution and haze permitting – Florence and its most important landmarks will be arrayed below in the broad Val d'Arno. It is worth continuing up right past the Basilica of S. Alessandro, which was constructed on an Etruscan base, to visit the church and monastery of S. Francesco, the site of the original acropolis. Instead of returning the same way, go right through the shady public gardens and downhill to the cemetery. Keep on to where Via Dupre forks left along the edge of the archaeological area. At the end, around the corner are impressive Etruscan walls in Via delle Mura Etrusche. To return to Piazza Mino, go back to the cemetery turn-off then keep straight ahead.

THE WALK

Start out in **Piazza Mino da Fiesole** (294m), named after the 15th-century sculptor and city son. Up in the topmost corner, the farthest away from the cathedral, take Via Verdi (red/white waymarking n.1). The narrow road passes houses and gardens and 5min uphill forks left to become Via de Montececeri, leading around east to an inspiring lookout. After a playground, Via degli Scalpellini (the stonecutter's road) takes over, soon a gravelly track south between high walls shaded by tall pines and oak trees. Past a Parco di Montececeri mapboard, continue on for the fork right for **Cava Braschi**. This brief detour leads to a fascinating walk-in quarry with huge columns.

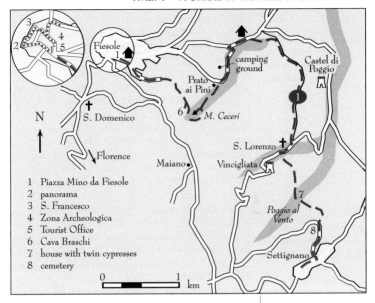

N

1 Piazza Mino da Fiesole
2 panorama
3 S. Francesco
4 Zona Archeologica
5 Tourist Office
6 Cava Braschi
7 house with twin cypresses
8 cemetery

0   1
|————|————| km

Thick overlying layers of marly terrain had to be cut through for the *pietra serena* to be reached.

Return to the fork and turn right past a cavity where *pietra morta* (suitable for fireplaces) was once extracted. Ignore a sharp fork left and proceed to the flat area alongside Cava Sarti, dotted with old stone huts for storing the masons' tools. Ahead a short climb leads to the cypress-bordered platform of 414m **Monte Ceceri** (40min) and more marvellous views over hills and countryside, villas and castles nestled amongst a rich variety of shrubs and trees. Perfect for a peaceful picnic. A stone marker commemorates Leonardo da Vinci and his early experiments with flying machines – his apprentices were apparently launched from here!

Where path n.7 drops right (for Maiano and its quarries), keep left (northeast) on n.1. The wide track dates back to 1932–3, part of the Italian Army's plan to place anti-aircraft guns on M. Ceceri; however it actually came into its own 11 years later when occupying German

41

Tourist Office Fiesole
tel.055/598720

Museo Civico, Zona Archeologica, Teatro Romano
The Roman amphitheatre was built to hold up to 3000 spectators, and is still used in summer for performances during the Fiesole Festival. The Archaeological Zone also includes an Etruscan temple on the lower level and remains of Roman baths, in addition to a small museum with Etruscan bits and pieces.

Accommodation
Fiesole: Villa Le Scalette B&B tel.055/5978484
Villa dei Bosconi tel.055/59578
Villa Sorriso tel.055/59027

forces bombarded Florence. It emerges from the wood at the houses of **Prato ai Pini** (371m). Turn right past a camping ground for a brief stretch of tarmac downhill to an intersection, and take the right fork. Not far along, opposite a luxury hotel (Villa dei Bosconi), a red/white path veers off right (east) into pleasant shady wood. Turning right onto a wider track, it curves south past properties, traversing olive groves well beneath Castel di Poggio, and ignoring turn-offs. After a sub-station a short climb through light wood emerges on a narrow surfaced road, where you head right for the church of **San Lorenzo** (290m, 1h20min). Immediately after the buildings, a path off left resumes its lovely way southeast amidst farms. Lovely views can soon be enjoyed back northwest to the curious castle of Vincigliata backed by Monte Ceceri. The mock medieval citadel was faithfully reconstructed in the mid 1800s on 11th-century ruins, by eccentric English gentleman Mr. Temple Leader. Its illustrious guests included Queen Victoria on 15 April 1888. A visit there led Henry James to conclude: 'The massive pastiche of Vincigliata has no superficial use, but, even if it were less complete, less successful, less brilliant, I should feel a reflective kindness for it. So disinterested and expensive a toy is its own justification; it belongs to the heroics of dilettantism'.

Continuing essentially southeast on good tracks alongside wood frequented by roe deer and boar, keep an eye out for waymarkings at the many junctions. Unsurfaced Via di Vincigliata is followed (left) for a short stretch, and leads to a house whose entrance is graced by twin cypress trees, on Poggio al Vento. Here branch left off the main track. On rather rough terrain, path n.1 drops steeply, coming out on tarmac in the vicinity of a cemetery. Keep straight ahead along Via Desiderio da Settignano then turn sharp right at an *Enoteca* (wine bar/restaurant) along Via S. Romano. This leads to the small square of **Settignano** (178m), suitably equipped with an outdoor café where bus tickets for the return trip are on sale.

2: Il Sentiero del Chianti: the Florence–Siena Long-Distance Path

Walking time:	20h45min – 4–5 days suggested
Distance:	75.2km/46.7 miles
Maps:	on pp.44–47, also Multigraphic 1:25,000 n.42/43 'Monti del Chianti' (but only as far as Monteluco), or Kompass 1:50,000 n.660 'Firenze-Chianti' (as far as Monteluco) & n.661 'Siena-Chianti-Colline Senesi' (covers Monteluco to Siena).

A breath of fresh air between crowded art cities. An original and enjoyable way for nature-lovers to reach Siena from Florence. 4–5 days' easy walking through vast uncultivated tracts of woodland high above the famous Chianti wine-growing countryside. The route follows the backbone of the Monti del Chianti, averaging 500–800m above sea level in altitude, and enjoys wide-ranging views over both the Chianti valley and reliefs to the west, while eastwards is the Valdarno backed by the mountainous Pratomagno ridge. On the way is the occasional isolated farmhouse, hamlet, tiny church and village, and even the odd villa, abbey and castle. On the final stages in descent towards magnificent Siena are classical silhouette lines of cypresses bordering lanes, quintessential olive groves and vineyards, laden late summer. A surprising variety of landscapes and vegetation.

Furthermore, you can wander for days and hardly meet a soul, maybe a mushroom collector or hunter. That's a special type of solitude in an area that sees thousands of tourists per year and to boot is a mere hop, skip and a jump from Italy's busiest motorway, the Autostrada del Sole. The itinerary rates as a nature and landscape rather than archaeological walk, though there is no doubt the Etruscans knew the area. The road that is known to have connected Chiusi with Montalbano transited via the

Access: San Donato in Collina, 13km out of Florence, where the walk starts, is served by SITA coach with departures from the main coach terminal in Florence (near the railway station). For alternative access and exit points, SITA also has regular runs to Siena along the main 'Chiantigiana' road (SS 222) via Greve in Chianti and Castellina in Chianti, with less frequently-served branches (usually excluding Sundays and holidays). The walk terminates at Due Ponti, a bus terminal on the outskirts of Siena, with frequent runs into town. The TRA-IN bus company serve the villages south from Gaiole covered in the later stages. Timetables are usually on display at bus stops. Details of runs are given at the relevant points during the walk description.

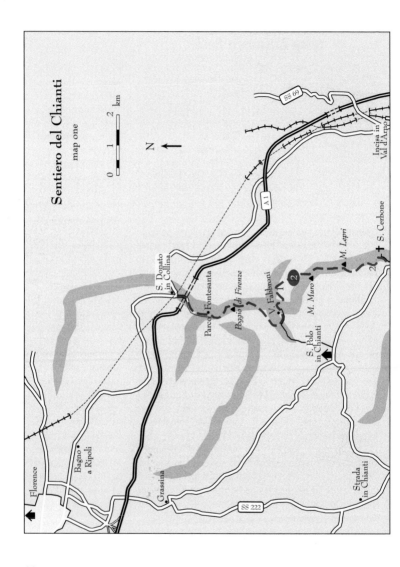

Sentiero del Chianti

map one

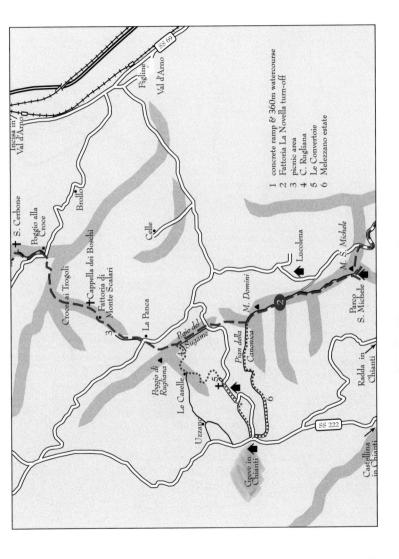

1 concrete ramp & 360m watercourse
2 Fattoria La Novella turn-off
3 picnic area
4 C. Rugliana
5 Le Convertoie
6 Melezzano estate

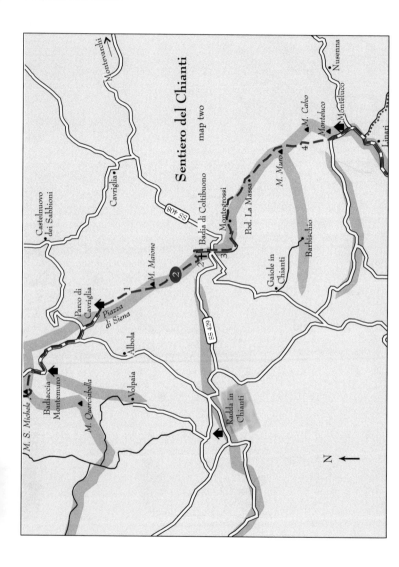

Sentiero del Chianti

map two

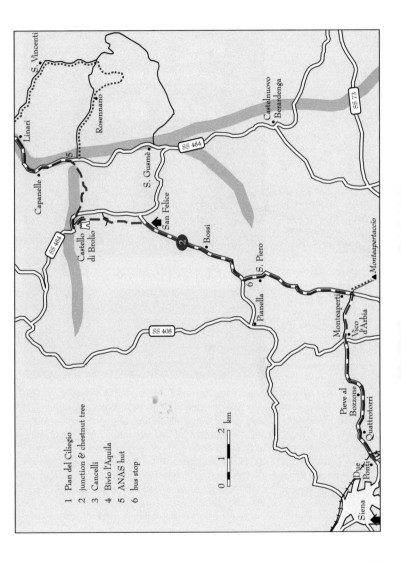

1 Pian del Ciliegio
2 junction & chestnut tree
3 Cancelli
4 Bivio l'Aquila
5 ANAS hut
6 bus stop

The black cockerel announces Chianti Classico land

Waymarking for the most part is white and red or orange paint stripes, numbered '00', like a pair of eyes. As the area is used by farmers and hunters, a multitude of other paths, signed and not, will present themselves. The best rule is to keep on the main track unless instructions or waymarking indicate otherwise.

Drinking water and picnic supplies should be carried as supply points are scarce. Villages usually mean drinking water and sometimes restaurants and shops (remember they close for long lunch breaks). Hotels and the like will usually provide packed lunches or at least a couple of sandwiches.

ridge in the Parco di Cavriglia, in the second stage. The very name Chianti in fact is believed to derive from the inscription 'Clunti' found recently on a cup in a late Etruscan settlement at Cetamura, not far from the Castello di Brolio. Siena, on the other hand, comes from Saina, the name of a patrician family from the same period. Though there is virtually nothing of Etruscan origin in the city itself, the Archaeological Museum contains finds from the vast province.

In the woodlands wildlife is plentiful starting with the wild boar, who leave muddy patches pitted with give-away hoof marks. You'll surprise birds with ground habits such as partridge and pheasant, especially early mornings. While its numbers are on the increase, the protected crested porcupine is elusive, though its tell-tale quills litter paths and woods. Even though no actual difficulties are involved, the continual ups and downs make for long and tiring stages, with accommodation possibilities few and far between at times. This is especially true of the first section – 7h30min as far as Parco San Michele (reducible to 6h15min by exiting to accommodation above Greve in Chianti). Though it would be a pity to miss this lovely solitary stage, it is feasible to slot into the itinerary by way of the convenient alternative access route from the township of Greve in Chianti. Shorter chunks of the walk can of course be bitten off at many points for conversion into day trips and loops – details are given throughout the description but the possibilities are endless.

Accommodation takes the form of hostels, private rooms and farm premises, in addition to the more numerous hotels and villas in lower villages and townships and reachable with detours off the main ridge route. They can be found at the end of the walk description. In summer it is a good idea to phone well ahead to book a bed, and in low season (winter) to ascertain whether or not they are actually open.

THE WALK

San Donato in Collina to Poggio alla Croce – 3h (12.3km/7.6 miles)

The coach from Florence will deposit you at the small village of **San Donato in Collina** (388m, general store). Take the 'Strada dei Montisoni' downhill southwest. It crosses over the Autostrada del Sole (A1) in its tunnel, though you wouldn't know it. Keep left at the cemetery, where the asphalt terminates. '00' is marked with red and white paint stripes on poles, walls and rocks, and several other itineraries also start here. Once through the olive groves, keep right at the next two junctions. In common with 'Percorso Natura 3' the route climbs on the edge of a wood on a narrow asphalt road, soon a winding dirt track. After a turn-off to a property (C. Gamberaia, 549m), it's around to a picnic area, Parco Fontesanta (30mins). '00' now turns up diagonally left on a track marked for P. Firenze/P. Croce. It's up through a beautiful chestnut wood past a huddle of television repeaters to emerge at Poggio di Firenze (693m). A crest offers sweeping views southwest. Bordered by masses of broom shrubs with scented yellow blooms, the wide stony track continues south in gradual then rather abrupt descent. Back in chestnut wood, keep right at junctions and alongside fenced-in properties, and you emerge onto a cypress-lined avenue. (1h20min total).

Exit route: the right branch of this farm road drops to San Polo in Chianti (242m) in about 30min as it is a little over 2km. Transport and shops are available, as are accommodation and meals. Then either re-enter the walk at the same point or take the SITA bus to Poggio alla Croce and slot in there.

Go sharp left (east). Not far along this pleasant dirt road passes beneath an arch belonging to abandoned **Villa Fabbroni** (543m) set amongst olive trees. Monte Muro is soon visible ahead southeast. Further on, a concrete ramp leads downwards to cross a small water-course at 360m, covered by thick undergrowth. Keep to the main track as it climbs steadily south now through an oak wood (regular red and white markings) up the northern flanks of Monte Muro. Thick chestnut takes over again, sheltering clumps of delicate mauve cyclamens which show up clearly against brilliant orange-red autumn leaf hues. Autumn walkers risk continual bombardment by miniature green-brown hedgehogs, alias falling chestnuts.

Once you reach the 550m level, the track levels out somewhat and the outlook opens eastward. Ahead on modest Monte Lepri (605m) you pass through one of area's many private game reserves (Robbiana Novella) where the light mixed wood is brightened by meadow saffron. A further drop between olives and vines comes out onto asphalt near the Fattoria La Novella estate (total 2h30min).

This is the first taste of the lovely Chianti landscape, complete with picturesque properties, grape vines and cypresses. Keep straight ahead on the surfaced road for a brief stretch, as the '00' soon branches off right on the edge of the field via an old track through wood. You skirt the ubiquitous antennas and pass the sanctuary of San Cerbone (563m) before joining a surfaced road. This quickly leads below the cross that gave the nearby village its name, and past restaurant/bar Le Due Lanterne, probably the most interesting attribute of quiet **Poggio alla Croce** (496m). Not far on is an intersection equipped with a welcome bench and drinking fountain.

Exit route: turn down right for the main road and SITA bus stop, for rare connections with San Polo in Chianti or Figline Val d'Arno.

Poggio alla Croce to La Panca – 1h45min (5.8km/3.6 miles)

From the intersection go straight ahead across an overpass, then around left past abandoned buildings and houses (not as shown on the Multigraphic 1:25,000 map). There is occasional hard-to-find waymarking for a dirt track which climbs and winds west through yet more beautiful chestnuts and pretty heather clumps. The frequent muddy patches sport clear hoofprints and scratchings left by wild boar. At the highest point (some 670m) another gradual descent begins, amongst blackberry thickets this time. At the path junction known as Croce ai Trogoli (a reference to 'trough'), path n.20 drops right (northwest) to San Polo in Chianti. Ignore it and keep straight on to the old shrine Cappella dei Boschi (more signed paths branch off east).

Not far around right is the eerie looming bulk of **Fattoria di Monte Scalari** (1h10min, 698m, and an exit path n.23 for Celle to the east). It was once a flourishing Romanesque abbey, however according to the locals its present state of utter abandon is due to a curse, as no-one ever manages to complete restoration work without a disaster befalling.

Further on past a prominent oak tree and picnic area the dirt road begins its winding descent to the quiet village of **La Panca** (487m). The name 'the bench' presumably refers to the one outside the bar-cum-general store, briefly left along the road. There is also a rather pricey restaurant (Trattoria Le Cernacche) and bus stop (though runs to either Florence or Figline Val d'Arno are extremely rare).

La Panca to Parco San Michele – 2h45min (8.4km/5.2 miles)

Cross straight over the road and continue in the same direction (south) along the eastern flank of Poggio di Rugliana. As it becomes a dirt track, path n.18 veers off right but '00' becomes a path climbing through curious sheet layers of crumbly pink-green rock. Several broad muddy sections are negotiated beneath pine trees. At 30min from La Panca a motorable dirt track is reached (599m). Monte San Michele is now SSE from here, whereas a suitable exit route presents itself (making accommodation over 1h closer than Parco San Michele).

Exit route to Greve in Chianti (1h45min) Go right along the dirt road to some old buildings where you keep left to pass a new house (C. Rugliana). Start winding down westward, taking the right branch at the next junction. Narrower and steeper soon, the route (n.22) drops left into an olive grove (yellow marking) to reach a dirt road below Le Caselle. This is a particularly picturesque area with views over characteristic Tuscan houses atop hills punctuated with cypresses and vineyards.

Keep left down the gravel road then take the turn-off for 'Castiglione' (the main track proceeds to Uzzano). Soon after the private driveway, just before the road starts climbing once more, a path drops down right (south) to cross a stream. Swing up past the magnificent villa Le Convertoie (370m). An asphalt drive leads to a small chapel (il Chiesino) on the corner of the main road (1h).

5min downhill from here is the entrance driveway for Agriturismo Anna, La Camporena.

Further downhill as the road curves left, take the pleasant dirt track right (southwest) through several olive-growing properties. Just after it joins the asphalt, go first left for the tourist office otherwise straight ahead for the supermarket and SITA bus. (40min from the Chiesino). The nearby *centro* of **Greve in Chianti** (236m) means well-stocked wine shops, pricey hotels and funnel-shaped Piazza Matteotti, alias car park, dominated by the statue of Giovanni da Verrazzano, navigator and local son. His claim to fame dates back to 1524 when he became the first European to sight what would later become New York, where a bridge now bears his name.

Access from Greve in Chianti to Parco San Michele (2h40min) From the town centre follow the road due east and turn right past the tourist office (signposting for 'Parco

San Michele') then left at the next junction. You climb east to the delightful Melezzano estate (364m) where the asphalt terminates. Amongst light scrubby vegetation which affords very little shade from the sun, you pass a small quarry and several properties, then the countryside opens out on Pian della Canonica as you near the crest and junction where '00' joins up from the left (610m, total 1h20min from Greve). For the remaining 1h20min see the following description.

From the **Rugliana** junction the main '00' route proceeds SSE along the wide dirt road via Poggio del Sugame. In 25min it cuts across the narrow road to Greve (532m). Straight ahead a cart track climbs gradually through light woods of oak, not to mention swathes of broom, black-berries and sweet oregano on the edges of the path. At 629m a panoramic stretch offers views both sides. Open fields follow where your passage might surprise partridge, before joining the wide dirt road from Greve in Chianti (30min more, 610m). Left now in a wide curve to cut the western flank of lookout point Monte Domini, though the path itself offers virtually uninterrupted views from here on. Still SSE along the wide sunny panoramic crest amidst bright wild flowers, ahead is a 'forest' of antennas and repeaters on the mount which precedes Monte San Michele. 40min from the 610m junction you reach a fork (740m) where the road is surfaced.•

Only 40min to go from here. '00' proceeds right at the 740m fork and climbs as a dirt road the rest of the way. Past the hill and antennas is a brief descent before veering right into a delightful wood. You finally reach the entrance to **Parco San Michele** and continue on for the tiny stone church and renowned restaurant, not to mention the spacious hostel Ostello-Albergo Parco San Michele (892m). It is a quite beautiful setting, amongst old chestnut trees and pines and there is a children's play-ground as well as ample picnic areas.

(Total walking time from San Donato in Collina – 7h30min).

• **Detour to Lucolena** (1h return) Continuing straight ahead, then left at the next junction, will see you on 2.5km (30min) narrow winds through a beautiful green zone to the village of Lucolena (542m) where you can be restored and stay overnight.

Parco San Michele to Parco di Cavriglia – 1h30min (5.8km/3.6 miles)

Backtrack to the actual entrance gates to Parco San Michele and take the dirt road up right. Soon left a (marked) path penetrates into deep dark conifers to bear right to the top of Monte San Michele 892m, occupied as usual by TV transmitting apparatus – no views at all, despite its being Chianti's highest mount. Keep right on the track (red and white marking) which soon drops to a 5-track intersection. Take the first left, SSE to then wind eastward through mixed wood, another favourite area with hunters. You join the tarmac at 730m, and turn down right. Nearby is the tiny hamlet known as **Badiaccia Montemuro** (706m, 50min from M. S. Michele), after the erstwhile mighty fortified abbey of the Camaldose order. Now it boasts but a diminutive church for the 19 inhabitants, together with a bar-restaurant (light refreshments also available) and private rooms.

The quiet road leads around east-southeast some 2.5km (30min) to the turn-off left for **Parco di Cavriglia,** a camping ground on the corner. A further 5min of asphalt lead to the entrance (where a small access fee is occasionally charged). The 600-hectare park was set up by the Cavriglia Council in 1970 and is a combination of nature park, zoo, picnic area, verging on the bizarre. Apart from food (restaurant only, no shops) and accommodation, and a couple of short trails including one for 'Tombe Etrusche', it offers little to hold the walker's attention. Along past the large parking area and 'Tavola Calda' (self-service type eats), take the track up for the 'Albergo' hostel-cum-hotel. Set on Poggio la Guardia (701m), the incongruous building is hidden away in deep silent wood.

Parco di Cavriglia to Badia Coltibuono – 1h45min (5.5km/3.4 miles)

Starting from the hostel, this stretch of '00' coincides with the Park's itinerary n.3. The wide track, SSE for the most part, follows an old Etruscan–Roman route along a panoramic crest known as Piazza di Siena – not that any paving is visible, or waymarking when it comes to that.

Other evidence of Etruscan presence in the area comes from evidence found at nearby Albola and some tombs.

Beech wood provides light but suitable cover for hunters' hides the minute the Park is left behind. Keep to the higher track (ignore the turn-off left after 20min), and climb through broom through the Pian del Ciliegio (Cherry Plane, 720m). Thick ferns on the edge of a conifer plantation compensate for the lack of cherry trees. A slight descent on the easternmost flank of the central ridge leads through undulating chestnut wood which abruptly gives way to towering pine trees and cool dark walking – and a Sentiero del Chianti signpost at last.

Stick to the main track as it passes to the right of M. Maione. Further ahead is a more varied and dense mixed wood which makes for pleasant shady walking. At a prominent junction with a huge gnarled chestnut tree, a bullet-riddled signpost directs you down left.

Exit to Radda in Chianti (1h20min) The right branch of the track here leads west to join the surfaced road SS 429 for the 7km to Radda in Chianti (accommodation, buses and tourist office).

Not far around the track now are the stately buildings of **Badia di Coltibuono** (628m) in an evocative setting. The Benedictine monastic complex dates back to the 8th century, and had a chequered history. Nowadays it is part of a wine estate. Its fine Romanesque abbey church was built in 1050. Walkers will have to be content with external viewing as the church only opens for mass on Sunday afternoons. The local vintage can, however, be tasted at the nearby restaurant Da Giannetto.

Badia Coltibuono to Monteluco – 2h45min (8.8km/5.5 miles)
Follow the curves of the road down past the shop (only local wine, honey and oil on sale) and cross straight over the road.

Exit: The SS 429 road leads to Radda in Chianti in 8km, whereas the SS 408 means 5km for Gaiole in Chianti, though there is a slightly shorter route via secondary roads that soon head due south off the road.

The curious fortified hamlet of Cancelli

Gaiole offers Siena and Florence bus connections and a tourist ofice, but no accommodation.

Cancelli, a photogenic tower, originally a fortified house is passed, then a small quarry. The eye sweeps over the rolling expanse of the Chianti hills now, with Radda's towers visible west, and the modern spread of the township of Gaiole closer southwest. The dusty track leads past the hill known as M. Grossi recognisable by its ruined tower, and curves into the quiet farming village of **Montegrossi** with its own odd scattered ruin (639m, 30min from Badia di Coltibuono).

The ensuing stretch is long, solitary and particularly delightful. Keep to the main dirt track, then left at the signed junction (5min) which indicates Monteluco amongst other places. The oak wood soon thins and the landscape opens up with masses of wild roses.

Further on signed path n.56 forks off right for the fortified village of Barbischio and Gaiole, a further alternative access/exit.

At the next intersection, marked by a lone oak, turn right and keep on southeast. The abandoned farm Podere La Massa in a marvellous position soon presents itself

(661m, total 1h15min from Badia di Coltibuono). Further around (past turn-off for n.37 left for Mancioni) the track flanks a small vineyard before curving towards yet another Monte Muro, the third encountered so far. Open shadeless terrain is crossed as you wind up to another superb panoramic zone, which takes in the Valdarno at the foot of the vast Pratomagno range, while looking back northwest is the Badia di Coltibuono and Monte San Michele as well.

You coast for a while, keeping to the main track along the crest. A brief descent leads to a fork where you go right (the left branch is n.39) and start another climb towards Monte Calvo. A wider track is joined (referred to as 'Bivio l'Aquila' as Podere Aquila is signed off to the right). This scenic route follows the westernmost flank of Monte Calvo, with the picturesque village of Barbischio below right. The tall conifer forest accompanies you down to another dirt road at a wayside shrine (the village of Starda is 3km left). At the nearby tarmac turn left (in the direction of Nusenna) and a little over 15min will see you at hospitable family-run hotel La Pineta on **Monteluco** (834m). 2h45min total from Badia di Coltibuono.

Apart from the towering pines, the setting is a little disappointing as there are no views and enormous TV transmitting equipment and associated apparatus dominate. The good news is that the restaurant is both highly recommended for its vast range of dishes including game in workman-size servings, and reasonable prices. Picnic supplies are also available – the last before San Felice. Don't bother taking the track behind the hotel up to the actual top of Monteluco, as it's closed off for yet more private TV broadcasting reasons.

Monteluco to Castello di Brolio – 2h (9.7km/6 miles)

From the nearby intersection, take the Siena road (also referred to as the San Gusmè road) southeast downhill. Traffic is usually light so you can enjoy yet another magnificent mixed wood inhabited by fallow deer, as you leave the high ridges and start the long descent to Siena. Not far down is a rough road.•

• **Side trip: San Vincenti-Rosennano circuit** (2h) The turn-off left (ESE) leads to the village of San Vincenti, the start of the recommended circuit waymarked n.57. It runs on quiet country roads via San Vincenti (520m) then loops around to climb back up west via the idyllic farming village of Rosennano (547m, grocery shop) on its panoramic outcrop. Through thinnish wood it's back to the road, briefly downhill of the turn-off for Castello di Brolio as follows. Allow approx. 2h.

After the San Vincenti road, the next turn-off is sign-posted for a peaceful hamlet, Linari (666m).

On the ensuing stretch you are rewarded with a vast sweep of countryside dominated by the clear volcanic outline of Monte Amiata to the south. A series of thickly wooded hills with the rare hamlet is the norm, much wilder than the wine and olive concentrations of the Chianti zone just over the ridge east. As the road curves west then south, the view opens up to the west as well, and the towers of far-off Castellina and Radda are visible WNW. The panorama continues from a ridge featuring Capanelle, a picturesque cluster of houses surrounded by vineyards, and offering the first views to Siena itself southwest. As the road traverses thick wood enlivened by noisy jays and magpies, a signposted track (with no mention of Brolio though) forks off to the right, opposite a dark red hut belonging to the road authority (ANAS). (A little over 1h from Monteluco).

You coast through the wood for a while before passing a house. Here you drop sharp right amidst a damp wood punctuated by the unusual white blooms and edible green-red berries of the so-called strawberry tree. The track ends at a road. Around to the right you soon reach a church and a multitude of minor roads, in full-on wine-growing country now. Unless you want to stop at the shop to stock up on local wines such as the Brolio variety or attempt to catch the elusive Gaiole-Siena bus, take the first sharp left to enter the **Castello di Brolio** estate (529m). Go through the stone pillars which commemorate the roadworks under Grand-Duke Leopold II in the 1800s, and up a cypress-lined driveway. Nearby is the unpretentious, highly recommended Ristorante da Gino.

Walkers can cut the corners of the driveway, then take the paved path that leads up alongside an impressive wall to the castle entrance.•

• Guided visits to **Castello di Brolio** are possible including the ramparts and chapel. The Ricasoli family took over the castle way back in the 12th century, though the Sienese army destroyed it in the 16th century, meaning further reconstruction. The red brick castle you see today was the work last century of Baron Bettino Ricasoli. A pioneer in the wine world of Chianti, he was also involved in reclaiming the Maremma and constructing the railway lines around Siena in the mid 1800s.

Castello di Brolio to Monteaperti – 3h30min (12.4km/7.7 miles)
Note: this stage can be shortened considerably if buses are used on the later sections.

Chianti vineyards surrounding Castello di Brolio

From the castle entrance proceed straight ahead on the dirt road. It starts its descent south alongside grape vines belonging to the castle vineyards and with more views over full-blooded Chianti countryside and hilltop villages. Real picture postcard stuff.

Still on the main track, after curving past a couple of houses, '00' breaks off left through dry oak wood on a rougher path (15min from the castle). Vines and wood studded with juniper shrubs alternate until you eventually join a narrow surfaced road to enter **San Felice** (396m, 1h30min from Castello di Brolio). (A convenient twice-daily bus joins the hamlet with Siena via Castelnuovo Berardenga, except Sundays and holidays.) A good part of this delightful village has now been taken over by an exclusive many-starred hotel complex. There are peaceful ivy-covered buildings and a jewel of a church on the perfect piazza, not to mention a *generi alimentari* grocery shop.

You rejoin the quiet road heading south for **Bossi** (326m) whose well-restored buildings line the road. Just in case it had slipped your mind, roadside boards remind that 'siete nel mondo del gallo nero' (you are in the world of the black rooster), namely the Chianti

59

Classico trademark. Not far down you join another side road (turn right) and shortly an intersection and bus stop-turnaround point (2h30min from Castello di Brolio).

While a road (right) goes via Pianella to Siena, you go left, south. With a bit of luck, though, you'll be able to hop on one of the regular buses going the same way (fewer on Sundays and holidays). This will save you footing the 5km (allow 1h) south via the hamlet of San Piero to the Monteapertaccio turn-off. The landscape is quite frankly surprising. You unexpectedly find yourself on the edge of the pale Siena 'crete' countryside, with rolling fields filled with yellow and ochre clay earth. A stark and beautifully dramatic contrast to the woods and vineyards encountered so far.

Have the bus drop you off downhill from small modern **Monteaperti** village (229m), at the junction for the actual Monteapertaccio hill, opposite a cenotaph and school.

Detour to Monteapertaccio (45min return) A dusty dirt track heads east through the fields aiming for the seemingly insignificant hillock SSE topped with tall evergreen sentinels. Marked by a memorial stone, it was the scene of a tremendous battle in 1260 between the Sienese, whose victory was both unexpected and short-lived, and the Florentines, whose army was superior. Contemporary historians, Dante included, wrote of the nearby watercourse, Torrente Arbia, as flowing red with the blood. A mound tomb of a prominent Etruscan family was also discovered in the vicinity in the 1700s.

Monteaperti to Due Ponti – 1h45min (7.6km/4.7 miles)
Note: this stage can be shortened if local buses are taken. The dirt road due west crosses the infamous Torrente Arbia where herons are sometimes seen, before climbing to the tranquil villas of **Vico d'Arbia** (265m) on their isolated crest. The asphalt unfortunately restarts 5min on, where you continue in the same direction following signs for Siena. The surroundings are characteristic Chianti once again, undulating terrain carpeted with green and

Glorious sunset on the Chianti ridge

lines of cypresses and scattered farms. The towers of Siena are a little closer now.

Some 35min on is the Pieve al Bozzone (206m) junction – another bus line into Siena (except Sundays and holidays).

On foot, keep following the signs for 'Due Ponti' along the ups and downs of this back road. A watercourse is crossed, then the village of Quattrotorri (272m) before the final descent across the railway line and into **Due Ponti** on the main road. You'll need to buy bus tickets at the tobacconist's before picking up a city bus that will take you direct to the centre of **Siena** and the marvellous square known as Il Campo.

Tourist Office Florence
tel.055/23320

Tourist Office Greve in Chianti
tel.055/8546287

Tourist Office Radda in Chianti
tel.0577/738494

Tourist Office Siena
tel.0577/280551

3: Castellina to Radda in Chianti

Walking time:	3h30min + 30min for Montecalvario tomb visit
Distance:	17km/10.6 miles
Map:	on p.64, also Multigraphic 1:25,000 n.42/43 'Monti del Chianti' or Kompass 1:50,000 n.660 'Firenze-Chianti'

Access: Both Castellina in Chianti and Radda in Chianti are fairly well served by the SITA Florence–Siena line, excluding Sundays and holidays. Drivers should take the scenic SS 222 Chiantigiana (Siena–Florence) for Castellina, then the SS 429 for Radda. Each township has ample car parking outside its historic walled nucleus.

The two attractive medieval Chianti League hill towns of Castellina and Radda are joined by this pleasant and varied route. The first actually boasts Etruscan origins and an important ancient road that ran from Volterra to Arezzo is known to have touched on the fortified town, enhancing its commercial importance. In addition to its graceful medieval buildings, Castellina in Chianti has a unique artificial 'hill' on its outskirts, actually an Etruscan tumulus that dates back to 4th century BC and containing four sizeable underground burial chambers. The appellation Montecalvario is due to a shrine which once graced the top, the last station of a medieval Via Crucis. It was not actually until 1507 that the 50m diameter tumulus itself was discovered, to widespread amazement. It is said to have inspired a drawing of a mausoleum attributed to Leonardo da Vinci, and kept in the Louvre. Systematic excavation and study of the Etruscan tomb had to wait until the beginning of the 20th century. The complex is believed to have served an aristocratic family, but does not appear to have been terminated. The whole thing is somewhat rundown and bare nowadays – tomb robbers were at work well before official exploration was carried out. A torch or head-lamp is handy for exploring the interior chambers.

Nowadays picturesque and quiet except when animated by market days, Castellina in Chianti owes its well-being largely to the production of Chianti wine along with a little tourism. There is a small exhibit of local Etruscan finds in the main square.

WALK 3 – CASTELLINA TO RADDA IN CHIANTI

After the compulsory visit to Montecalvario, the itinerary passes through largely uncultivated countryside, with isolated farms set back off the road amidst light woods of oak, cypress and pine. Wild flowers and herbs are everywhere. Apart from a brief stretch of dusty road, it is essentially a delightful wander on undulating tracks and paths. The splendid Romanesque church of San Giusto in Salcio features on the final leg to Radda in Chianti, arguably the most attractive of the Chianti hill towns.

While the itinerary is described as a one-way traverse connecting the two towns (return possible by bus), it can easily be converted into shorter loops. The best alternative idea, though it means some asphalt at the start, is to leave Radda in Chianti heading west along the SS 429 road for Castellina. Soon after La Croce intersection (10min), head off downhill south on the narrow minor road for Ama. Just over 2.5km of wooded curves later, you cross a watercourse and take the dirt track to San Giusto in Salcio. Allow 40min this far. From here follow the main description for the cart track to Radda, meaning approx. 2h for the entire trip.•

THE WALK

For the main part of the walk, traverse the township in a southerly direction then head past the warehouse-like wine cooperative along main road SS 222 in the direction of Siena. Some 10min along, turn left up Via dei Castagni, which has a small chapel on its corner. It soon becomes a dirt road with several houses before entering a light oak wood. As it starts to climb, take the lane on the right (south) at the first curve. After a small vineyard keep right at a fork. A brief climb and you wind down to join a wide unsurfaced road, near the entrance to Villa Casalecchi (20min).

Turn left here (east). There is very little traffic. A series of gentle up and downs proceed through open terrain, almost bare at times. The gaze ranges over wild bushy countryside, flowered in spring with wafts of sweet-scented aromatic herbs in summer. A cypress-lined stretch leads to the turn-off south for **Badiola** (30min from

• **Montecalvario tomb visit** (30min return time) Montecalvario, the enormous Etruscan tumulus-cum-hill stands on the northern edge of **Castellina in Chianti** (578m). The vast smooth rounded shape is visible over the rooftops from the edge of the township, its profile a line of low trees. From the area below the medieval Rocca and church take the street downhill to the junction with the SS 429 and follow the right branch (for Radda) a short way. A faded yellow/black sign for 'Tombe Etrusche' indicates the climb left, where Hotel Colombaie occupies the opposite corner. The entrance gate is always open. An individual entrance corridor or dromos leads to each of the four burial chambers which face the cardinal points. Each has a different layout and composition, and as a rule were constructed using so-called 'false' or step vaulting. Return to Castellina the same way.

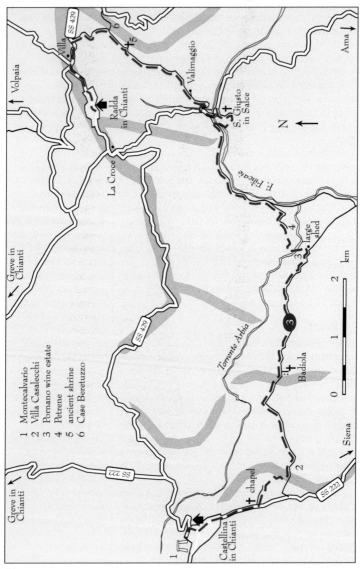

1 Montecalvario
2 Villa Casalecchi
3 Pornano wine estate
4 Petrene
5 ancient shrine
6 Case Beretuzzo

Casalecchi). It's worth the brief detour to the minuscule church and lone house, still inhabited. Back on the main track the panorama is peacefully pretty, and there are continual sweeping outlooks that take in traditional houses scattered through the woods, and the occasional clearing for olive or grape cultivation. The road, rougher now, starts a long winding descent and passes the access track for the **Pornano** wine estate, visible below. This inner valley is both very still and particularly dry. Keep on down through the delicate broom to the large shed at the intersection (368m, 1h30min from Castellina). Here the dirt road for Radda bears right (southeast) but walkers can cut the corner.

Go down left (north) ignoring turn-offs for properties, to cross the concrete bridge. Take the next turn-off right (while the track you've left continues to Poci). It climbs out through the fields and vines belonging to the isolated house of Petrene (396m) then drops down the narrow access track to join the dirt road heading north once more. The following stretch can be dusty as it serves local farm vehicles. However it runs alongside the Fosso delle Filicaie stream and there is welcome shade in the form of willows. In a little over 2km the track curves east below the village of San Giusto in Salcio.

Either continue along the road, turning right at the nearby junction for San Giusto, otherwise you can leave the road near a power pylon and cut across the stream to a steepish path up alongside vines. **San Giusto in Salcio** (419m, 2h20min total) is a delightful shady spot for a rest and refurbishing drinking water, as well as worthy of an exploratory wander. The 11th-century church occupies the site of an ancient Etruscan temple. Radda is now visible on its vantage hill to the north, with the start of an urban sprawl on a minor scale on its surrounding slopes.

Take the track down north to join the tarmac briefly, keeping left. Once over the bridge, keep an eye out for the first lane off right, signposted for the Valimaggio wine estate. The track climbs quickly, and you keep left at the estate driveway, circling below the main homestead, in a northeasterly direction. A superb panoramic ridge is soon gained, and several curious constructions such as towers,

Tourist Office Radda in Chianti
tel.0577/738494

Accommodation

Radda in Chianti:
Hotel/restaurant
Il Girarrosto
tel.0577/738010

Pensione Pistolesi
tel.0577/738556

La Bottega di
Giovannino
tel.0577/738056

Castellina in Chianti:
Il Colombaio
tel.0577/740444 (3-star)

a castle and a villa present themselves on distant wooded slopes. This is by far the quietest part of the itinerary, and there is a riot of wild flowers and masses of herbs. Following a slight ascent, a curious ancient wayside shrine is found at a minor junction – keep straight on. Three cypresses are the backdrop for a round stone base topped by a cross.

A little further on, the track passes the turn-off for a set of houses (Case Beretuzzo, 500m) and, bearing left, begins its descent through thicker wood. Ignore the directions left for Canvalle Agriturismo and keep on downwards. A picturesque tower-cum-house is passed, then the bottom of the valley reached. Straight up ahead you emerge on the tarmac road next to Villa Miranda. The township of **Radda in Chianti** is but 1km uphill now – follow the road signs. The final climb means lovely views ranging over to Volpaia (north) as well as towards Monte San Michele in the far background. Total 3h30min from Castellina in Chianti.

The tiny historic town centre, once an impressive stronghold of the Chianti League (it acted as the chief seat in 1415), is both fascinating and quiet, and after a well-earned rest deserves a strolling visit for the 'cammi-namento medievale' (medieval walkway) and square with its Palazzo Comunale whose facade is set with ceramic shields.

You can catch the bus back to the starting point or enjoy a peaceful overnight stay here.

4: Volpaia

Walking time:	3h
Distance:	11.8km/7.4 miles
Map:	on p.68, also Multigraphic 1:25,000 n.42/43 'Monti del Chianti' or Kompass 1:50,000 n.660 'Firenze-Chianti'

Access: Radda in Chianti can be reached by SITA bus (Florence–Siena line) all days except Sundays and holidays.
Drivers can take the panoramic SS 222 for Castellina in Chianti then turn east on the SS 429 for Radda in Chianti. There is ample parking outside the town walls.

Volpaia is one of those delightful medieval villages in the Chianti area that seem oblivious to the hectic rhythms of the twentieth century. It can be reached in a straightforward rewarding day's stroll from the hill town of Radda, which in itself deserves a careful visit. The itinerary follows country lanes and paths and only a short section of asphalt, with a series of gradual ups and downs (totalling some 400m in both ascent and descent). There are rolling expanses of fields and vineyards of course (wine tastings possible at many estates), but surprisingly also many tracts of woods which shelter fallow deer and foxes – the name Volpaia is actually a reference to foxes. In addition to the well-preserved historic buildings of Volpaia, the walk takes in the Romanesque church of Santa Maria Novella. An interesting longer circuit is easily made by continuing on the dirt road past Santa Maria Novella then looping back down to Volpaia, adding at least 1h45min–2h to the total walking time.

THE WALK

Leave **Radda in Chianti** (533m) west by way of the road for Castellina in Chianti. Ten minutes downhill at La Croce inter-section take the minor road furthest right. Thence you'll need the first turn-off to the right (signpost for Sass-osi). A track proceeds alongside a couple of houses and straight through past a private swimming pool to a wire fence on the edge of wood. An over-grown path follows the fence in descent and emerges onto tarmac (391m, 30min from Radda). Take the road signposted for

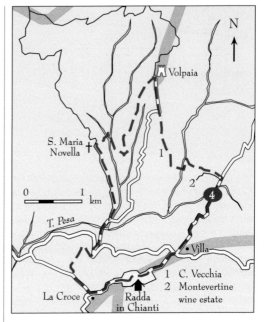

One of the first note-worthy buildings in **Volpaia** is the curiously-named Commenda di Sant'Eufrasino, actually a deconsecrated church, used for the occasional exhibition these days. Narrow alleys, along with other simple stone buildings characterise this unspoilt village, which occupies an excellent panoramic position. The one bar-cum-food store also serves delicious home-style Tuscan lunches in a small square in the shade of the 13th-century donjon, a reminder of the long military history.

1 C. Vecchia
2 Montevertine
wine estate

Volpaia, across Torrente Pesa, then leave it to keep north on the dirt road for Santa Maria Novella. About 20min up this shady way is the hamlet and graceful 12th-century church of **Santa Maria Novella** (478m) set off the road amongst olive trees and worthy of closer inspection.

Back on the road, just before the cemetery a rough track heads off right (east) down into wood. An old stone bridge crosses the first of two small watercourses. The path climbs SSE, brightened by tiny delicate cyclamen flowers in the undergrowth. Ignore turn-offs. A sharp veer north leads to a wider vehicle track (CAI signpost for n.52, 1h15min total).

This proceeds north through vineyards and past several houses undergoing restoration. The final stretch commences with a shrine then a cypress-lined avenue, Viale del Nonno (Grandfather's Avenue) – a grandiose approach to the village of **Volpaia** (617m, 1h40min total).

The delightful medieval village of Volpaia

Suitably refreshed, take the narrow scenic road downhill south out of the village. Some 500m as it curves right (553m), take the furthest right of the two lanes that present themselves. This is private property so it is essential walkers do not stray off the path. Bordered by low cypresses, it drops quickly and crosses straight over a wider track between two small houses, still heading south. The going is a little rougher and steeper now. Shortly below a lovely restored house on the edge of a wood (Casa Vecchia, 446m), leave the newly surfaced track for the old cart track (left) that heads down through the wood. It passes between olives and vines to reach a group of houses, where you turn left (east) to the bottom of the valley. The terrain is open here, and once over the watercourse (approx. 30min from Volpaia) a modest poplar plantation takes over. After an abrupt left (not shown on the Multigraphic map), the track winds right and climbs into wood once more. You pass the driveway for the **Fattoria di Montevertine** wine estate (regular wine tastings), then continue east to join the tarmac (376m), where you turn right.

The towers of Radda can now be seen on the hill southwest, and as the road climbs the ridge there are lovely views of the countryside. This final stretch involves some 3km of tarmac, a climb of 200m, and 40min in all. It transits via the Villa intersection, before the last climb to **Radda in Chianti** once more (1h20min total from Volpaia).

Tourist Office Radda in Chianti
tel.0577/738494

Accommodation
see Walk 3

5: Environs of San Gimignano

Access: Lying on the southwestern edge of the Val d'Elsa that runs from Empoli to Siena, San Gimignano is most easily reached from Poggibonsi, only 11km away. The walled town centre and its narrow streets are closed to non-essential traffic, but there are ample car parks outside. TRA-IN buses provide regular daily connections with Poggibonsi and its railway station for ongoing services to Siena and Florence.

Walking time:	5h45min – 4h15min with a car
Distance:	24.3km/15.2 miles – 16.4km/10.2 miles with a car
Map:	on p.72, also Multigraphic 1:25,000 San Gimignano, Volterra or Litografia Artistica Cartografica 1:25,000 Volterra, San Gimignano, Casole d'Elsa

San Gimignano 'of the fine towers', one of Tuscany's perfectly preserved and most visited medieval hill towns, traces its ancestry back to late Etruscan times. A number of necropolises have been explored in the vicinity, including the Poggio del Comune hill, and the odd find is conserved in the town's museums. But who needs an excuse for a wander through the lush countryside that nourishes the vines that produce Vernaccia, the renowned local dry white wine? Its earlier, presumably fuller-bodied version, reputedly prompted Michelangelo to say that it 'kisses, licks, bites, thrusts and stings'.

San Gimignano owes its unusual name to a 4th-century bishop from far-off Modena who was summoned, in one legendary account, to drive away the barbarians and save the city. Another story relates that an altar boy from Colle di Val d'Elsa had his eye on the venerated man's precious ring, and managed to filch it during his funeral. Much to his chagrin, however, the whole finger came off as well and he fled in a blind panic, to halt later in a church. The doors mysteriously locked fast and he was trapped inside until the holy relic was lain to rest. It has been suitably preserved in the frescoed interior of the Romanesque cathedral of San Gimignano ever since.

A quick word is in order on the town's history and unique trademark array of towers, recognisable from a great distance. Constructed by patrician families for storage purposes and even the odd prison, they were also symbols of power and prestige. A total of 72 stood out against the skyline back in the 13th century, and a good 15 have survived. The only tower open to the public, Torre Grossa in the Palazzo del Popolo, begs to be climbed for its marvellous panoramas over the countryside. The passage of the Via Francigena, a medieval pilgrim route, brought prosperity to the town before the terrible scourge of the Black Death which swept through on several occasions. Poverty and consequent lack of development could be the reason why the town and its towers have retained their essential medieval aspect.

The fields and woods are populated by a host of wild animals such as pheasants, shy porcupines and fallow deer, as well as a plethora of wild boar, too shy to show themselves. The latter are more easily seen in the streets of San Gimignano posing staidly alongside the sausages and hams they contribute to.

Nothing useful in the way of shops or refreshment points is encountered along the way, so before setting out a visit to the town's bakeries is in order. Delicious heavy-duty spicy biscuits such as Cavalucci and Ricciarelli, together with the omnipresent Panforte, crammed with dried and candied fruit, honey and nuts make eminently suitable walking fare.

Another 'must' in town is the 1h stroll 'Passeggiata delle Mura' that circumnavigates San Gimignano by way of the outer walls.

THE WALK

At the southern end of **San Gimignano** (324m), cross Piazzale Martiri di Montemaggio, which doubles as the bus terminal. Between the Carabinieri and a parking station. a narrow road drops west, soon becoming a good dirt track lined by vines and olive trees, offering some interesting angles back to the town and towers. Ahead is the ample, low-lying, smoothly rounded spread of Poggio del Comune.

At a bench in the shade of two noteworthy cypresses, turn left (southwest) through fields of sunflowers and across a malodorous stream, Botro dele Volte. You then need the right fork at the nearby farm for the climb to

A rewarding day can be spent on this varied walk through the picture-post-card cultivated countryside, rolling hills and woodland rich in Mediterranean species cloaking Poggio del Comune. Included is a visit to Castelvecchio, an atmospheric crumbling medieval castle and settlement. The complete circuit is rather lengthy but follows easy farm tracks waymarked with red and white paint stripes for the most part. In all some 500m in ascent and descent are covered.

Those with a car can drive to San Donato and cut the walk time to 4h15min and the height gain/loss to 300m. Moreover a shorter variant is possible by limiting the walk to Castelvecchio and returning the same way – allow 3h30min return from San Gimignano, or 2h from San Donato.

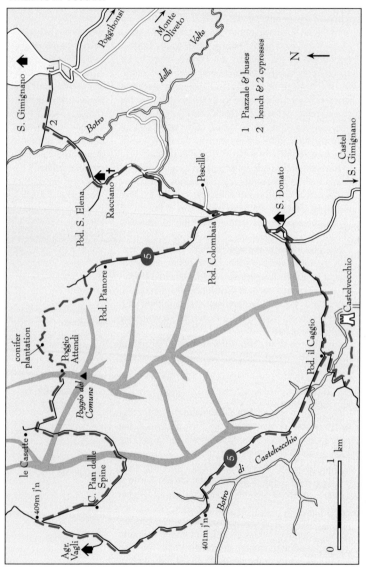

S. Gimignano

Poggibonsi

Monte Oliveto

Volte

delle

Botro

2

1 Piazzale & buses
2 bench & 2 cypresses

N

Pescille

Pod. S. Elena

Racciano

S. Donato

Castel S. Gimignano

Pod. Colombaia

5

Pod. Pianore

Castelvecchio

conifer plantation

Poggio Attendi

Pod. il Caggio

Poggio del Comune

le Casette

C. Pian delle Spine

409m j'n

5

Castelvecchio

di

Botro

401m j'n

1 km

Agr. Vagli

0

Podere S. Elena and a gravel lane left along a ridge with great views back onto San Gimignano, its landmark towers looking for all the world like fully-fledged skyscrapers. All around the orderly countryside spreads out in a patchwork of colours. Keep left for the tiny hamlet of **Racciano** (304m, 30min), complete with miniscule chapel and restaurant. The way soon drops past prestigious vineyards to join a broader surfaced road (turn right) for a climb through broom and holm oak woods. Shortly after the turn-off for Pescille is a track off to the right adjacent a farm, Podere Colombaia, where the return route emerges. Not far afterwards is the detour for the charming sleepy hamlet of **San Donato** (357m, 1h).

Continue through to the main road, turn right then first left (southwest) for a broad muddy bulldozed lane through light wood with pockets of juniper and rock roses, not to mention the curious strawberry trees. As it bears west, you see the surviving towers of Castelvecchio high above a deep valley. Some 20min in from the road is Podere il Caggio, set in a clearing carved out of the wild wood. Take the plunging track left down to ford Botro di Castelvecchio then up the other side. Go left at the junction through cyclamens and tree heather for the marvellously desolate site of **Castelvecchio** (382m, 1h45min). A massive crumbling tower is followed by a surprising string of ruined stone houses and even a faltering Romanesque church with a covered underground cistern. The castle and settlement date back to at least 12th century, but only 7 families remained in 1458, and no subsequent history was recorded.

Return to Podere il Caggio and this time take the left fork (northwest) through felled woodland and into the realms of the Riserva Naturale Regionale di Castelvecchio, skirting the base of Poggio del Comune. Signs of the hordes of wild boar are everywhere – hoof-prints criss-crossing the muddy lane on excursions. There is the odd clearing, then soon after crossing the Botro di Castelvecchio once more, a T-junction is reached with a broader track (401m, 2h45min) – go right beneath the towering army of maritime pines. Vast fields of sunflowers are passed and the views open up towards low-set Poggio del Comune.

The fine towers of San Gimignano looking for all the world like skyscrapers

Tourist Office San Gimignano
tel.0577/940008

Accommodation
Le Vecchie Mura
tel.0577/940270

Private rooms c/o Celati
tel.0577/940185

Foresteria Monastero di San Girolamo
tel.0577/940573

Fattoria San Donato
tel.0577/941616

Not long after Agriturismo Vagli the marked route branches right (409m, 3h10min) on a rough narrow track climbing steadily SSE past stone houses (C. Pian della Spina). Some 20min up as it starts to level out, keep your eyes skinned for an unobtrusive branch left through rich red earth. Further along in the wood at a concrete pylon, keep right as per waymarking (close to Le Casette on the map). The ensuing crossroad means a left turn and short climb to **Poggio Attendi** and its residence (584m, 4h), detoured as per arrows. On the other side, go straight down a lane (no waymarking on this tract), which quickly peters out and narrows heading northeast at first following an old mossy stone wall. A small conifer plantation is traversed, then a clear hunters' path drops steadily east through damp wood hung with ivy. About half an hour from Poggio Attendi you will hopefully emerge on a broad track where you go right. Red/white paint stripes reappear and point you left down a path to an abandoned property, Podere Pianore (434m), well below Poggio del Comune now. From here on a vehicle track leads south through dense wood. The final leg features rock slabs pitted with fossils, and views of San Gimigano once more. A total of 5h wonderful walking and you emerge on the road at Podere Colombaia. From here it's 45min back to **San Gimignano** as per the first stage of the walk, otherwise right for San Donato.

6: Volterra City Route

Walking time:	1h30min + extra time for visits
Distance:	5km/3.2 miles
Map:	on p.77 + detailed city map from the tourist office

There's something slightly forbidding about Volterra, its bleak stone medieval centre almost cowering in the shadow of a menacing Medicean fortress. Amidst a harsh and unfertile landscape, the geographical isolation it chose on a lofty capacious rock platform crumbling at the edges and gradually surrendering its past to eroded gullies, sets it apart from archetypal Tuscany, and obliges would-be visitors to effect considerable detours off the classical Tuscan trail. But there's more to Volterra than meets the eye, an Etruscan heart beneath the cold exterior. Perhaps to compensate for its exposed position at 540m above sea level, buffeted and infiltrated by icy winds, this erstwhile Etruscan city affords the trickle of visitors a warm welcome, attentive hospitality and a wealth of experiences from all stages of its past.

Volterra in fact claims a history that goes back at least 3000 years. In Etruscan times it was Velathri, one of the 12 great cities of the confederation, with a domain that took in a vast area stretching both inland as well as coastwards. Evidence of settlement from early 9th century BC has been unearthed on the city outskirts in the shape of tombs and cinerary urns, while the 6th century left the ruins of its central acropolis. 4th–2nd century BC turned out to be the most prosperous Etruscan period for Volterra. In addition to minting its own coins, it produced a characteristic type of ceramic, firstly with red figures and later varnished black ones, which was exported throughout Etruria and as far afield as Corsica and Liguria. A prosperous trading centre, Volterra owed much to the proximity of rich mineral deposits, primarily copper and alabaster. As a visit to the museum will tell,

Access: Volterra is reachable by way of the scenic winding SS 68 from Colle di Val d'Elsa. Those arriving from Cecina on the coast will need the lower stretch of the SS 68 as it heads east inland across the plain to Saline before climbing the final 9km to the town. From the north there is also the SS 439 from Pontedera (39km). Note: only residents are allowed car access to the city centre; everyone else must use the official parking areas outside the central walled zone.

The TRA-IN bus company has plenty of runs from Colle di Val d'Elsa (connections with Poggibonsi railway station as well as the township of San Gimignano), in addition to the line southwest for the railhead of Saline, hence train connections for Cecina on the busy Livorno–Rome line. There are also direct coaches from both Florence and Pisa.

alabaster or 'Volterra marble', alias a variety of gypsum, an evaporite mineral found in clays and limestone, has long lent its marvellously luminous properties and range of soft coloured hues to Etruscan urns and statues. The tradition is continued by imaginative modern-day masters who craft the fragile translucent material into all manner of accessories for furnishing.

As regards the walk, it commences as an easy stroll within the present town limits taking in the acropolis, two original Etruscan portals and the museum. Once outside the innermost circle of medieval walls, the route proceeds along a quiet country road downhill to some tombs, and this stretch can be covered by car if desired.

THE WALK

Starting at the bus terminal and main entrance to Volterra, **Piazza Martiri della Libertà**, walk in towards the Albergo Nazionale, where D.H. Lawrence stayed in the 1920s while working on his fascinating *Etruscan Places*. Turn left and soon left again for Via Porta dell'Arco. At the bottom of this steep cobbled road stands the 4th century BC Etruscan gateway, **Porta all'Arco** (10min). Its massive masonry is intact on the lower layer, but erosion has disfigured the carved heads it bears of the city's divinities. 'Strange, dark old Etruscan heads of the city gate, even now they are featureless they still have a peculiar, out-reaching life of their own,' (D.H. Lawrence). The inner part of the gateway has grooves for a portcullis, quoted by Roman sources as an ancient invention.

Return uphill and back past the Albergo Nazionale, but continue straight ahead for the signposted **Parco Archeologico**. You'll find yourself in a pleasant public park, which is closed off at the easternmost end by the huge Medicean fortress, now a high security prison. Uphill on the highest point, the site of the 6th century BC acropolis, it is possible to view free of charge the meagre ruins of two Etruscan temples together with remains of Roman baths (25min total this far).

Leave the park by the far left (easternmost) exit, and take the flight of steps through to Via Don Minzoni. The **Museo Etrusco Guarnacci** is briefly right, at n.15. It is

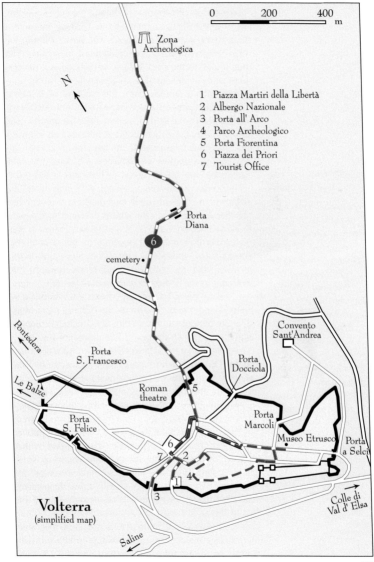

1 Piazza Martiri della Libertà
2 Albergo Nazionale
3 Porta all' Arco
4 Parco Archeologico
5 Porta Fiorentina
6 Piazza dei Priori
7 Tourist Office

Zona Archeologica

N

Porta Diana

6

cemetery

Pontedera

Porta S. Francesco

Le Balze

Roman theatre

Porta S. Felice

Convento Sant'Andrea

Porta Docciola

5

Porta Marcoli

Museo Etrusco

Porta a Selci

7 6 2

4

1

3

Volterra
(simplified map)

Saline

Colle di Val d' Elsa

77

dedicated wholly to local finds, and the core collection itself is historical, commenced in 1731 by Monsignor Guarnacci, a prelate of Volterra who presented it to the city. The overall effect is overwhelming to say the least, due in part to the sheer volume of material (a good 600 urns for example) but also, unfortunately, to the old-fashioned criteria employed for the majority of displays: objects are grouped according to type and decorative motifs, not a great help for visitors. After the ground floor which houses the earliest (3000–2000BC) burials followed by Villanovan examples in terracotta, come the astounding numbers of alabaster and tufa urns and sarcophagi intricately carved with scenes in bas relief ranging from processions, sacrifices, wild boar hunts and scenes from classical Greek mythology, to everyday life together with an inordinate number of scenes with departures in covered wagons. A sculptured image of the occupants in a reclining position, as per a banquet, adorns many, with facial expressions stern and disapproving, and the overall effect tends towards the grotesque as the bodies are stunted to fit the lid.

Pride of place on the upper floors goes to the celebrated slender nude known as the 'Ombra della Sera' (Shadow of the Evening), an elongated statue in bronze, which looks for all the world like a modern sculpture. Giacometti in fact is said to have drawn his inspiration from it. Once out of the museum, turn right along Via Don Minzoni-Via Gramsci, and right again at Via Guarnacci. Through a medieval gateway, Porta Fiorentina, the walk quits the innermost medieval area. Left is a huge Roman theatre, worth a stop.

Straight ahead, take Via di Porta Diana and short cut the wide curve. You pass the present-day cemetery which preceeds the imposing remains of another extant Etruscan entrance, **Porta Diana**. While the opening seems narrow for modern standards, it was clearly a double gateway flanked by the unmistakable original masonry, despite the loss of the arch, long gone. It stands at a considerable distance below the medieval portals and points clearly to the impressive size of the city in Etruscan times. In 4th century BC in fact the walls were extended for a total

Of the carved scenes Lawrence mused:

'It would be very interesting to know if there were a definite connection between the scene on the ash-chest and the dead whose ashes it contained. When the fish-tailed sea-god entangles a man to bear him off, does it mean death by drowning at sea? And when a man is caught in the writhing serpent-legs of the Medusa, or of the winged snake-power, does it mean a fall to earth... And the soul carried off by a winged centaur; is it a man dead of some passion that carried him away?'

length of 7km to enclose some 116 hectares, compared to the mere fraction – 26 hectares – occupied in medieval and modern times.

A short way downhill into luxuriant countryside, the view spaces left (west) to the far end of Volterra's crumbling plateau, with the stately isolated basilica of San Giusto presiding over remnants of Etruscan walls. Long stretches, along with countless tombs, not to mention churches, have been devoured by the ravines that resulted from repeated land collapses at the Balze cliffs.

The roadside banks are soon pitted with entrances to manmade underground caverns, namely tombs. Exploration of Volterra's underground riches was in full swing as early as the 1720s. The usual practice was to excavate a tomb, empty it of the contents (which ended up in private collections as well as the odd state museum), and fill in the hole so as not to waste agricultural land. Surrounding properties are dotted with the vestiges of a wide range of Etruscan tombs, but tall fences discourage visitors. One unique and curious exception was the famous Tomba Inghirami from the city's eastern flanks – complete with its 53 urns in alabaster, it was removed stone by stone and faithfully reconstructed in the garden of Florence's Archaeological Museum.

Of the thousands of tombs discovered in the immense necropolis on these slopes, just two can be visited today in the (signposted) **Zona Archeologica** (some 25min from the museum). They date back to the relatively late period, namely 3rd–1st century BC, but make for an interesting visit and are fitted with permanent lighting. The access paths are strewn with the white bell blooms of the strawberry tree, and thread their protected way through a fenced-off olive grove. Entrance is via flights of steep rock-hewn steps, then a slab door, all excavated in the yellowish conchiferous (shell-bearing) sandstone. The tomb closest to the road is an unusual round underground chamber ringed with benches where the sarcophagi once rested. Allow a further 30min back the same way to the city centre, without neglecting a look at the main square, **Piazza dei Priori**, studded with medieval edifices.

Tourist Office Volterra
tel.0588/86150

Accommodation
Convento Sant'Andrea
tel.0588/86028 (both single and double cells-cum-bedrooms available)

Hotel Etruria
tel.0588/87377 (3-star)

Hotel Nazionale
tel.0588/86284 (3-star)

7: Saline di Volterra, an Alternative Approach to the City

Access: see Walk 6 for access to Volterra. Saline, where the walk starts, can be reached by car from Volterra by following the SS 68 southwest. Alternatively from Cecina on the coast take the SS 68 eastward. By public transport from Volterra take the local bus for the short ride down to Saline. Otherwise from Cecina on the main Livorno–Rome rail line, several trains a day (or the odd substitute bus) still run as far as Saline.

Walking time:	2h15min
Distance:	10km/6.2 miles
Map:	on p.82, also Multigraphic 1:25,000 San Gimignano, Volterra or Litografia Artistica Cartografica 1: 25,000 Volterra, San Gimignano, Casole d'Elsa

'The small, forlorn little train comes to a stop at the Saline de Volterra, the famous old salt works now belonging to the State, where brine is pumped out of deep wells. What passengers remain in the train are transferred to one old little coach across the platform, and at length this coach starts to creep like a beetle up the slope, up a cog-and-ratchet line, shoved by a small engine behind. Up the steep but round slope among the vineyards and olives you pass almost at walking-pace, and there is not a flower to be seen, only the beans make a whiff of perfume now and then, on the chill air, as you rise and rise, above the valley below, coming level with the high hills to the south, and the bluff of rock with its two or three towers, ahead.

After a certain amount of backing and changing, the fragment of a train eases up at a bit of a cold wayside station, and is finished. The world lies below.'

The cog train that transported D.H. Lawrence to Volterra in 1927 is, alas, no more. High running costs combined with competition from buses led to its dismantling in 1958. It had been in service since 1912 carrying alabaster, timber and coal in addition to passengers. While the landscape is not exactly alpine, locomotives and mechanisms made in Switzerland were employed for the 9km line from Saline to Volterra, that climbed some 450m. Before that the journey from the railhead at Saline meant a good two hours by mail-coach up the endlessly winding road. Nowadays the rails have been removed leaving a clear and easy track for walkers. A novel way to reach marvellous Volterra.

So, when you've had your fill of Etruscan sarcophagi in the museum (as per Walk 6) and alabaster in the showrooms and feel like a peaceful stroll in the fresh air, head down to Saline. The stark surroundings are reminiscent of the 'crete' clay areas south of Siena and, though not a patch on classical Tuscan scenery, have strong historical appeal, especially for rail enthusiasts.

Cool times of the year are best, namely autumn and winter, as it can get hot here and there is hardly any shade along the way. There are several shops and restaurants at Saline, as indeed at Volterra, but nothing in between. The walk is described in ascent (while equally feasible in the opposite direction), and involves a climb of 480m, guaranteed smooth and gradual by the original railway gradient.

As far as the Saline or salt flats go, these are essentially vast inland lagoons isolated from the sea. Processing operations have been going on since the 18th century, and nowadays produce over half of Italy's salt.

THE WALK

From the actual railway station at **Saline** (72m) where the bus drops off passengers, go back across the level crossing and turn right along the main road (north). Not far on, past the houses as the road starts climbing, turn down right on Via Pia (10min – should the sign be missing, it's to the right of Via Fucini). It soon becomes a dirt track through the fields, and reaches the old railway track where you go left. It is easily recognisable by the allotments, kennels, chicken coops and miscellaneous sheds lining it, in combination with shrubs and trees. There are views up to faraway Volterra. On the nearby left slope there is the first of the *biancane*, low rounded eroded clay formations typical in this area. A bluish paper-thin outer layer of salt forms as their surface water evaporates. Rather a primitive landscape somehow. In contrast, on the bottom of the shallow valley (or *botro*) the train followed, the track is encased in thickets of

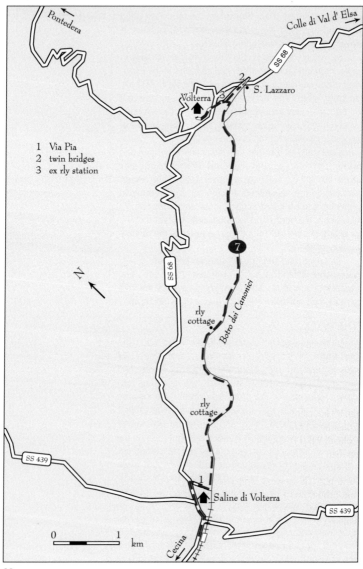

1 Via Pia
2 twin bridges
3 ex rly station

hawthorn and acacia, with wild roses, common toadflax and yellow broom.

Moving on past the first of a series of disused railway cottages, you are surrounded by the strangest, incredibly white hues on the furrowed undulating hills. The landscape is stark with limited colours, though not especially silent due to the squawking magpies that flash overhead trailing showy tails.

On this initial stretch the train's maximum speed was 40km/h, whereas on the part following the second cottage (50min) the rack-and-pinion was engaged and the train slowed to 15km/h at the most. Traces remain of the middle rail where the rack was fitted. The 10% gradient is a little stiff for walking, and will in all likelihood make you puff. The track passes a house then olives and vineyards. It is built up in parts, with several bridges across farm roads. Keep straight ahead even where farm tracks branch off.

As you come below the houses of **San Lazzaro** and the imposing fortress-prison of Volterra, the track suddenly drops down right – leave it for the narrow path which cuts across the hillside left. At this point (1h45min), known as Fonte Pipoli, the flank has crumbled, and the original track has disappeared. You proceed between tall rushes, then follow the path that climbs up to the left alongside a vegetable garden enclosure. The original track is rather too overgrown with brambles and the like to make for an easy passage. The path quickly emerges on the upper level close to the original station building, but it's imperative you go on right to see the twin bridges. Constructed at an oblique angle high over the road for Colle di Val d'Elsa, they enabled the locomotive to back up then haul the carriages into the station.

From the station building (ironically now used by the local bus company!), dominated by the Medici fortress, cut through to Viale della Stazione and up left straight through the intersection for the tree-lined approach to **Volterra** itself (555m).

Tourist Office Volterra
tel.0588/86150

Accommodation
Volterra: see Walk 6

Saline di Volterra: Hotel Africa
tel.0588/44193 (3-star)

8: *The Murlo Circuit*

Walking time:	4h
Distance:	13.7km/8.6 miles
Map:	on p.87, also Kompass 1:50,000 n.661 'Siena-Chianti-Colline Senesi' (partially)

The walk itself entails an overall 150m of both problem-free ascent and descent, and is essentially a long circuit on paths and cart tracks. It takes in Poggio Civitate and the panoramic crest south to the hamlet of La Befa. On its return northwards it makes use of the old railway line constructed in 1877 to transport coal (lignite) from the mine below Murlo right through both wars, until its closure in 1948. The actual rails and sleepers have been removed, leaving an excellent traffic-free walking route with the exception of a couple of narrow passages where the original track has crumbled away.

The tiny charming castle-cum-village of Murlo survives in a world of its own in an unusual corner of Tuscany, well off the beaten track. It sits isolated on a 300m ridge that neatly divides the typical pale clay 'crete' landscape to the northeast, from wild hills that extend southwest into the Maremma. The latter mean well-stocked woods which shelter an astounding range of edible mushrooms not to mention the ubiquitous wild boar, pheasants, fallow and roe deer, much to the delight of local hunters. The foundation of Murlo itself dates back to the 11th century, however American-led excavations on nearby hills as from the 1960s have unearthed some exceptional discoveries, proof of a settlement back in Etruscan times spread over 3600sq m. Dated at 7th–6th century BC, it encompassed a richly-decorated princely palace 60m in length and complete with a pediment decorated with terracotta statues such as sphinxes. The most curious of these were the trademark 'cowboys', bearded figures wearing huge broad-rimmed hats reminiscent of a sombrero. In spite of a fire that ravaged the buildings in late 6th century BC, the town was rebuilt and expanded. All the material used and objects discovered were produced locally, even though Murlo was linked by road at the time with Castellina in Chianti in the north and Roselle southwest. Proof of this was supplied by the 'rubbish dump' which yielded a plethora of broken ceramics, bone and ivory items. The high level of craft work is exemplified in exquisite and intricate granular gold jewellery and delicate earthenware bowls, their elegant handles depicting slender human figures. The site also yielded a necropolis, while several modest tombs came to light in the vicinity of nearby Vescovado.

As the actual excavation site on Poggio Civitate has been all but filled in to discourage visitors and vandals, a visit to the well-laid out museum at Murlo is compulsory. It's worth it for the building itself, once the Bishop's Palace, a solid square-based tower-like structure with inward tapered walls, now carefully renovated. The palatial Etruscan structure has been partially reconstructed on the top floor and includes the original roof tiles. A quick glance out of the panoramic windows will suffice to confirm that nothing much has changed in this sector over 3000 years, as the surrounding houses are covered with exactly the same materials. As Murlo was long isolated, experts believe that a great deal of Etruscan DNA may linger on in the veins of the local population. Ongoing studies by Turin University are comparing DNA from the blood samples of 50 local families with that taken from Etruscan skeletons. The inhabitants seem pretty nonplussed by all the fuss.

As far as practical aspects go, Vescovado means food shops, a modern hotel, restaurant and buses, but nothing else of great interest. Murlo on the other hand offers two cosy if pricey B&Bs and a highly recommended family-run eating place (bookings suggested), which also does snacks, handy as there are no food shops here. The quiet hamlet of La Befa also has accommodation and food, and can be used as an alternative starting point.

THE WALK

Below the walls of **Murlo** (317m), start from the car park shaded by two magnificent stately umbrella pines. Take the surfaced road past the turn-off for the Miniera, then turn right at the next intersection in the direction of Buonconvento. Some 1km along, after a wide curve to the right, turn right up a dirt track (past a sign forbidding entry to the non-authorised). Amidst olives, broom and Mediterranean scrub, a little way along is a restored farm building (Il Casino, 317m). After the buildings fork left up a narrow path which soon bears left at an abandoned quarry, and you climb through woodland towards a ridge.

Access: Murlo lies 2km south of Vescovado, reachable by minor but good roads from the Val d'Arbia and the SS 2 (Cassia) running south from Siena. There are signed turn-offs at Monteroni d'Arbia and in the vicinity of Lucignano d'Arbia. From the west, a scenic route for Vescovado branches east off the SS 223 (Siena-Grosseto) via Casciano. Furthermore, a smaller road links Buonconvento in the southeast with Murlo and Vescovado. The unsurfaced road for La Befa branches off this latter route at Bibbiano. Public transport is decent: several daily TRA-IN buses run from Siena via Monteroni d'Arbia (on the Siena–Grosseto railway) to Vescovado, and a council minibus covers the final 2km to Murlo. As a rule, the railway station of La Befa (usually referred to as the 'Stazione per Murlo' despite the distance) is served by the odd slow train each day (Monday–Saturday only) on the Siena–Grosseto line. ➤

➤ On Sundays (May–Nov) it is served by old trains thanks to the volunteer-run Treno Natura program.

(The area to the right/southwest is Poggio Aguzzo, where a sizeable necropolis was found.) Take care to proceed essentially SSE here as paths are faint and unmarked. Poggio Civitate is traversed, though the only signs of any excavation here are filled-in ditches – everything has been transferred to the museum for safekeeping and study. Pity, really. A roughish rock-based track eventually descends to a T-junction (45min) and a good dirt road. (Close-by to the left is a shrine to **San Biagio**, a useful reference point.)

As per waymarking for 'Comune di Murlo itinerario n.4', you head right downhill (southwest) in the vicinity of abandoned terracing. A ruined house is passed and the terrain becomes much drier and features juniper shrubs. A slight rise takes you past Podere Montorgialino with beautiful views SSE to the extinct volcano Monte Amiata preceded by the medieval spread of Montalcino. Nearby at an elegant lone pine, Murlo comes into sight NNW amid scrubby woods. Soon in descent past an old quarry (ignore turn-offs), the track is shaded in pretty woodland and curves south to round Poggio Giorgio. A stone wall and olive plantation precede a junction where you turn right. Once past a small farm (Podere Quato, 290m) the lane levels out. The wood is thicker and more varied now and includes holm and cork oak, colourful rock roses, broom, lentisc, juniper, heather, strawberry tree as well as cyclamens, You pass close to ruins of a 13th-century fortress then the church of **Montepertuso** (273m), now home to a youth community.

The track becomes a trifle rough on the ensuing steepish descent. At the bottom of the hill a road is joined (turn right) near a cross. Unless time is tight, ignore the turn-off for the Miniera and the next stage for the time being as ahead around the bend south is the hamlet of **La Befa** (151m, 2h). Important features for walkers include the locanda which offers B&B, followed by the historic and renowned bar/restaurant Osteria whose modest and not very inviting exterior belies a bustling kitchen that concocts homestyle fare, hearty game and rich mushroom dishes. Snacks are also available. For culture vultures, a 17th-century church is a little further on.

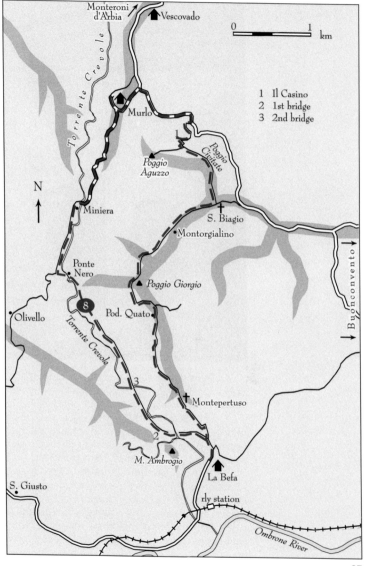

1 Il Casino
2 1st bridge
3 2nd bridge

A quiet corner in the
village of Murlo

La Befa's unmanned railway station is a mere 10min
stroll away downhill near the River Ombrone. Turn left
when you reach the railway line.

From **La Befa** backtrack 5min uphill to the turn-off
mentioned above. Go left (westward) one the lane
marked red/white (Siena Province long-distance route).
An open field is coasted in the shade of prominent Monte
Ambrogio (west), then Torrente Crevole crossed by way
of an iron footbridge. There's a brief length of cyclone
fencing to be followed before a branch right for the short
climb to the old railway, which comes in from the left via
a first old stone bridge. Ahead are some small-scale
eroded bare 'calanchi' ridges. Turn right (northwest) onto
the track for the second delightful stone bridge high over

Torrente Crevole. On this beautiful stretch it flows over smooth rock slabs in the shade of stately poplars, their foliage yellowing as autumn approaches. Light grey herons fish stealthily from the bank or perched on rocks. Ahead now, on the right-hand side of the river, the Mediterranean sclerophyll vegetation thickens and the atmosphere is somewhat desolate, though occasional openings offer glimpses of the watercourse and abrupt surrounding hills. A long cutting is followed by a zone with friable red-tinted Jasper rock and remains of marine organisms. The odd rockslide may need clambering over as the track hugs the hillside for a brief exposed stretch along the narrowing valley where the original track was once built up on columns. You proceed through thick scrubby maquis with frequent red/white paint waymarking on trees and stones. At approx. 1h from La Befa a newly reconstructed iron bridge (**Ponte Nero**) bears left to cross Torrente Crevole.

On the other side a lane proceeds in a shallow cutting, while across the valley is another of the series of characteristic isolated rounded knolls that abound in this area. The valley has opened up considerably now, with Murlo visible ahead (north).

Keep right (straight ahead) on the wider track encountered soon, which leads to the first of the many structures belonging to the old coal mine. The houses have been partially restored for the new inhabitants of **Miniera** (198m). After a brief stretch of tarmac, the road turns right across a bridge and climbs back to **Murlo**, accompanied by the sweep of the wild surrounding hills dotted with farms. A beautiful sight. Total 2h to Murlo from La Befa.

Accommodation

Murlo: B&B Il Castello tel.0577/814188

B&B L'Etrusco tel.0577/811102

Vescovado: L'Albergo di Murlo tel.0577/814033

La Befa: Locanda Il Palazzotto tel.0577/808310 (open mid-March to Oct)

9: Through the Sienese 'Crete' via Monte Oliveto Maggiore

Walking time:	5h + extra for monastery visit
Distance:	20.8km/13 miles
Map:	on p.93, also Kompass 1:50,000 n.661 'Siena-Chianti-Colline Senesi'

Access: Buonconvento can be reached from Siena by either TRA-IN coach or rail on the Grosseto line. By car you'll need the SS 2, otherwise known as the Cassia, the old Roman route to Rome.

The end point, San Giovanni d'Asso, is connected by an occasional TRA-IN bus with Torrenieri, from where more frequent services can be picked up for the return to Buonconvento.

A further option comes by way of a special train known as Treno Natura, run by volunteers on the Asciano–Monte Antico branch line. It generally functions on Sundays from April to December. Handy stations are at San Giovanni d'Asso and Torrenieri, which features a marvellous monumental railway building. ➤

The 'Crete' refers to the undulating chalky countryside southeast of Siena, recognisable from millions of postcards and calendars with its trademark cypress trees punctuating the ridges like exclamation marks. On the map it occupies a vast crescent, encompassing waves of hills rolling into infinity. Extremes of landscape offer stark contrasts between utter arid desolation and luxuriant harvests. Spectacular transformations are wrought by the seasons: pale clay slopes that are dull and bare in winter are painted fresh green by the spring, then flooded in summer by rippling golden seas of wheat dashed scarlet and violet-blue by poppies and cornflowers. Autumn colours return to the muted category, but then it is the vastness and emptiness of the stark windswept landscape that render it so attractive and somehow liberating.

On a geological plane this argillaceous terrain comprises a series of clay deposits from the Pliocene, 7 to 1.5 million years ago. Excessive exposure to the elements has led to weathering, a dramatic and common phenomenon on the higher reaches. Furthermore, an unusually high salt content combined with poor nutrient levels allow few plants to survive and consequently anchor the soil in the upper reaches. Though the terrain is not renowned for fertility, scattered sheep manage to eke a living from the meagre grass. Under the care of Sardinian shepherds, the hardy flocks have long been a good bet here and are responsible for the tangy *pecorino* cheese. At the start of the walk is the low-key township of Buonconvento, which nonetheless traces its history back to the 12th century, though several place names in

the vicinity indicate earlier Etruscan origin. This curious elongated brick-walled town was evidently named after a 'good meeting place of peoples' who settled to exploit the fertile land at the confluence of the Ombrone and Arbia rivers. It went on to become an important point on the medieval Via Francigena, one of the pilgrim routes leading to Rome. However the principal historical and artistic highlight of the walk comprises the 14th-century monastery complex of Monte Oliveto Maggiore high up in the hills. Curious natural lighting effects endow the buildings with warm honey-coloured hues when the background is soft green, in contrast to the flame-red of the bricks against a stark sky. Many visitors flock to purchase the monks' herb liquor as well as olive oil and honey, though most queue to see the *Life of St. Benedict* cycle of Renaissance frescoes. These were begun by Luca Signorelli, though the majority were painted by Sodoma, as the former rushed off to commence work on Orvieto cathedral. Even walkers not interested in the artistic aspects will enjoy the visit due to the very position of the monastery, adeptly described by an illustrious ecclesiastical visitor in the 15th century, Pope Pius II de' Piccolomini, who wrote:

Typical pale clay landscape in the rolling 'Crete' hills

➤ It is also possible to slot into the walk at Monte Oliveto Maggiore itself then follow the walk either to Buonconvento or San Giovanni d'Asso During school terms a bus runs from Asciano via Chiusure to Monte Oliveto Maggiore and back, but be warned, it consists solely of an early morning then early afternoon run.

'If you ask about the form of the hill it occupies, observe a chestnut leaf. Ruinous crags that fall away sharply and very deep abysses, the sight of which cause you to shudder and instil horror, obstruct access from any direction but the narrow tongue of earth, the entrance to which is defended by a solid tower, with a moat and drawbridge.'

While rather long for a single day, the complete walk is very rewarding, though accommodation is now available at Chiusure. A fair amount of climbing – 250m in ascent alone – is involved, but with gradual gradients. Make an early start if you intend visiting the monastery since it closes for lunch. Shorter variants are possible by excluding the monastery and/or Chiusure, cutting several hours off the total time, as can be seen from the map. Otherwise from the monastery follow the road to return to Buonconvento – hitchhiking is always feasible. Spring or autumn are the most suitable times of year. Attempting the walk in hot summer weather is inadvisable as there is very little shade along the way. A chilly winter's day, on the other hand, would guarantee an invigorating experience as the crests are windswept to say the least.

The route sports occasional faded red and white waymarking and several 'Treno Natura' signposts, thanks to enthusiasts who mapped out walks in the area some years back, to link up with train lines.

As usual the basic rule of self-sufficiency applies in terms of food and drink, though refreshments and meals can be got at Chiusure, Monte Oliveto Maggiore and San Giovanni d'Asso. Remember there is no drinking water between villages.

The quiet township of Asciano, founded by the Etruscans, lies on the northeastern edge of the 'crete' and is worth a stopover for its museum which contains finds from numerous necropolises in the area.

THE WALK

From the railway station at **Buonconvento** (146m), take the main road north to the turn-off right for Monte Oliveto Maggiore. Over the level crossing and 20min out of town, a dirt road turns right, signposted for Armena. It leads

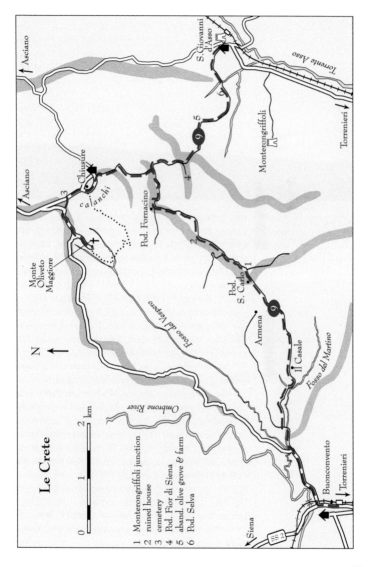

Le Crete

N ←

0 1 2 km

1 Monterongriffoli junction
2 ruined house
3 cemetery
4 Pod. Fior di Siena
5 aband. olive grove & farm
6 Pod. Selva

Spring paints the 'Crete' countryside emerald green

east between hedgerows then over a bridge. At the ensuing fork, you'll need the right branch, through fields which slope gently towards the watercourse, lined with poplars, the perfect habitat for the area's fine white truffles. The track climbs to a crest and a farm (agriturismo 'Il Casale'), followed shortly afterwards by a further farm. Keep to the right of this second group of buildings and onto a rougher path northeast, skirting furrowed fields. A vast panorama opens up to take in Montalcino (south), Chiusure (northeast), and the massive russet brick monastery complex of Monte Oliveto Maggiore below it. Silhouetted cypress trees hold their own on the ridges, amidst an intricate network of fishbone crests.

The entrance to a property (**Podere San Carlo**, 333m, 1h15min) is passed, in an especially windswept position. Keep straight ahead at the next junction (a Treno Natura variant turns down southeast for Monterongriffoli and thence San Giovanni d'Asso). Then, as the vehicle track curves left in descent, leave it for the rougher cart track right (still northeast) climbing the ridge. The landscape quickly becomes wilder with plunging ravines nearby. The crest is surprisingly sandy and hosts masses of tough broom and an amazing array of aromatic herbs. The monastery appears deceptively close from here. Keeping to the main track, you climb past a ruined house, then drop past a small-scale conifer plantation to emerge near a couple of houses (**Podere Fornacino**, 320m, 1h45min total). Go right onto the wider cypress-lined vehicle track, which now effects a rather circuitous route east to detour the deep gorges and bizarre 'calanchi' gullies.

Before your eyes is an astonishing instance of survival – an elevated 'peninsula' hosts a single house and ever-diminishing olive grove out on their own in the middle of a yawning chasm, joined to the 'mainland' by a precarious dirt road and slender crest bridge.

Over a rise is the turn-off at approx. 400m (2h10min total time) for the descent track for San Giovanni d'Asso you'll need later on. Ignore it for the time being and keep left on the clear road downhill (northwards) towards Chiusure which never seems to get any closer (30min to go). A couple of farms precede the final uphill section. Keep left on the approach so as to enter the village via the tiny square which houses a telephone booth, drinking fountain and the Paradiso bar/restaurant which doubles as the food store for **Chiusure** (401m, 2h40min from Buonconvento). This somewhat dilapidated red brick village probably counts its blessings as a matter of habit as another day passes without it sliding into the awesome ravines at its very feet.

Now, for the most straightforward extension to the Monte Oliveto Maggiore monastery, from the square at Chiusure take the narrow street up to the main road, hence the main road left (north). You follow a high narrow ridge that affords dramatic views over the surrounding countryside, rife with deeply eroded gullies on the southern side, subject to weathering by sun and rain. Soon after the cemetery (where a faint and often slippery path cuts the corner) the road veers south and continues dropping to the 273m location of **Monte Oliveto Maggiore**, amongst pine and olive trees (30min from Chiusure).

Return to Chiusure the same way (grand total of 3h40min this far).•

For the gentle descent route towards the destination of San Giovanni d'Asso, leave Chiusure via the unsurfaced road you arrived on. Return southish for 30min to the 400m turn-off mentioned earlier on. Namely, where the track bears right (west) signposted for 'Il terzo frantoio',

• **Alternative access to Monte Oliveto Maggiore** (1h30min return).
A longer and much more tiring, not to mention dramatic alternative to the road consists in the track from Chiusure that leads southwest along a narrow ridge past two farms. It then drops steeply to cross a watercourse before a final climb to the monastery (45min). Only for the fit.

Tourist Office Asciano
tel.0577/719510
(May to October)

**Tourist Office San
Giovanni d'Asso**
tel.0577/823101

**Tourist Office
Buonconvento**
tel.0577/806834

Accommodation
Buonconvento:
Albergo Roma
tel.0577/806021

Chiusure:
Podere Le Piazze
tel. 0577/707269 or
0577/707267.
A lovely rustic-style B&B
run by the monastery

St Giovanni d'Asso:
La Locanda del Castello
tel. 0577/802939

you branch off left (east at first), as per the red and white paint stripes. Over a rise the track heads south through beautiful rolling fields. Far-off Montalcino comes into view southwest, then San Giovanni d'Asso itself southeast. The open ploughed fields offer fleeting glimpses of shadowy sheep, their presence betrayed by tinkling bells. Pockets of dark green wood shelter timid roe deer along with porcupines, who scatter quills behind them as though to punctuate their skill at being elusive. The winding cream-coloured track is often lined by broom and aromatic herbs, and a further eroded zone is passed. Keep left at the fork near wooden railings (Provincial path marker n.5).

Once over a rise the track traverses a spectacularly panoramic zone, and where it bears right along a further crest towards a prominent farm (**Podere Fior di Siena**), leave it and keep straight ahead downhill on the rough path. It's not far to an abandoned olive grove and farm. After a gate the track proceeds through shady oak wood, and a wide curve southwest at first, emerging below the recently restored Podere Selva. You join its access track in proximity to an elegant ancient pine, then drop to cross a watercourse.

The jealously guarded poplar plantation and reserve is the 'breeding ground' of the local renowned white truffles – this area boasts the highest percentage per inhabitant of truffle 'hunters' in Italy! Keep to the main track on the final uphill stretch past a farm entrance, then right at the next two forks. This will hopefully bring you out on a narrow asphalt road, where a left turn means the lone holm oak at the base of towering red brick walls, then a final left up Via Roma leads quickly to Piazza Gramsci and the bus stop. **San Giovanni d'Asso** (310m, 1h20min from Chiusure) is dominated by a curious 13th-century castle-cum-palace, recently converted into a top-notch hotel. Nearby is the delightful Romanesque church of S. Pietro in Villore. The railway station is 10min left downhill.

10: Montalcino to Sant'Antimo

Walking time:	2h15min
Distance:	9km/5.6 miles
Map:	on p.98

The walled town of Montalcino can be seen from miles around on its lofty scenic ridge. It gives the impression of supervising the spread of gentle hills which are dedicated to the production of Brunello di Montalcino. This renowned and full-bodied red wine, together with the younger Rosso di Montalcino, accounts for 1400 cultivated hectares of what, incidentally, also happens to be beautiful walking country.

The captivating township is a pure medieval delight, with six gates leading into the easy-going centre, dominated by the imposing 14th-century Rocca. But here too there are rumours of ancient origins, confirmed by evidence of Etruscan-era settlements, tombs included. A collection of miscellaneous items is on display in the archaeological museum. Castelnuovo dell'Abate, near the walk's end, also yielded several tombs last century. However the destination of this walk is the graceful Romanesque abbey church of Sant'-Antimo, rich in both history and art. According to legend it was founded as a Benedictine monastery in AD781 by no less than Charlemagne, in gratitude for deliverance from an epidemic which threatened his troops on their way north from Rome. The crypt has survived from that period, while the church as it is now dates back to 1118. Exquisitely carved alabaster capitals top the columns that run around the nave, and they are embellished with a curious bestiary such as griffins, eagles and dragons, continuing outside on the external wall of the apse. All can be admired to the accompaniment of Gregorian chant, courtesy of the resident Cistercian monks who hold regular services. The church's saint, Antimus, was a native of ancient Bithynia (present-day Turkey) in Asia

Access: Just south of Buonconvento on the SS 2 (Cassia), drivers will find signposting for the 14km climb to Montalcino. Coming from the opposite direction on the SS 2, a signposted road from Torrenieri climbs 9km. TRA-IN has plenty of direct buses daily from Siena to Montalcino. They transit via the railway stations of Buonconvento (Siena–Grosseto line) and Torrenieri (on the Asciano–Monte Antico branch line – see Walk 9 for details).

The minor TRA-IN bus run Montalcino–S.Angelo (Monday–Saturday only) can also be used to save doing the initial 3km of the walk. Ask to be let off at Le Ragnaie.

From Castelnuovo dell'Abate at the end of the walk, it is possible to return to Montalcino by a further TRA-IN bus (except Sundays). This village is also connected with the Monte Amiata railway station (on the Asciano–Monte Asciano branch line).

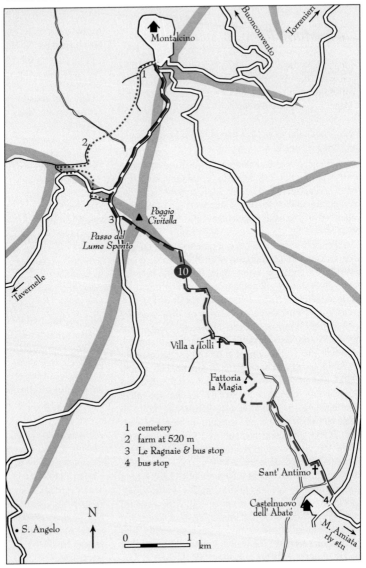

Montalcino

Buonconvento

Torrenieri

1

2

Poggio
Civitella

3

Passo del
Lume Spento

Tavernelle

10

Villa a Tolli †

Fattoria
la Magia

Sant' Antimo †

4

Castelnuovo
dell' Abaté

M. Amiata
rly stn

S. Angelo

1   cemetery
2   farm at 520 m
3   Le Ragnaie & bus stop
4   bus stop

N

0   1
km

Minor. His evangelising fervour and responsibility in the destruction of a pagan temple earned him a grisly martyrdom in 4th-century Rome.

As far as the walk itself goes, it begins with a stretch along asphalt then crosses some beautiful open countryside with stunning 360-degree views on the way to Sant'Antimo, in the vicinity of another quiet medieval village, Castelnuovo dell'Abate. Wide tracks are followed for the most part, with only the odd steep stretch on roughish terrain, making this itinerary both suitable and warmly recommended for everyone.

The walking time given is one-way, with the return trip by bus from Castelnuovo dell'Abate. If you do it in the opposite direction, add a little extra for the uphill sections.

An alternative is given to avoid the surfaced road in the first section, and while it involves half an hour more than the main route, follows quiet farm roads and paths, and there are lovely views westward. The waymarking (red and white markings for Siena Province route n.2) tends to be a little erratic.

THE WALK

Leave **Montalcino** (514m) via the southernmost gate below the Rocca. Take the road for Grosseto and follow it south for approx. 3km. After a rise, preceding the panoramic Passo del Lume Spento (621m), is the Agriturismo **Le Ragnaie**. Left is the wide gravel road you need, marked for Fattoria La Magia and Villa a Tolli among others (40min this far).

Alternative route to Le Ragnaie (1h10min)

From the Rocca end of Montalcino, follow the road for Grosseto but take the first right, Via del Poggiolo (Siena Province signpost for route n.2). Downhill, the asphalt ends after the cemetery, and you keep straight ahead uphill after passing a turn-off. At the ensuing rise the marked path leaves the lane to head right (southwest) downhill through a wood which becomes progressively damper and moss-ridden as you go. After a minor watercourse a lower cart track is joined around the base of the

The graceful Romanesque abbey of Sant'Antimo

hill. As the wood thins there are views across beautiful swathes of rolling countryside, both wooded and cultivated. Keep left at a fork and up past a large farm (at approx. 520m), where a wider vehicle track is joined. Past sturdy chestnut trees is a T-junction – go left up to the tarmac (ignoring the Tavernelle turn-off right), and keep your eyes peeled for a waymarked lane off left. It shortly curves south to cross the road, and proceeds by way of a rough track skirting a field to some ancient oak trees. Keep left at the next gravel road and follow it as far as the nearby asphalt, namely the road from Montalcino. Turn right, then after a brief rise, Le Ragnaie is just round the corner.

Southeast now, ignore all detours and stick to the wide main track between the woodland clothing modest Poggio Civitella on your left, and fields edged with tangles of laden blackberry plants. The horizon opens up quickly with stunning views ranging to the Apennines far off to the west, then the patchwork spread of the light green-yellow clay of the 'crete' hills, including the red brick monastery of Monte Oliveto Maggiore visible NNE.

Ahead, over to the east are the proud and prominent fortresses of Rocca and Ripa d'Orcia. Dominating the scene in this direction of course is the impressive volcanic bulk of Monte Amiata with its gentle and thickly wooded slopes.

The wide track gradually winds down past several farms to the historic hamlet of **Villa a Tolli** (532m, 1h15min total), its main lane lined with old farm buildings festooned with colourful creepers. Keep left at the cross (drinking water opposite), unless you detour right to the tiny church. Through woodland next, the lane continues to the entrance drive for Fattoria La Magia. Here take the rough lane down to the left between wild thickets of fragrant broom on one side and an orderly olive grove on the other. The village of Castelnuovo dell'Abate soon comes into view on its isolated knoll, and a view of the perfect grey stone abbey of Sant'Antimo framed by trees. Down at the bottom of the hill, keep left at the two consecutive junctions and onto a lane alongside a watercourse shaded by willows. The **Abbazia di Sant'Antimo** is not far away now, isolated in beautiful countryside at 318m, its escort comprising the most perfectly formed 'paint brush' cypresses in Tuscany (total 2h). Time seems to stand still here.

After an attentive visit to the abbey, take the unsurfaced access road southeast for 15min to reach the Montalcino-Castelnuovo dell'Abate road, opposite the renowned restaurant 'Osteria Basso Mondo'. The bus stop for Montalcino is on the corner. The right branch leads up into the old medieval centre of **Castelnuovo dell'Abate**, worth a visit in its own right.

Tourist Office
Montalcino
tel.0577/849331

Accommodation
Montalcino: Albergo Il Giardino
tel.0577/848257

Private rooms:
Affittacamere Anna
tel.0577/848666

Castelnuovo dell'Abate:
Locanda S. Antimo
tel.0577/835615

11: Bagno Vignoni and a Scenic Loop

Access: Bagno Vignoni lies on a side road off the SS 2 (Cassia) a mere 5km south from San Quirico d'Orcia, a hub for public transport. Regular RAMA buses run via Bagno Vignoni before proceeding south to Abbadia San Salvatore on the wooded flanks of Monte Amiata. San Quirico d'Orcia, on the other hand, is served by the TRA-IN bus connections northwest via Buonconvento towards Siena, or eastwards via Pienza to the main Florence–Rome valley.

Walking time:	3h
Distance:	8.8km/5.5 miles
Map:	on p.103, also Multigraphic n.40-41 1:25,000 'Massiccio del Monte Amiata' or Freytag & Berndt WKI30 1:50,000 'Chianciano-Val di Chiana-Monte Amiata'

This walking itinerary both commences and concludes at Bagno Vignoni. It is a magnificent circuit that follows the banks of the River Orcia, before climbing through thick wood to take in the castle of Ripa d'Orcia. From there it returns to the spa resort the long way round, namely along an immensely panoramic ridge lane that touches on the minuscule hamlet of Vignoni Alto. Some 200m in height gain and loss is involved, though nothing excessively steep or difficult. Some sustenance and liquid refreshment is advised if you plan to do the recommended full circuit. There are woods thick with Mediterranean species, while open fields and hillsides are covered with shrubs such as broom which fills the air with its profuse scented blooms in summer. Other colours come from rock roses and wild gladiolus, trampled by the wild boar and porcupine, known frequenters of these woodlands. The placid river, on the other hand, encourages willows and poplars, and several varieties of aquatic fowl indulge in fishing along this stretch.

THE WALK

From the bus stop at **Bagno Vignoni** (306m), walk all the way through the car park to where it widens and a channel carrying the still steaming water from the spa baths runs valleywards. Next to the railings a narrow path clambers down the rock flank where centuries of lime-stone precipitate have transformed it into a gigantic slab of cake with thick icing dribbling down it in slow motion.

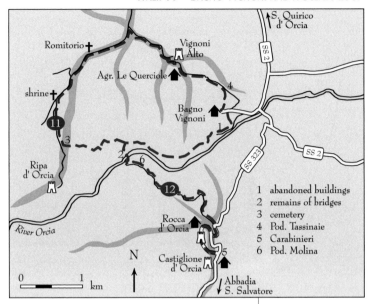

A few old caves once housing mills are passed, then a rock bath for a free warm dip.

(Should this path be too steep for your liking, return to the access road for Bagno Vignoni and follow it downhill for a few minutes to where a lane forks off towards the river. This will bring you out at the base of the cliff, and hence the main route.)

The wide track heads southwest through light wood then disused buildings and overgrown dump belonging to the travertine quarry. Keep to the main lane and ignore side paths. After a rise over a rocky surface, it narrows to a path through undulating wood, and is marked by the occasional faded red arrow. You pass along the lower edge of a field, then are plunged back into wood. On emerging at a wider track and a field, keep left towards the water and the junction with the route from Castiglione d'Orcia that has just forded the **River Orcia** (see Walk 12). An old suspension footbridge hangs forlorn, its floor boards in tatters, while a short distance downstream are

Vignoni Alto

'Mystical' and 'timeless' are easily applied to the historical spa village of **Bagno Vignoni**. Those familiar with Tarkovsky's films will recognise the foggy bath from his haunting work Nostalghia. In cool weather in fact steamy vapours rise in clouds from the surface of the water, an eerie sight. Bagno Vignoni has been renowned since Roman times for its hot curative waters. A good 36 springs gush from a depth of 100m below the ground at 50°C. The square owes its present design and elegant porticoes to the Medici family and Renaissance times. The village itself is very quiet and includes several B&Bs, top grade hotels and a handful of restaurants.

the ramparts of the road bridge that was washed away by the flood waters some 70 years ago (40min this far). The river's flow is soon constricted by the towering cliffs below Ripa d'Orcia, and it picks up strength for the westward course to join the River Ombrone, ending up in the Tyrrhenian Sea near Grosseto.

A little way back from the actual bank, a wide track starts winding and climbing its way west, marked by bright red and white paint stripes. The dense wood here consists of holm oak, the strawberry tree, lentisc and bay trees. Unfortunately they block any views and the half hour ascent on this medieval way tends to be a little monotonous. So you'll be pleased to reach the modest cemetery and a wide unsurfaced road along a crest (429m, 1h10min this far). The countryside has opened up considerably here, and views are wide-ranging.

Turn right here and continue north climbing gradually along the scenic ridge past farms. Fifteen minutes on is a shrine near a turn-off. Keep to the main track as it curves northeast through fields edged with aromatic herbs and past an old hermitage, the Romitorio, amid a cluster of upright pencil cypresses. This long stretch offers unbeatable views of the vast spread of the rolling clay-

The Renaissance porticoes and historic spa of Bagno Vignoni

based Siena 'crete' hills which extend northwards. WNW is Montalcino on its ample hilltop, whereas due south is conical Monte Amiata.

At the ensuing junction the road forks – take the right branch southwest for Vignoni Alto (whereas the northern track leads towards San Quirico d'Orcia).

It's a mere 10min downhill to the fork off left for the delightful tranquil hamlet of **Vignoni Alto** (493m, 2h40min total). A massive square-based tower dominates the cluster of restored houses and drinking fountain, while the panorama also takes in the ridge northwest with the Renaissance towns Pienza and Montepulciano.

To continue the descent, return briefly to the fork that led you into Vignoni Alto, and turn left past the cemetery then several more properties and the lane for friendly and wonderfully scenic Agriturismo Le Querciole. The dirt road is also pleasant and panoramic. Soon after an isolated house (Pod. Tassinaie, 363m) on a corner as the road curves and becomes steeper, take the path off right for the final drop back to the baths, which are virtually below you now. After a stretch alongside a wire fence, go right along Via Amerighi to reach the memorable central square-cum-bath of **Bagno Vignoni** once more (30min from Vignoni Alto). Though the historic 'tub' is closed to bathers, the hot pool at the Hotel Marcucci is open to non-guests, and makes for a relaxing way to conclude this marvellous walk.

Tourist Office San Quirico d'Orcia
tel.0577/897211
(seasonal)

Accommodation Bagno Vignoni:
Hotel Le Terme
tel.0577/887150 – atmospheric 'summer house' for Pope Pius II, built in the 15th century

Hotel Posta Marcucci
tel.0577/887112 – luxury establishment that incorporates the modern-day spa

B&B La Locanda del Loggiato tel.0577/888925

Agriturismo Le Querciole
tel.0577/897408

12: Fortresses in the Val d'Orcia

Access: Castiglione d'Orcia can be reached by branching off the SS 2 (Cassia) 5km south of San Quirico d'Orcia. The SS 323 covers the final 3km climb.

RAMA buses serve the route from San Quirico d'Orcia, continuing on to Abbadia San Salvatore in the south on Monte Amiata.

See Walk 11 for the access to Bagno Vignoni (p.102).

Walking time:	1h40min + time for visits
Distance:	5.7km/3.6 miles
Map:	on p.103, also Multigraphic n.40-41 1:25,000 'Massiccio del Monte Amiata' or Freytag & Berndt WKI30 1:50,000 'Chianciano-Val di Chiana-Monte Amiata'

The landmark fortresses of the Val d'Orcia are visible from all over the countryside south of Siena. Ripa d'Orcia with its castellated outline is covered in the previous walk, whereas a short distance across the river is dominating Rocca di Tentennano. It once controlled a vast territory and key passages of the well-trodden medieval pilgrim way to Rome, the Via Francigena. Nowadays the first image that comes to mind is to describe it is that of a stump of a multi-stage rocket, not a fortress at all until you get up close and appreciate its commanding position. The massive Rocca di Tentennano, which also incorporates the hamlet of Rocca d'Orcia, was built on solid limestone on the edge of the sea of clay that accounts for a great part of the Val d'Orcia. Constructed around the 1200s it witnessed endless take-overs and feuds between the powerful Salimbeni clan and the Sienese among others. After the area was absorbed into the Tuscan Grand Duchy in the 16th century, the fortress fell into disuse.

To its south is the Rocca of Castiglione d'Orcia partially concealed from view and less dramatic. It was owned by another strong family, the Aldobrandeschis. Cocooned by a pleasant cypress-studded park, it is worth a look, as is the lower medieval part of the town. Its maze of medieval alleyways merits a lengthy wander and there are several tiny 12th-century churches.

There are rumours of Etruscan tombs in the proximity of both fortresses, though nothing in the way of evidence. Nearby San Quirico d'Orcia, however, professes Etruscan origins, and it is hard to imagine that this stunning corner of south Tuscany, previously central Etruria, was unfamiliar to this ancient people.

The rolling countryside is studded with orderly rows of olive trees in fields that turn emerald green overnight after rain. Colour contrasts with the yellow-orange autumn shades of deciduous trees can be breathtaking. The walk itself takes in the first Rocca then the underlying hamlet. It follows wide lanes and an old medieval route, descending a good 300m, a little steeply at times. After crossing the River Orcia, it proceeds to the historic spa resort of Bagno Vignoni, a memorable spot. It is not particularly recommended in the reverse direction as the climb can be hard going on a sunny day, so be warned! Midwinter is not an advisable time to visit due to the elevation – snowfalls are not unknown and the panoramic position exposes the area to biting winds. While the walk rates medium on the difficulty scale, a word of warning concerns the River Orcia, forded via a concrete causeway. In normal conditions it's a matter of taking off your shoes and splashing your way over, however persistent heavy rain can swell the watercourse and make this unsafe. This walk is a perfect supplement or alternative to the previous itinerary which starts at Bagno Vignoni.

Waymarking for the first half of the itinerary is covered by the Province of Siena system – freshly painted red and white stripes along with the occasional signboard and (fairly useless) map.

There are food shops, bars and restaurants at both Castiglione d'Orcia and Bagno Vignoni.

THE WALK

On the northern edge of **Castiglione d'Orcia** (517m), opposite the Carabinieri station, is a road signposted for the Rocca di Tentennano, only 5min away. Continue straight through the car park and up the ramp to the entrance for the restored central tower. Even without climbing to the highest point, the views are brilliant and space over the Val d'Orcia northeast and the hilltowns of Pienza, Montepulciano and beyond, the vast expanses of

The charming cobbled square of Rocca d'Orcia

the clay country of Siena northwards, as well as north-west to the hillside sprawl of Montalcino. Monte Amiata and its vast wooded slopes are best seen from higher up. Closer are picturesque fields where orderly rows of sombre olive trees contrast with crops, golden or emerald green depending on the season.

From the Rocca, keep left and down the twisting cobbled streets past the miniature churches of the exquisite and beautifully preserved medieval hamlet of **Rocca d'Orcia** (499m). Siena's Saint Catherine is said to have spent time here in meditation. Be sure to see the charming cobbled square with its raised cistern (plus restaurant and lodgings). Then continue around north circling the hill and to the stone exit archway where the narrow road drops to a junction (20min this far). Keep left on the tarmac for a couple of curves. Five minutes downhill next to a house a lane turns off left, marked with the red and white waymarking of the Provincial Path n.1, actually the route of a well-trodden medieval way. Northwest for the most part it drops below Rocca d'Orcia, whose houses seem to cling to the rock face for all they're worth from this angle. You pass a farm with yapping dogs and head towards the river. North now, your destination is visible – the historic spa resort of Bagno Vignoni and its old quarries, while on the ridge above is the tiny hamlet of Vignoni Alto. West is the majestic Ripa d'Orcia castle.

After an isolated farm, Podere Molina (258m), the track quickly reaches the banks of the **River Orcia**, past a ruined mill all but hidden in the undergrowth off left (total 1h to here). The route fords the river by way of a concrete causeway in normal conditions. Downstream are the remains of the road bridge swept away by flooding in the 1930s. To complete the picture is a dilapidated suspension bridge. Resign yourself to taking off those shoes! Herons and other feathered fishers are not an uncommon sight on the water's edge.

On the other bank, red and white waymarking on rocks points you up right. Where a decent track starts climbing up left (see Walk 11), turn right instead. A wide track leads briefly uphill and flanks a field, but you soon leave it for a path right into light wood, guided by the occasional faded red arrow. Another field is skirted then more ups and downs through trees, before finally emerging onto a wider track with a rock base. This is the edge of the disused travertine quarry zone, and keeping straight ahead, you pass long abandoned masons' workshops. Further along is a bizarre rock face plastered with limestone precipitate left by the waters exiting the spa resort. At its base is a sizeable rock bath where hot soaks can be had for free. It's possible to leave the track here and clamber up the cliff by way of a narrow path, coming out close to the main parking area and bus stop of **Bagno Vignoni** (306m, total 1h40min). Should this final stretch look too precarious, keep to the lower track which climbs gradually to the surfaced access road for the spa, where you turn left.

It is now compulsory that you make your way to the central square, alias Roman bath of this exquisite historical spa village, before returning to Castiglione d'Orcia by bus. (See Walk 11 for more information on Bagno Vignoni.)

**Accommodation
Castiglione d'Orcia:**
Albergo Le Rocche
tel.0577/887031

Rocca d'Orcia:
Foresteria Il Borgo
tel.0577/887280 (upper price range)

Bagno Vignoni:
see Walk 11

13: Monte Cetona

Access: the signposted turn-off for the starting point, Fonte Vetriana, is to be found on the SS 478 about halfway between Sarteano and Radicofani. A couple of LFI buses a day on the Chiusi–Radicofani line use this road and you get off at the Fonte Vetriana junction. You can cover the last 1km southeast to the hamlet by driving carefully on the gravel track, or allow 15min on foot.

Sarteano, as well as Cetona, is also served by the LFI Chiusi–Montepulciano bus which detours to the villages.

Walking time:	4h
Distance:	15km/9.3 miles
Map:	on p.111, also Freytag & Berndt WKI30 1:50,000 'Chianciano-Val di Chiana-Monte Amiata' or Kompass n.662 1:50,000 'Chianciano Terme' (partially)

Monte Cetona is a modest 1148m mountain southwest of Chiusi, whose inhabitants use it as their weather beacon – a cloud cap concealing the peak is a harbinger of bad weather and vice versa. Not far from Tuscany's borders with both Umbria and Latium, its isolated position on the western edge of the Val di Chiana makes it particularly panoramic. The wooded flanks are crisscrossed by a dense network of paths and tracks, well used by local people on their forays to gather wood and mushrooms, or hunt in autumn, activities long practised in the whereabouts. The eastern flank of Monte Cetona in fact has a wealth of prehistoric cave sites, such as Belverde where a good 25 caverns are open to the public. With finds dating back as far as an impressive 80,000 years, they rate among the oldest in Central Italy. The Archaeological Museum in Perugia holds the bulk of the material unearthed here in the 1950s: an astonishing array of spear heads, scrapers, earthenware, a primitive pair of compasses, grinding stones and cereals, then bones from animals such as the leopard, cave bear and even a rhinoceros! Modern day walkers should limit their expectations to encounters with the harmless smooth snake which suns itself in clearings and fleeting glimpses of roe deer and wild boar in the wood.

As far as the Etruscans were concerned, prior to the rise of the neighbouring city of Chiusi, an early Villanovan settlement occupied the upper reaches of the mountain. Several minor towns and villages in the

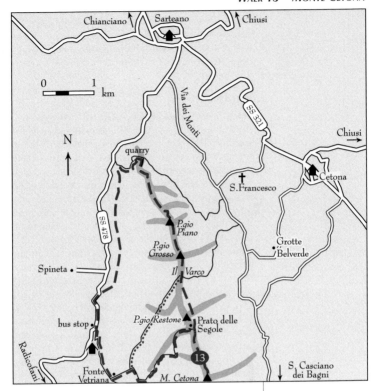

vicinity also boast Etruscan origins, Cetona and Sarteano
included. The latter has a scattering of tombs and, with
Chianciano Terme, shares the highly valued mineral
waters that have continued to attract flocks of visitors
through the ages.

It is worth doing the walk at almost any time of year,
except perhaps midwinter when it sometimes snows and
summer when haze can spoil the views. Spring or late
autumn can be especially beautiful. A climb of some
400m and descent of 600m are involved, but it is all very
gradual and on wide paths and tracks. Buy picnic food
before setting out, namely in the nearby towns, as Fonte
Vetriana has no shops. Carry your own drinking water as

the karstic terrain means none can be found along the way. As well as the itinerary described here that follows a lengthy loop to return to Fonte Vetriana, a shorter round trip is feasible by cutting downhill from Il Varco – allow 2h15min in this case.

THE WALK

The hamlet of **Fonte Vetriana** (707m) is coming back to life as the odd city dweller returns to enjoy a summer sojourn in their grandparents' home and indulge in horse-riding. Monte Cetona is ahead east, its massive summit cross clearly identifiable. Just before the main group of houses and opposite the washing troughs and fountain that gave the place its name, is a track marked red/white for the '*vetta*' (peak), though rust has all but consumed the writing. This winds and climbs northeast. The wood is made up of hornbeam and a variety of oaks, and autumn colours can be spectacular, not to mention the array of spring orchids in the clearings. (Some 15min up, a forestry track branches off NNE – the shorter variant returns this way.) Keep right (SSE) for the time being and stick to the main track, ignoring turn-offs, including an MTB route. Swinging around northeast the track approaches the main crest, close to Poggio Restone and its cluster of aerials. 50min total will see you at an ample clearing which goes under the strange name of **Prato delle Segole**, namely 'Meadow of Onions' (997m), often lined with orderly stacks of firewood.

Monte Cetona's constituent limestone is more obvious now in the form of karstic depressions and patches of light-coloured rock beneath the vegetation. The Rocca (fortress) at Radicofani can be seen WSW now, with the cone of extinct volcano Monte Amiata in the background.

Still on the main track you bear right (south) up the wide wooded crest – mostly beech with tiny bright cyclamens nestling in the undergrowth. The track peters out to a path and though there is no waymarking on this stretch you can't go wrong. You climb out at the colossal iron cross on **Monte Cetona** (1148m, 1h15min this far). The summit was long a site for religious practices back in

Reminders of old farming ways at Fonte Vetriana, with Monte Cetona in the background

ancient times, while a castle, now all but disappeared, stood here in the Middle Ages. The views are wonderful all round of extensive woods and rolling countryside and, visibility permitting, range from the Lago Trasimeno (northeast) preceded by Chiusi and the Val di Chiana, to Lago di Bolsena (south). Faraway sounds like dogs barking waft up.

Go back to the **Prato delle Segole** junction and leave the main track for the clear path over the ridge and diagonally north. Marked by regular if faint red and yellow marking, it cuts through the damp wood which has been colonised by a host of mushrooms and fungi. It descends gradually keeping to the right (east) of the main crest. The township of Cetona can occasionally be glimpsed below. The odd clearings encountered in this area were once used by charcoal burners. After 20min you come out on a wide forestry track and the 853m saddle known as **Il Varco**, the Opening (total 2h).

Shorter variant to Fonte Vetriana (30min)
To complete the round trip, from Il Varco turn left (SSW) on the forestry track. It's a lovely panoramic descent and coasts through woodland. After 20min where the track is

Tourist Office Cetona
tel.0578/238153

Tourist Office Sarteano
tel.0578/265312

Accommodation

Fonte Vetriana:
Agriturismo La
Ghiandaia
tel.0578/265169

Self-catering c/o
Agriturismo Il Borgo del
Lupo tel.0578/265929

Cetona: rooms c/o
Osteria Vecchia
tel.0578/239040

Sarteano: Albergo
Roberta tel.0578/265636

barred to unauthorised traffic, you're back on the track described at the start of the walk and continue southwest back to Fonte Vetriana once again.

From **Il Varco** the main itinerary cuts straight across the saddle proceeding in a northerly direction through the trees. Following faded red and yellow markings, it climbs and winds along this marvellous sunny ridge taking in Poggio Grosso (896m) and even a dolina or two. Some 20min from Il Varco is a clearing (**Poggio Piano**, 833m). Not far on the path turns decisively down right then resumes its northerly direction on the eastern side of the ridge now. The wood is thicker here and roe deer are not an unusual sight. The route becomes a shady avenue, with ruts left by sleds and carts, and it widens into a rough vehicle lane at a house. There are occasional glimpses of Sarteano NNE illuminated by the sun in the afternoon.

An electricity pole is passed, then further downhill is a T-junction with a wider vehicle track (710m, 2h50min total time). The metal net fence on the other side encloses a **quarry**.

Here a left turn will take you in a wide curve and down past a municipal dump.

Exit to Sarteano: Only minutes below is the Sarteano–Radicofani road. Unless you manage to pick up a rare passing bus, 40min on foot are all that separate you from the medieval village of **Sarteano** (573m) with its 15th-century castle.

(This last leg to loop back to the start point takes 1h.) Bear left (south) at the lane alongside a pine plantation. 15min along, where the track veers left and is barred by 'proprietà privata', keep straight on. A concentration of cypresses soon precedes a junction in view of the main road – go straight ahead, SSW now. Past a gate, an older lane takes you down to join the tarmac for a final brief stretch left to the turn-off for **Fonte Vetriano** once more.

14: Chiusi and Poggio Gaiella, the Legendary Mausoleum of Lars Porsenna?

Walking time:	1h30min
Distance:	5.6km/3.5 miles
Map:	on p.117, also Freytag & Berndt WKI30 1:50,000 'Chianciano-Val di Chiana-Monte Amiata' or Kompass n.662 1:50,000 'Chianciano Terme'.

'He was buried under the city of Clusium, in a spot where he has left a monument in rectangular masonry, each side whereof is three hundred feet wide, and fifty high, and within the square of the basement is an inextricable labyrinth, out of which no one who ventures in without a clue of thread can ever find an exit...'

This account by Roman chronicler Pliny the Elder refers to the mausoleum of Lars Porsenna. The legendary Etruscan king of Chiusi from 6th century BC was best known for his siege on Rome to avenge and reinstate tyrannical Tarquinius Superbus, the last king the capital knew. Despite the extravagant nature of the description of his tomb, which goes on with a complicated list of tiers of huge pyramids and intricate structures, long-standing rumours equate it with Poggio Gaiella, a modest hill which doubles as a gigantic burial mound or tumulus. However, nothing in the way of above-ground structures has ever been found as confirmation. Close to the surface, however, are layers honeycombed with a veritable labyrinth of low, backbreaking passages and burial chambers. It has actually been dated as 2nd century BC, and experts say the modest dimensions of the internal tombs suggest they belonged to people from low social classes.

Despite the fact that archaeological investigations in the area commenced way back in the 15th century, the Poggio Gaiella hypogeum complex was not excavated

Access: Chiusi is located on the main Florence–Rome thoroughfare, the Val di Chiana, accessible from the A1 autostrada via the Chiusi–Chianciano exit. Alternatively there is the SS 71 that connects Arezzo via Lago Trasimeno to Orvieto and beyond, then the SS 146 from the west and the Val d'Orcia.

The Chiusi Scalo railway station is used by slow trains on the Florence–Rome line, in addition to a useful branch line Chiusi–Asciano–Siena.

For the start of the walk itself, several LFI buses run daily to the lake from the railway station and Chiusi Città (except Sunday and public holidays). By car, follow signposting for 'Lago di Chiusi', which lies 5km north of Chiusi Città. It is also possible to drive as far as Poggio Gaiella – the turn-off for the unsurfaced track is signposted along the lake road.

Chiusi's **Museo Nazionale Etrusco** was opened in 1870 with items donated from private collections. It has a relatively modest but varied series of exhibits from local tombs, as the bulk of the finds ended up in the Palermo, Florence and Vatican museums. On display are intriguing locally-produced Canopic ash urns with human-shaped lids named after their Egyptian counterparts, small sphinx-like statues and a *glirarium*, a huge terracotta jar pierced with holes evidently for breeding dormice, a delicacy at Roman feasts. Many objects were made from *pietra fetida* or 'stinking stone', a brittle type of limestone found here which emanates a strong unpleasant smell when first cut, but which hardens on prolonged contact with air.

until 1839. A report, courtesy of George Dennis (1848), refers to a monumental girdle of stone blocks circling the base, as well as painted internal tomb decorations, a hint of aristocratic burials perhaps. An air of abandon reigns nowadays, though limited restoration work was under way at the time of writing. By circling the hill many entrances can be visited, but much has crumbled and collapsed and tunnels and passages are blocked. Closer inspection would mean crawling into the maze of underground passages, armed with care, a torch and even a ball of string – not recommended if you suffer from claustrophobia. From the outside it's still very evocative in its peaceful setting.

Lars Porsenna's final resting-place has still not been found, but there is no lack of candidates for the honour, such as the Cuccumella tumulus at Vulci with its maze of tunnels. In local lore, a hoard of treasure is also included – a hen with a brood of 5000 chicks, accompanied by 12 horses, all in pure gold! The aura and mystery surrounding the king later induced Grand Duke Cosimo I to claim direct descent, and he had the title of Magnus Dux Etruriae conferred upon himself.

The starting point of the actual walk, modest Lago di Chiusi, has a camping ground and restaurants. A quiet spot as motor boats are not allowed, it is the realm of fishermen and bird watchers. The former go for the perch, pike, tench, carp and eels, the latter to observe the kite, buzzard, kingfishers, herons and a variety of ducks. Long ago the body of water was the scene of a ceremony akin to Venice's famous Ascension Day custom of wedding the sea (the lake in this case) with a ring, the task performed by the Chief Magistrate in lieu of a Doge.

The walk essentially amounts to a stroll, with very little climbing involved. The destination is fascinating, and all in all a delightful day can be spent in the area.

As regards the nearby town of Chiusi, the orthogonal layout confirms its Etruscan origins, as do the numerous tombs found throughout the surrounding countryside. Probably known as Clevsi or Camars (later Clusium in Latin), it was a prominent member of the twelve-city federation, its heyday the 6th century BC. The favourable

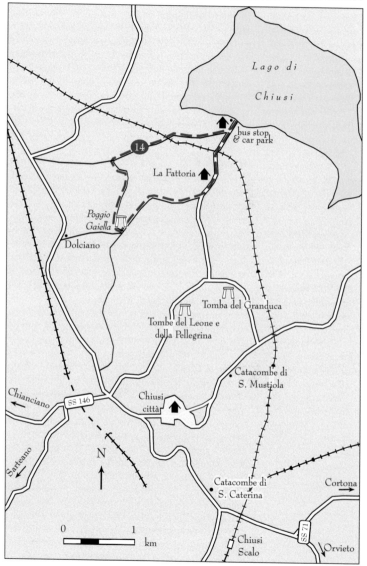

Tombs: A custodian from the museum will accompany you the 2km outside town by (your) car to open up the 3rd–2nd century BC Tomba della Pellegrina (Tomb of the Pilgrim) discovered in 1928. It belonged to an Etruscan patrician family, the Sentinate, and still contains several sarcophagi decorated with scenes from mythology. Nearby is the Tomba del Leone (Tomb of the Lion), similarly excavated in the sandstone. The famous frescoed Tomba della Scimmia (Tomb of the Ape) is unfortunately no longer open to the public since its painted surfaces have seriously deteriorated because of too many visitors over recent years. Several other modest tombs in the vicinity can be visited freely – look out for the yellow signs.

geographical situation on the Val di Chiana thoroughfare led it to play a decisive role later in expansion northwards towards the Po plain. Visitors are offered a wealth of ancient evidence by way of the historic Etruscan Museum and some tombs with massive stone-slab hinged doors, though the few chambers actually open to the public cannot be compared with those of Cerveteri or Tarquinia. In addition several early Christian catacombs are accessible. Further information is given after the walk description.

THE WALK

From the bus stop and car park on the southern shore of **Lago di Chiusi** (251m), walk past the camping ground and restaurants, back up the road. Turn into the first dirt lane off right (west) which passes through fields, heading diagonally towards the railway line. The underpass (10min) brings you out facing the low wooded hill, Poggio Gaiella. Keep right along the muddy track flanked by a clay embankment. A good 10min along, take the first track off to the left (SSE), and keep left at the next junction to reach the edge of an oak wood. A couple of minutes into the trees turn right to climb on another wide track. It's a couple of winds to a motorable dirt road with a farm on your right. More important is the solitary pine tree on the left corner and a faded yellow sign that announces **'Poggio di Gaiella'** (300m, total 35min this far).

Diagonally up left now through the field and olive trees are the openings to the maze of excavated passageways and tunnels that run through the hill. It's worth walking all the way around the hill to inspect and explore the various entrances (allow about 15min). A strange two-winged greyish transparent type of fly can often be observed inside, evidently endemic to Chiusi's tombs.

Back at the pine tree on the road, turn left (northeast) along the lane. There are lovely swathes of wood edged with broom and alive with chirping birds. The lane curves right to descend briefly alongside a field dotted with delicate pale yellow common toadflax which contrast with the bright clumps of cyclamens amidst the trees opposite. Several curves and a couple of farms later and you join

3rd century BC patrician sarcophagi decorated with scenes from mythology, Tomba della Pellegrina, Chiusi

the road that links Chiusi with the lake (15min from Poggio Gaiella to this junction). To return to the starting point, go left (northeast) along the quiet asphalted road. Past a restaurant/hotel (La Fattoria) and over the railway line, some 20min will see you back at the lake side (total 1h30min).

Other Visits

Museo della Cattedrale, Piazza Duomo. Apart from a display of cathedral-type items from Tuscany's oldest church, you can visit the Etruscan underground passages and wells beneath the bishop's garden and the main square. By the time of publication, excavations should have extended as far as the bell tower, connecting by way of the 1st-century BC barrel-vaulted cistern. Through the museum it is possible to join a guided tour to the **Catacombe di Santa Mustiola** 1.5km away. On an earlier Etruscan burial site, these were in use 3rd–5th centuries AD. Despite the fact that her cousin was Emperor Claudius in person, Mustiola, a 3rd-century virgin and martyr, was arrested for her prison visits to Chiusi's other saint, Ireneo. She suffered torture then beheading as a result of her rejection of the Roman prefect's proposal of marriage. Saint Mustiola's remains were transferred to the town's cathedral in the 1700s following the chance discovery of the catacombs during excavation work on a well. The similar complex of the Catacombe di Santa Caterina lies on the southern side of town towards Chiusi Scalo.

Tourist Office Chiusi Città
tel.0578/227667

Accommodation
Chiusi Città:
Hotel La Sfinge
tel.0578/20157

On the lake road:
La Fattoria
tel.0578/21407 (3-star)

Chiusi Lago:
Private rooms c/o Pesce d'Oro camping ground
tel.0578/21403

15: The Heights of Cortona and a Franciscan Retreat

Access: The SS 71 between Arezzo and Lago Trasimeno passes the foot of Cortona's hill, and several clearly sign-posted roads wind up to the town. Otherwise from the A1 *autostrada*, take the Val di Chiana–Bettolle exit and proceed on the Perugia *superstrada*, then the appropriate exit for Cortona. The closest railway station for Cortona is Camucia, from where regular LFI buses climb the short remaining distance to the town. At the Sodo intersection at the end of the walk, another LFI bus covers the final 3km return to the town.

Walking time:	4h + extra for monastery and tomb visits
Distance:	15.3km/9.6 miles
Map:	on p.124, also Litografia Artistica Cartografica 'Sentiero 50 dal Trasimeno alla Verna' 1:25,000

Cortona is a quintessential Tuscan town, where virtually every hotel room looks over the characteristic jumble of red-tiled roofs. In a blend of medieval and Renaissance architecture, the buildings seem to cascade down the hill-side, with surprisingly steep narrow streets and flights of steps threading through the maze. This is not a town for the weak-kneed, nor is it a typically Etruscan site for that matter, despite its dominating position over the strategic Val di Chiana. No typical tufa platform here. However, one vaguely level area well above the present town has revealed traces of an ancient acropolis, now the site of a Medicean fortress. The ground is compact stratified sand-stone, not particularly suitable for excavation, and in fact the few Etruscan tombs in the whereabouts are above-ground structures rather than underground chambers. There are also interesting lengths of extant defensive walling in huge rectangular stone blocks, such as those outside the Porta Colonia in Via delle Mura Etrusche. They probably date back to 5th century BC, though are believed to have been reinforced in anticipation of the arrival of Hannibal and his troops several centuries later. To no avail, however, as the invaders laid waste to the city at the time of their overwhelming defeat of Roman forces on the shores of Lago Trasimeno (see Walk 16).

Though details about Cortona's past are somewhat sketchy, its Etruscan name has persevered all but intact – from Curtun. Formerly an Umbrian stronghold, it swiftly became one of the most powerful centres in the Etruscan

The woods and the old paved way above Cortona

city-state league from 8th century to 4th century BC, after which it entered into an alliance with Rome. The Middle Ages meant the usual turbulence, then relative calm during the great artistic blossoming of the Renaissance which included Luca Signorelli whose masterpieces include the frescoes in Orvieto's cathedral. Another marvellous painter and city son was Pietro di Cortona.

A visit to Cortona leaves long-lasting impressions that range from the wonderful views encompassing the broad expanse of the Val di Chiana backed by a mountainous ridge and bordered by Lago Trasimeno in the southeast, as well as the cawing jackdaws, acrobatic swallows and the unforgettable wafting perfume of the stately lime trees in the lower part of town.

It is essential that walkers carry picnic supplies and drinking water as there are no bars or shops en route except for those at Santa Margherita and Torreone, not far from the start. One tasty suggestion are the local loaves: *ciaccia con ciccia* (pronounced 'chacha con cheecha') are baked with a sort of bacon, while *con formaggio* is with cheese.

If desired, those with a car can shorten the walk by 1h starting out from Torreone. On the way back, leave the walk at Le Celle and return to Torreone via the narrow 2km surfaced road. A further cut of 45min is possible by eliminating the upper extension to Monte Cuculo.

THE WALK

From Piazza della Repubblica, the main square of **Cortona** (494m), it is naturally an uphill route on Via Santucci, behind the supermarket. The broad pedestrians-only lane climbs stiffly through a covered passage to emerge close to the hospital entrance on via Berrettini, named after the artist also known as Pietro di Cortona. Straight ahead you soon pass a huge old circular well in Piazza del Pozzo, then enter triangular Piazza Pescaia. Keep left and up past the church of San Cristoforo, then right onto Via Santa Croce. This paved lane winds up through cypresses and a lovely picnic area, to the church of **S. Margherita** (620m, 20min). Dedicated to the town's 13th-century saint, this mock Romanesque building, featuring a magnificent rose window, was completely reconstructed in 1897. Several 19th-century writers, including Henry James, waxed lyrical about the atmosphere and views.

(The lane that climbs from the café leads to the Medici fortress and more panoramas.)

Head out on the road through the old walls, their cracks overflowing with perfumed golden wallflowers. The Alta Sant'Egidio mountain looms northward. Red and white waymarking for n.561 is now evident, and you are pointed to the cypress-bordered lane to the right of the road. There's a level stretch then broad curves downhill with wide-ranging views over the wild hills including Monte Cuculo, northeast. You veer left to **Torreone** (589m, 30min total) and its snack bar.

Straight across the road from the hotel, path n.561 (signed as 'Strada basolata') continues NNE alongside a tiny old church. Scattered properties are passed on the very gradual ascent, believed to be the course of an old Roman road. Ignore all turn-offs and stick to the main track which proceeds amongst alternating flowering wild fruit trees, olive trees and dark conifers, all alive with bird song. Rock roses, tree heather and masses of broom

The itinerary described here is quite a kaleidoscope of history and nature. It climbs through the town itself and follows an old paved way through woods and extraordinary explosions of wild flowers, to a panoramic ridge 900m above sea level. The ensuing descent touches on a perfect Franciscan retreat, before emerging on the valley floor at Sodo, the site of two impressive Etruscan tumulus tombs. The return to Cortona is by bus. The paths are easy to follow thanks to clear waymarking and numbering, courtesy of the Arezzo branch of the Italian Alpine Club. This is particularly helpful as the area is crisscrossed by a dense network of forestry and hunters' tracks. Though no actual difficulty is involved, it does mean a fair climb (a total of 400m in ascent and 700m in descent) – the only really steep ➤

brighten the way and wild strawberries can be expected in summer. Soon after a shrine the track reverts to its older rough state and enters a thick chestnut wood. A total of 1h from Cortona will see you at a small watercourse, where n.561 leaves the main track. This is the start of a delightful authentic flagged way from the Middle Ages. With a perfectly calculated gradient it winds up into a peaceful wood of tall dark firs, where the drumming of woodpeckers echoes. Once over a second minor watercourse, it crosses open moor-like terrain which will mean a host of wild orchids and aromatic herbs.

A dirt track is crossed (coinciding with the n.563 junction needed for the descent). Keep straight ahead through the final stretch of chestnut wood followed by open terrain and overgrown terracing. You emerge onto a quiet surfaced road opposite a **cenotaph** and pine copse which conceals a pleasant shady picnic area (911m, 1h30min).

For the **extension to Monte Cuculo**, some 45min return from this spot, take the first lane off right (SSE) virtually opposite the cenotaph. Marked n.50 (the long-distance route from Lago Trasimeno to La Verna), it quickly narrows to a path and proceeds along the lovely lightly wooded ridge, with several scenic openings over the wild hills. After an isolated house a brief drop leads to a panoramic saddle (920m) and ruined stone hut, just before **Monte Cuculo**, a popular hangout with hunters judging from the spent cartridges littering the ground. The vast outlook down the mountain and across the broad Val di Chiana plain extends past pale-coloured Montepulciano (southwest) to the prominent peak of Monte Amiata as well as Monte Cetona (SSW).

Return the same way to the **cenotaph** (2h15min total) thence path n.561 downhill as per the ascent. It is believed that St. Francis used this route on his way between the various monasteries dotted throughout these hills. After 10min the dirt road is reached – turn right here for n.563. A couple of minutes and bends downhill, branch left onto a rougher track through beautiful chestnut and oak wood. At yet another junction, keep left (southeast) to where a group of largish pines herald a well-signed turn down right. Here a clear path winds its

➤ sections being those within the realms of the town itself! Late spring (May–June) is the best time for the flowers on the mountain flanks, but any time of year is feasible, apart from midwinter when snow and icy winds are the norm

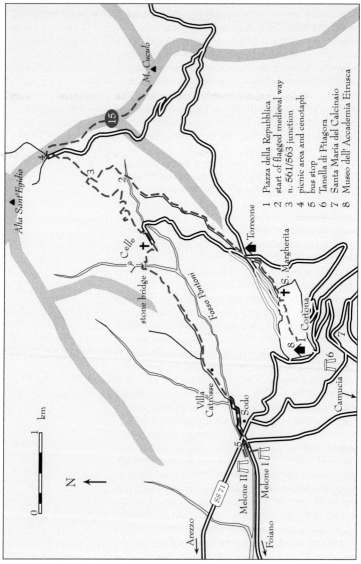

1 Piazza della Repubblica
2 start of flagged medieval way
3 n. 561/563 junction
4 picnic area and cenotaph
5 bus stop
6 Tanella di Pitagora
7 Santa Maria del Calcinaio
8 Museo dell' Accademia Etrusca

way through typical Mediterranean vegetation and eventually comes out at restored properties that include a swimming pool. Keep on the narrow access road, then turn right as you meet the surfaced road from Cortona. Very shortly, an entrance drive is reached for to a picturesque group of simple light-coloured stone buildings that make up the idyllic Franciscan retreat called **Le Celle** (553m, just over 3h total). The monastery dates back to the early 13th century and its guests have included such renowned holy figures as St. Anthony of Padua and St. Bonaventura from Bagnoregio. Visitors can wander around inside and even see the spartan cell used by St. Francis, but are reminded that it is a place of prayer and silence the rule.

For the final 50min leg to Sodo, facing the main entrance to Le Celle, keep left down the lane as per red/white waymarking. This drops down to a beautiful spot where the Fosso Pontoni stream is crossed by an elegant stone bridge constructed in 1728 under the auspices of the visionary Grand Duke Leopold, and restored in 1995.

The lovely shady path climbs briefly through cypresses then leaves the realms of Le Celle to return to mixed wood heading southwest. Two small streams are crossed then terraces and olive groves, and the path joins a wide farm lane in gradual descent cutting the flank of the southwest outlier of Alta S. Egidio. Cortona reappears south across the valley. About 40min from Le Celle n.563 passes beneath the arch belonging to 17th-century Villa Catrosse (311m), constructed for a prominent family from Cortona, and complete with chapel and ornamental gardens. In spring this leg means a series of splendid flowering cherry trees.

After crossing Fosso Pontoni once more, keep left along a surfaced road, which quickly leads to the five-way intersection including the SS 71, just below the hamlet of **Sodo** (260m, 3h50min).

(The bus stop for the return to Cortona is just over the bridge right, on the Arezzo road.)

For the nearby 'Ipogeo Etrusco' continue straight ahead (southwest) along the left bank of the canal, on the

The idyllic Franciscan retreat of Le Celle, Cortona

road for Foiano. First left, a lane leads to the **Melone I** tomb-mound, enclosed by fencing. The grassed earth tumulus, 60m in diameter, was discovered in the 1920s and is covered by trees and creamy-coloured lords-and-ladies spathes. A guided visit arranged through the museum (see below) takes you through 6th–4th century BC sepulchral chambers which open off the entrance corridor, while inscriptions in Etruscan characters indicate the family names of the erstwhile occupants.

Back at the five-road crossroads, turn left over the bridge and sharp left again. This lane along the watercourse leads to the **Melone II** tumulus and its burial chambers, open for visits most mornings. However a unique altar platform and monumental stone steps guarded by massive sculpted figures discovered in 1990, can be admired from outside any time.

From here, the easiest way to return to Cortona is by bus. Anyone interested in a further unusual Etruscan tomb should ask to be let off at the **Tanella di Pitagora** (the Lair of Pythagorus), shortly before the junction marked by the weathered Renaissance church of Santa Maria del Calcinaio. Set in its own miniature grove of cypresses, this 2nd century BC burial monument is a curious struc-ture on a massive 8m circular travertine base. Its slab walls house niches for cinerary urns. It was long held to be the final resting place of the Greek mathematician Pythagoras (6th century BC) but this was because the town was confused with the Greek colony of Crotone much further south in Calabria. Here too it is necessary to pre-arrange a visit through the museum (see below).

Back in **Cortona**, the Palazzo Casali in Piazzale Signorelli houses the **Museo dell'Accademia Etrusca**. The Academy was founded in 1727 and has a modest, rather jumbled collection from various eras, the highlight of which is a 5th-century BC Etruscan bronze oil candelabra. George Dennis was particularly taken with it: 'Were there nothing else to be seen at Cortona, this alone would demand a visit'.

Tourist Office Cortona
tel.0575/630352

Museo dell'Accademia Etrusca tel.0575/630415
for visits to the Melone I and Tanella di Pitagora tombs.

Accommodation Cortona:
Albergo Athens tel.0575/630508

B&B Le Gelosie tel.0575/630005

Ostello San Marco (IYH hostel) tel.0575/601392

Torreone:
Corys Hotel tel.0575/62232

16: In Hannibal's Footsteps Above Lago Trasimeno

Access: the northern shore of Lago Trasimeno can be approached by way of several directions and means. By car via a branch of the A1 *autostrada* (for Perugia) which runs along the northern shore as does the SS 75b, or the SS 71 (Arezzo–Chiusi) via the westernmost edge. Trains follow similar routes, with the junction for the Perugia–Foligno branch line at Terontola – you need the station for Passignano sul Trasimeno. APM buses from Perugia serve the villages around the lake including Passignano, except on Sundays. At the end of the walk you'll need an LFI bus (daily service) from Ossaia to Terontola station, where a train will take you back to Passignano.

Walking time:	5h30min
Distance:	21.3km/13.3 miles
Map:	on p.131, also Litografia Artistica Cartografica (Florence) 1:50,000 'Sentiero 50 dal Trasimeno alla Verna'.

The shores of the glittering expanse of Lago Trasimeno, Italy's fourth largest lake, are lined with picturesque thickets of reeds interspersed with water lilies. These provide nesting grounds for water fowl that feast on the wealth of fish in the shallows. The backdrop of pretty hills is covered with olive groves and vineyards, which produce very drinkable reds and whites, which come under the appellation Baccio del Trasimeno. Scientists believe the lake is the relic of a vast body of water that covered the area in Pliocene times, while picturesque stories tell of Jupiter casting thunderbolts into its depths, setting the entire surface aflame!

As far as archaeological evidence is concerned, proof of settlement dating back to the Iron Age has come to light, a spillover from Chiusi, together with later 3rd–2nd century BC burials from the Perugia side. Around this time Etruscan hydraulic engineers carried out extensive drainage work involving the marshlands in the neighbouring Val di Chiana, transformed into the 'granary of Etruria'. The lake, fed by rainwater, was given an artificial outlet – an underground channel attributed to the Romans, and which connected with the River Tiber below Perugia. It was re-adapted in the 15th century, and extant lengths are still visible near San Savino on the eastern shore. In the 1700s flooding became a constant problem and a plan was put forward to drain the lake completely. Overwhelming local opposition managed to thwart the idea despite government approval in 1865. Co-starring with the lake, however, the protagonist of this unusual itinerary is none other than Hannibal, the charismatic general from Carthage intent on bringing the Romans to their knees. Having traversed Spain and the Alps, Hannibal and miscellaneous troops such as Gauls, Spaniards and members of tribes who joined forces along the way, together with a single surviving elephant, were gradually making their way down Italy. Roman Consul and General Flaminius Gaius was hot on their heels, and, unwisely ignoring the string of bad omens that beset his camp that morning, fell into the masterful ambush set for him on the shore of Lago Trasimeno on the morning of June 21st, 217BC. The Romans approached from the west through the Passo di Borghetto where the hills reach right down to the water's edge. Once inside the natural amphitheatre and confused by a thick mist that enveloped them, they came under lightning attacks by troops concealed around the hilly flanks. Fifteen thousand Romans fell without even having time to draw their swords, Flaminius included, compared to a mere 1500 on Hannibal's side; 6000 were taken prisoner. Many local place names survive as reminders of the battle: Ossaia for bones, Sanguineto for blood, and Sepoltaglia for burials. The scattered Etruscan settlements in the area were allied with the Romans at the time, and Cortona, for example, is reported to have reinforced its ramparts in anticipation of attack. Passing through in the 1870s Henry James commented: 'Between Perugia and Cortona lies the large weedy waste of Lake Thrasymene, turned into a witching word for ever by Hannibal's recorded victory over Rome'.

Nowadays railway lines and freeways run along two sides of the lake, but the hills along the northern edge offer some excellent solitary walking. This itinerary follows in the footsteps of Hannibal and his allies. The departure point is the lakeside township of Passignano sul Trasimeno, of Etruscan origin, and whose name comes from Passum Jani, Pass of Janus. You climb high up into typical Mediterranean woods which provide shelter for elusive boars, foxes and porcupines. Ridges are followed for the most part, meaning extended scenic sections with

There are further walking possibilities in the area along routes marked by local groups with yellow triangle signs. Ask at the tourist office for the relevant green leaflets (*Itinerari Regione dell'Umbria* – in Italian), but do not attempt them without a good map as the descriptions are threadbare to say the least.

A suggested follow-up to the walk is a swim in the Trasimeno. Several modest beaches are dotted around the shores. As the depth of the lake never exceeds 6m, the March–October water temperature averages out at 21°C.

stunning views over the lake and distant mountains in addition to the wild hills inland towards the Apennines. Marvellous places for the troops to hide and prepare their attack. The walk is rather long and the extended shade-less stretches make it unsuitable for hot summer weather, though gentle breezes often keep the crests cool. Carry plenty of drinking water as refurbishment possibilities are few and far between. The second leg from Gosparini onwards is the prettiest and late spring wonderful for wild flowers. Several escape routes are given to shorten the day. There is red/white banded waymarking and numbering at fairly regular intervals, courtesy of the Arezzo Alpine Club. Other intersecting tracks and paths are encountered continuously, and a little care needed at the many junctions. A fair amount of climbing (some 680m) and descending (650m) is involved, though walking is mostly on good tracks. The first half follows the start of path n.50, the 106km route from Lago Trasimeno to La Verna, the Franciscan retreat above Arezzo, feasible in five days' walking. After that, branch path n.565 takes you through the ancient battle zones.

THE WALK

From the railway station at **Passignano** (265m), walk towards the castle in the old town centre, whose narrow old traffic-free streets deserve a wander. From the car park in Piazza Trento e Trieste directly below the tower, red/white waymarking for n.50 indicates the way north up a flight of steps before skirting the old walls. You turn left up a quiet surfaced road, lake views improving with every step. Keep straight on at the crossroads where a house is smothered in lilac, and up through olive groves which give way to broom and oak. Stops to admire the glittering spread of the lake, its three islands and the snail-like ferry, let you get your breath back as the going tends to be pretty steep. Past a couple of isolated houses, some 35min from Passignano (approx. 480m), leave the asphalt for a lane off left, northwest. (The 'Sentiero 50' map omits the continuation of the asphalt.) The vegetation is wilder here and includes more maquis-type shrubs and trees, while porcupine quills are scattered underfoot. You

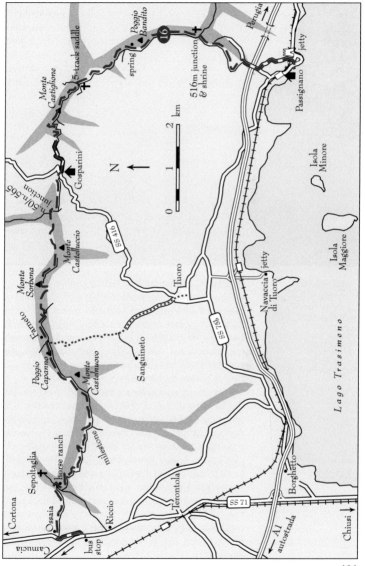

Lago Trasimeno and its islands from above Passignano

emerge on a wider track close to a conifer plantation, and bear downhill alongside an open grassy bowl full of sheep and wild orchids. 50min total means a junction marked by cypress trees and a shrine (516m), where you take the wide gravel track in common with the diamond-marked path n.3. After climbing past more pines, the track levels out and offers lovely panoramic walking and grazing horses, not to mention spreads of wild flowers. A brief detour up right to Poggio Bandito 604m (signposted 'Punto Panoramico') is feasible. Soon afterwards is a spring covered by stone slabs, theoretically suitable for drinking. At the junction close-by (1h25min), leave the wide track and keep straight ahead on a rock-base path past a farm. A level stretch through a picturesque glen, home to cuckoos, is followed by a brief climb brightened by pretty rock roses, then wood once more. A house and shrine precede your arrival at a saddle alias 5-track junction (1h45min). Shortly you'll need the fork right via a rougher track for the climb to **Monte Castiglione** (804m), disappointing as it is occupied by a modern villa and fenced-off parkland (2h10min).

Head down the wide track, but leave it at the first bend for the older way which curves down west through pretty mixed wood. The lake comes back into view, while you wend your way along a short stretch of asphalt through a rash of new houses to the road pass at **Gosparini** (606m, 2h30min). In addition to a hotel, there's a *trattoria*, bar and grocery shop.

Straight over the road route n.50, a lane now, follows the broad crest, whereas a little way along, n.3 veers left down a cypress-lined lane on its descent to Tuoro – a feasible escape route.

Keep straight ahead (westwards) along a single row of cypresses to join a wider track and the start of low fencing. A short way uphill, keep an eye out for the 674m path junction (2h45min) where your new path n.565 branches off left (due west) along the ridge. (N.50 sticks to the lane and heads northward for the Franciscan retreats above Arezzo.) This point is also the Umbria–Tuscany border. You go through a gate of sorts, hence beautiful pasture land which affords the magnificent spread of the lake in its entirety, as well as Passignano and the headlands. Cortona is visible WNW as is Alta S. Egidio and its aerials northwest. A stunning spot. The route leads towards the wooded profile of modest Monte Castelluccio, and at a fork and stone marker, takes the faint middle path straight up the grassy slope and into an oak wood. You don't actually touch the top of the mount, but skirt its northernmost flanks, through thick beech wood, the perfect setting for violets and anemones in spring.

At a saddle marked by cypresses a further track is joined, and you coast westwards along a ridge again. Soon at Monte Sorbena (694m) is a sharp turn left at a 'Pericolo d'incendio' sign (fire danger) down a rough path through scrubby dry vegetation that includes tree heather. Below you south now is the fatal (for the Romans) battle plain and these hills and ridges are the very places the Carthage army and allies hid until their well-timed ambush. Go right at the bottom and continue to a saddle (560m, 3h45min), **Farneto** on the map, and a favourite spot with hunters. Far beyond the lake Monte

• **Escape route to Tuoro**
(50min)
Take the narrow dirt road that winds its way southwards through the thick wood right into the midst of the ancient battle ground. After some 2.3km you pass close to Sanguineto, a reference to blood, then proceed for 1.5km on a quiet surfaced road to the peaceful village of Tuoro sul Trasimeno (309m, 50min), where Hannibal lives on in statue form. Buses pass here, but the railway station is a further 2km (20min) down on the lakeside.

Tourist Office
Passignano sul Trasimeno
tel.075/827635

Accommodation
Gosparini:
Hotel Cima
tel.075/844331

Passignano sul Trasimeno: Hotel Del Pescatore
tel.075/8296063

Cetona and Monte Amiata can be seen southwest. You are also right over the township of Tuoro and knowing that the main route continues for another 1h45min snaking its way along the undulating crest, an alternative exit is feasible here.•

The main route proceeds westwards in ascent once more, to Poggio Capanno (597m) – yet another renowned scenic point. After the track has levelled out somewhat, there are more mild up and downs past Monte Castelnuovo, then at around 560m (4h20min), n.565 leaves the main track which starts its descent towards Sanguineto – keep straight ahead on a rougher lane which touches on the Umbria–Tuscany border once more. Take the right fork at a milestone dating back to 1768 to reach an isolated house, passing round to its left. Keep a careful eye on waymarking on the next stretch, as there is a maze of secondary lanes. Vineyards are not far ahead, then a conifer plantation. You climb to a junction and iron cross next to a horse paddock, where a dirt road drops left for Riccio. Keep right and past a horse ranch in the direction of the picturesque church of **Sepoltaglia** set among cypresses on its separate outcrop, and visible a long way back. It is worth a detour, time permitting. After a couple of brick stations of the cross the marked path veers off left at a 463m fork (5h5min) before the church. This is where n.565 finally commences its last descent accompanied by hosts of the purple poppy-like flowers of the crown anemone. Once out of the wood, a shrine, orderly olive groves and vineyards are passed, before the modern-day cemetery and the road through the quiet village of **Ossaia** (292m). Turn left for the main road SS 71. The bus stop for Terontola is a little further along to the left on the opposite side of the road (5h30min grand total).

17: Isola Maggiore

Walking time:	45min
Distance:	2.2km/1.4 miles
Maps:	on p.131 and p.136

Access: See Walk 16 for details of how to reach Lago Trasimeno. To get to the island itself, the closest point of embarkation is Navaccia di Tuoro, though there are also sailings from Passignano or Castiglione del Lago on the western shore. Departures are virtually hourly throughout summer, and the trip takes about 10min.

For car-less visitors, Tuoro is served by frequent trains on the Terontola–Foligno branch line, and the railway station is particularly handy for the ferry jetty.

Set on vast Lago Trasimeno, diminutive Isola Maggiore boasts a picturesque fishing village where lace-making is still practised, monuments to Saint Francis who landed there one stormy night in 1211, and pretty walks through olive groves and along the wooded shoreline. The island lies a short distance from the northwestern edge of the lake and despite its name – Isola Maggiore means the greatest island – is the second largest, though a mere 800m in length. For anyone passing through the area with a half day or so to spare, the following stroll around the island is warmly recommended. The ferry trip over the vast calm expanse of water is fun and Isola Maggiore peaceful, not to mention car-free.

Weekends are best avoided as the entire population of Perugia seems to come to the Trasimeno to relax and the island can get crowded, though most visitors limit themselves to the village and don't necessarily venture out on the paths.

No difficulty at all is involved in this varied itinerary, perfect for all walkers. It's a good idea to be equipped with picnic supplies though you won't regret a meal of the tasty grilled lake fish in one of the island's modest restaurants. Visitors wishing to savour the calm atmosphere at length can even stay at the island's single hotel, where advance booking is advisable in summer.

THE WALK

From the landing stage on **Isola Maggiore** (260m), turn right (south) away from the village which is spread out along the western edge of the island. Follow the main road briefly then take the lane that climbs diagonally and decisively above the houses. Keep straight on past a

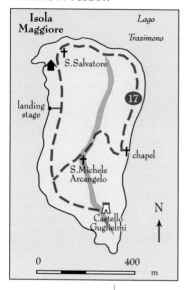

Isola Maggiore

Lago Trasimeno

† S.Salvatore

17

landing stage

† chapel

† S.Michele Arcangelo

Castello Guglielmi

N

0   400
m

Tourist Office
Castiglione del Lago
tel.075/9652484

Tourist Office
Passignano sul Trasimeno
tel.075/827635

Accommodation
Isola Maggiore:
Hotel Da Sauro
tel.075/826168

Tuoro:
Volante Inn
tel.075/826107

Passignano:
see Walk 16

turn-off, and all the way to private Castello Guglielmi in a commanding position on the point (15min). It was constructed in the 19th century on the site of a convent. A path drops to the shore.

Return the same way to the turn-off then go right (east) for a brief ascent to the 15th-century church of S. Michele Arcangelo which houses some beautiful frescoes, should you be lucky enough to find it open. At 309m this is the highest point on the island, and there are lovely views between the cypresses and ancient olive trees to the mountainous ridge north above Tuoro. The flourishing vegetation also includes asphodels and towering giant fennel plants. Imported ponies often graze here, at work as the island's non-polluting lawn mowers. This is a perfect spot to enjoy a picnic beneath ancient trees, before a path with crisscross fencing takes you down to the eastern coast and the **chapel of San Francesco** (30min total). A little further along the shady shoreline is a statue and shrine where the saint is believed to have landed on that stormy night, to spend time in solitary meditation.

The wide path continues around the island's pretty northern perimeter and eventually climbs a little before the tiny Romanesque church of **San Salvatore**. The village is just around the corner now, the stone walls of its restored 15th-century houses draped with drying nets, while the traditional fishing craft lay on the placid lake virtually at their doorstep.

A leisurely 45min in all should see you back at the jetty for the return ferry to Navaccia di Tuoro.

18: Perugia City Walk

Walking time:	2h + visits and miscellaneous stops
Distance:	5.5km/3.5 miles
Map:	on p.139 + detailed city map from the tourist office.

A mention of the magnificent city of Perugia in Umbria elicits reactions and associations that range from: the turbulent Middle Ages, Perugino alias Pietro Vannucci and Raphael's master, the famous 15th Umbrian school of painting, the renowned university for foreigners, and last but not least the *Baci Perugina* (kisses, literally) which are moreish hazelnut-filled chocolates. The Etruscans rarely rate a mention, and the city's Etruscan and Roman remnants play second fiddle to the multitudinous medieval and Renaissance delights, though the role of these early civilisations was particularly instrumental in shaping the city. Perugia is strategically located on the west bank of the River Tiber, the ancient boundary between Umbria and Etruria, and boasts a history that extends back over three millenniums. The original founders were the Iron Age Umbrian tribe, and the Etruscans took over from them around 6th century BC, transforming the settlement into a powerful member of their league of city-states. The centre was encircled by 3km of protective walls of travertine blocks, though of modest dimensions compared to those at Cortona, for example. The Etruscan city, possibly called Peiresa or Peithesa, became a close ally of Rome early on, which ensured the prosperity enjoyed in the 3rd–2nd centuries BC. However the civil wars during the struggle between the successors of Julius Caesar took a heavy toll. Fire destroyed a good part of the buildings, its population was starved into submission, and the entire senate massacred along with numerous others.

Perugia is eminently suitable for a walking visit, the twists and turns of its myriad laneways revealing mysterious corners apparently unchanged since olden times. Keys to the kaleidoscopic past are continually encountered

Access: Perugia can be approached by car from several directions. From the north via the A1 autostrada, take the Val di Chiana exit, thence coast Lago Trasimeno on the SS 75b. From the south, leave the A1 at the Orte exit and follow signs for Terni, thence the SS 3b. Once in the immediate vicinity of the city, park at the first car park you see, to avoid wasting time getting lost in the maze of streets. The main car parks are connected to the upper historical city centre by either escalator (scala mobile) or elevator (ascensore), modern amenities grafted comfortably onto the ancient mass. Traffic is banned from the city centre, apart from deliveries including tourist drop-offs.

The main railway station is well below the city, southwest, and frequent shuttle buses (those with numbers not letters) will take you up to centrally located Piazza Italia in a quarter of an hour or so. There are heaps of coach services to and from various parts of Umbria.

in a sort of historical stratigraphy. The extant sections of wall, on the other hand, mark the city's progressive expansion. The walk itself is confined to the city and is an easy stroll through the traffic-free centre. The variety of locations touched on is simply amazing – from the underground realms of the Rocca Paolina fortress, narrow medieval laneways, vast panoramic parks, an Etruscan well – without neglecting the medieval and Renaissance marvels of this fantastic city. Picnic supplies are hardly necessary as there are inviting bars, cake shops, bakeries, grocery shops and taverns on every corner.

The city's altitude of 500m above sea level combined with its proximity to the Apennines explains the not uncommon winter snowfalls, which make for spectacular photographs and play havoc with the traffic. However the snow is usually short-lived and any time of year is suitable for a visit, with the exception perhaps of July when crowds come for the Umbria Jazz festival.

Note: in addition to this city itinerary, a visit to the extraordinary underground tomb, the Ipogeo dei Volumni, is not to be missed. It can be found at a short distance from the city centre, right under the motorway! Details are given at the end of the walk description.

THE WALK

Start out from the southwestern corner of **Piazza Italia** and take the first leg of the escalator down into the surprising underground labyrinth of the **Rocca Paolina**. Very little is left of this erstwhile massive 16th-century fortress which bore witness to plenty of bloodthirsty events when Perugia belonged to the Papal States. Originally incorporating ten churches and 400 houses, with connecting tunnels throughout the city, it was gleefully demolished on the Unification of Italy in 1861. Go left along the extraordinary underground medieval way Via Bagliona. There are plenty of nooks and crannies to explore, including 3rd–2nd century BC Etruscan masonry. The way leads out through **Porta Marzia**. The base of this monumental doorway dates back to Etruscan times and, like others, bears the inscription 'Augusta Perusia' from the time the city came under the Romans and was

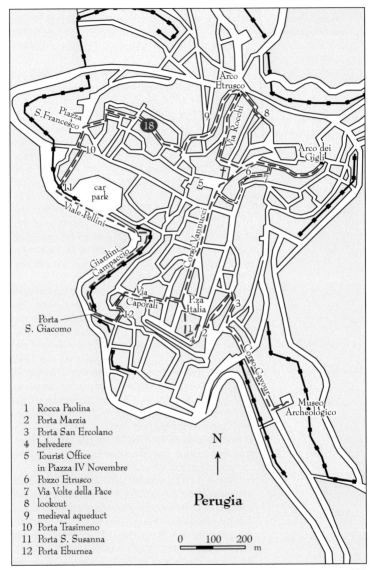

Arco
Etrusco

Piazza
S. Francesco

Via Rocchi

18

9

8

Arco dei
Gigli

10

7   6

11

car
park

5

Viale Pellini

Corso Vannucci

Giardini
Campaccio

Via
Caporali

P.za
Italia

3

Porta
S. Giacomo

12

1
4   2

Corso Cavour

Museo
Archeologico

1   Rocca Paolina
2   Porta Marzia
3   Porta San Ercolano
4   belvedere
5   Tourist Office
     in Piazza IV Novembre
6   Pozzo Etrusco
7   Via Volte della Pace
8   lookout
9   medieval aqueduct
10   Porta Trasimeno
11   Porta S. Susanna
12   Porta Eburnea

N

Perugia

0   100   200
                      m

139

Ipogeo dei Volumni, Ponte San Giovanni is easily reached on the FCU bus from Piazza Italia, daily except Sundays and holidays.

One of the largest and best preserved articulated tombs from 2nd century BC, it belonged to a leading family, the Velimna, or Volumni in the Latin version.

renamed Perusia. The ornate upper arched level features colonnades, busts of various divinities plus their horses, and the city's later 3rd century AD appellation 'Colonia Vibia'.

Outside the main walls now, turn left up the street and continue for a few minutes to a flight of steps on your right which leads down out through another extant Etruscan arched entrance reconstructed in the Middle Ages. It is known as Porta San Ercolano, after the 6th-century bishop whose resistance to Totila's Huns cost him his life. The story goes that after decapitation, his head miraculously returned to his body and reattached itself. The church dedicated to Ercolano is the unusual towered building on your right.

Straight ahead the way downhill soon becomes Corso Cavour, and passes the site of an ancient amphitheatre down to the right. Keep on through the crossroads for the crumbling Gothic style church of San Domenico. In to the left is the entrance to the erstwhile convent, now the **Museo Archeologico Nazionale** (15min this far).

Highlights are exquisite gold jewellery, hammered bronze panels, stelae and Etruscan inscriptions. The outstanding piece, however, is kept at the Florence Archaeological Museum: the Arringatore (Orator) is an elegant bronze statue of an Etruscan noble dressed and posing as a Roman aristocrat. The museum is worth a visit as it gives a good idea of the large number of interesting sites that have come to light in and around Perugia as well as the settlements dotted along the shores of Lago Trasimeno. Recent finds are on display in a temporary exhibit, including those from the tomb of the Cutu family in Monteluce on the city outskirts. Its cinerary urns, stuccoed then painted, may have been the work of the same craftsmen responsible for the famous Volumni ones.

Return to Piazza Italia the same way (30min total). As you emerge from the escalator, keep left for the Giardini Carducci and an extraordinary belvedere, a must on a clear day. The view inspired Henry James to declare: '[Perugia] ... ought to figure in the gazetteer of fond memory as the little City of the infinite View'. A plaque over the road in the corner puts names to the mountains such as the prevalently limestone range of the Monti Sibillini featuring snowbound Monte Vettore southeast, Monte Cetona to the southwest, beyond which is distant Monte Amiata.

Back at Piazza Italia once more, embark now on Perugia's main thoroughfare and showcase, Corso Vannucci. Named after the artist Pietro Vannucci, this was the city's main north–south axis in Etruscan times, and curiously, the current width of 15m corresponds closely to that of the central street in Etruscan settlements such as Marzabotto (see Appendix). Past the breathtaking Palazzo dei Priori (which demands a separate visit) is Piazza IV Novembre, with the tourist office tucked in around to the left. The square started out as the main intersection between the east–west and north–south axes in Etruscan times, then was paved by the Romans for the forum, complete with a monumental fountain. The magnificently sculpted 13th-century Fontana Maggiore was recently restored.

Around to the right of the cathedral is Piazza Danti, site of weekend markets and the entrance to the **Pozzo Etrusco**, the famed Etruscan well, on the right (45min this far). This extraordinary example of hydraulic engineering has a 450,000 litre capacity, is still fed by natural springs and is 35m deep and 5m across. Excavated in the agglomerate rock then partially lined with travertine slabs, its construction coincided with that of the acropolis, 4th–3rd century BC, and was obviously built to last – the overhead trusses weigh 8 tons each!

Back on street level in Piazza Danti, keep right through Piazza Piccinino and past the hostel along narrow pedestrians-only Via Bontempi which takes you into the amazing medieval heart of the city and the Arco dei Gigli. This modest old gateway is set at an angle to the original Etruscan walls, well inside the present city limits. Unless you opt to wander further through this fascinating maze, backtrack a little then turn down left at the sign for Trattoria La Botte. This leads into an unusual covered street, Via Volte della Pace, where time seems to have stood still since the Middle Ages. You emerge into Piazza Matteotti, then take Via Calderini to return to the cathedral hence Piazza Danti (1h).

George Dennis (1848) exhorted people to visit the Ipogeo dei Volumni:

'Let the traveller on no account fail to see the Grotta de' Volumni... one of the most remarkable in Etruria... It was soon after its discovery that I found myself at the mouth of this sepulchre. Never shall I forget the anticipation of delight with which I leapt from the 'vettura' into the fierce canicular sun, with what impatience I awaited the arrival of the keys, with what strange awe I entered the dark cavern – gazed on the inexplicable characters in the doorway – descried the urns dimly through the gloom – beheld the family-party at their sepulchral revels – the solemn dreariness of the surrounding cells. The figures on the walls and ceilings strangely stirred my fancy. The Furies, with their glaring eyes, gnashing teeth, and ghastly grins – the snakes, with which the walls seemed alive, hissing and darting out their tongues at me – and above all the solitary wing, chilled me with an undefinable awe, with a sense of something mysterious and terrible...'.

Keep left across the square and take the last street on the right, Via Ulisse Rocchi. This is reputed to be the oldest street in the city, part of the north–south axis, boasting Etruscan origins some 2500 years ago. Between its narrow precincts you leave this inner city area via the impressive double oblique arch of the **Arco Etrusco**. Though the arch itself was not actually Etruscan, the lower section dates from 2nd century BC, while the later addition features the words 'Augusta Perusia' after the Roman colony. The towers and loggia alongside belong to the 16th century (1h10min this far).

Outside the towering walls is Piazza Braccio Fortebraccio, which means 'arm strongarm', the name of a *condottiere* from the Middle Ages. It's worth taking the 10min detour right up the steep street that runs southeast alongside a church, and continue via the flight of steps to the lookout at Piazza Rossi Scotti and a ruined fortress. This was one of the main sites of the Etruscan settlement of Colle del Sole, probably named for a pagan temple to the sun located in the vicinity.

Perugia's impressive Arco Etrusco

From the Arco Etrusco, keep left following Via C. Battisti. It quickly curves southwards and crosses another

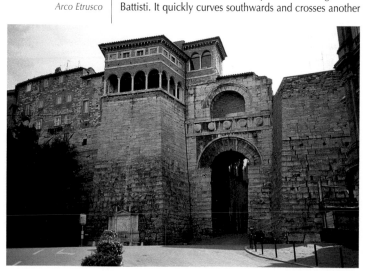

of Perugia's landmarks, the medieval aqueduct, now a walkway. At nearby Piazza Cavallotti, excavations have unearthed stretches of ancient roadway, but special permission is necessary to visit the site. Keep right through Piazza Morlacchi and proceed straight ahead downhill, turning left at the bottom, as per the line of the old Etruscan walls. Steps lead to a pleasant grassed area alias **Piazza San Francesco** in front of the curiously skeletal church of the same name which is flanked by the more solid Oratorio di San Bernardino and its ornate facade. This is believed to be the site of the Etruscan acropolis (1h30min this far).

Go south from here along narrow Via Curiosa which emerges just below ancient Porta Trasimeno. By taking Via della Sposa downhill you'll leave another walled area through Porta S. Susanna. Walk left along busy Viale P. Pellini past the car park and escalators, and just before the road tunnel (Galleria Kennedy), climb the steps into the pretty wooded park, Giardini del Campaccio, at the base of towering walls. Follow the path along right via the erstwhile moat, alias the original Etruscan boundary.

Having rounded the narrow corner, ignore the path variant that climbs left to a dead end, and drop to the side road hence through Porta San Giacomo. After that, the first narrow lane on your left, Via del Paradiso, is a steep series of steps back to the walls. Keep right to the interesting gate known as **Porta Eburnea** alias Arco della Mandorla. Dark fragments of the ancient masonry are still visible in this Etruscan entrance as are the usual inscriptions from Roman times. The archway was long held to be of good auspices, and members of the medieval Baglioni dynasty would leave the city this way on their way to battle.

Back in the inner city area, head up right on Via Bruschi, then Via Caporali, past highly recommended Osteria Garibaldi. A dog leg turn left then right up a final flight of steps will bring you out in **Piazza Italia** once more (2h total).

Tourist Office Perugia
tel.075/5723327

Accommodation
Hotel Etruria, Via della Luna 21
tel.075/5723730

Hotel Piccolo, Via Bonazzi 25
tel.075/5722987

Centro Internazionale per la Gioventù (non IYHF hostel), Via Bontempi 13
tel.075/5722880

Access: By car you'll need the SS 1 (Aurelia) that runs all the way down the Tyrrhenian coast. From the south, take the exit for Piombino and continue west to the actual outskirts of Piombino, before a secondary road turns north signposted for Baratti and Populonia. Some 5km along, keep a look out for a final turn-off left (west) which brings you out right on the Golfo di Baratti. If you approach from the north, leave the SS 1 at San Vincenzo, where a coastal road will take you 12km south for the minor turn-off right (west) for Baratti.

There are ample parking areas in the vicinity of the Parco Archeologico, in addition to the beachfront and port areas at Baratti. By public transport, the occasional ATM bus from Piombino comes as far as Baratti, with a stop right outside the Parco, and even proceeds as far as hilltop Populonia (except Sundays). Piombino in turn can be reached by train via the branch from Campiglia Marittima on the main Livorno–Rome line.

19: Baratti and the Populonia Promontory

Walking time:	2h + 1h for necropolis visit
Distance:	5km/3.2 miles
Map:	on p.147, also Multigraphic 1:25,000 'Isola d'Elba'

The splendid sweep of the Golfo di Baratti is lined by a wonderful spread of a beach, backed in turn by a flourishing stand of magnificent umbrella pines. The westernmost extremity of the gulf is dominated by a high rocky headland where the turrets of Populonia are silhouetted at sunset. As from 7th century BC, this promontory hosted powerful Pupluna, the sole Etruscan city-state on the coast. At its heyday the inhabitants numbered 25,000, slaves included, and the city was later encircled by defensive walls of large uneven blocks, stretches of which are still standing. The name, which appeared on the coins minted here, is derived from Fufluns, alias Bacchus, probably for the fertile vineyards. The actual port was in the sheltered bay below, and it witnessed intensive trade with Sardinia, Corsica, Marseilles and Greece. An Etruscan ship lies submerged off the point, and may have gone down on an outward voyage to the nearby island of Elba, which yielded vast quantities of iron ore and copper. After timber supplies were depleted on the island itself around 3rd century BC, smelting work continued on a greater scale on the mainland close to the port, and the old industrial area complete with furnaces can be visited. This period coincided with the advance of Rome and the consequent fall of many Etruscan cities. Under a pact, Populonia supplied Rome with mammoth quantities of iron for weapons during the Second Punic War (which ended with the defeat of Hannibal at the hands of Scipio in 202BC). Slag quickly mounted up to a height of 20 metres around the industrial area, burying an ancient necrop-

The unusually broad patrician Tomba dei Carri, Baratti archaeological site

olis. It was not until the 1930s, when a mining company from Piombino realised that modern methods could extract a lot more iron from the scoriae, that the monumental cemetery came to light once more. Some 2 million tons of material were removed, and the highly profitable venture lasted right up until the 1960s. The tomb structures inevitably suffered at the hands of the heavy earth-moving equipment, though most had already caved in under the immense weight of the slag. However thanks to extensive restoration, a very interesting range of tombs can once more be appreciated in the realms of the Parco Archeologico di Baratti e Populonia. The most memorable are huge round-based tumuli whose inner chambers can be reached via backbreaking passageways. One of the oldest (7th century BC) is the 28m diameter Tomba dei Carri, where a patrician family was interred along with two ritual chariots. All these above-ground structures were built with the local sedimentary rock known as *alberese*, a fine-grained compact variety of limestone, and there are also several sarcophaguses on the site in dark volcanic *nenfro* stone.

As you'll gather from the numbers of hunters who tramp through the area in autumn, the wild woods on the broad headland, which extends all the way south to Piombino, provide refuge for wildlife ranging from red and fallow deer to pheasants and the elusive wild boar, wreakers of havoc wherever they pass. On the other hand, the gardens and scrub around Baratti come alive with the flickering pinpoints of light from magical fire-flies, an unforgettable experience on a summer evening.

The itinerary described here starts with the guided visit to the San Cerbone necropolis, named after the 6th-century bishop of Populonia (see Walk 20). It then follows two of the Park's marked loop pathways climbing through dense Mediterranean wood and maquis thick with flowering species. A further guided visit is recommended to the Necropoli delle Grotte, a series of underground burial chambers dating back to 4th–2nd century BC. Several have painted dolphin and wave decorations.

Two compulsory follow-ups to the visit through the Parco Archeologico (for which an entrance fee is applicable), are Populonia and the 'Pineta'. See descriptions later.

On the practical side, refreshments are available inside the Park, at the Baratti beach and marina areas, as well as low-key Populonia, though a picnic is always a good idea for the quiet spots. There are several picnic areas with benches in the Park itself.

THE WALK

After the guided visit around the **Necropoli di San Cerbone** (allow 1h) take the track past the Visitor Centre for '**La Via delle Cave**'. It flanks Campo all'Arbia, a meadow thick with purple and yellow wild flowers in spring, as well as sturdy bushes of white tree heather with its tiny sweet-scented bell blooms. At a toilet block the path leads to the edge of wood, for an easy climb through the lovely dense wood of glossy holm oak. Not far in is an abandoned *cava*, the first of a series of erstwhile limestone–sandstone Etruscan quarries. With helpful informative panels, the path makes its way to a *belvedere*, with lovely views across the gulf and the Val di Cornia. It

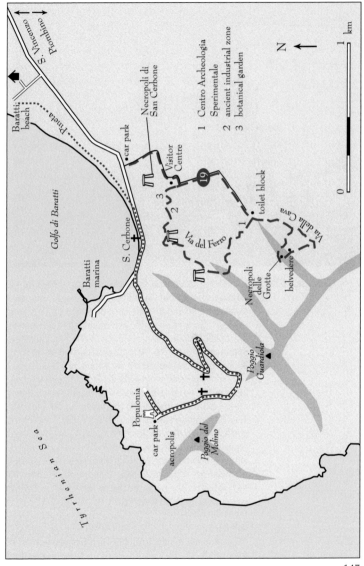

Key:
1 Centro Archeologia Sperimentale
2 ancient industrial zone
3 botanical garden

The castle at Populonia

also looks down into the elongated cut where burial chambers accessible via narrow steep passageways were excavated (Necropoli delle Grotte, guided visit). A loop takes you back to rejoin the ascent path, for the return to the toilet block. Turn off left for the Centro di Archeologia Sperimentale, where visitors can engage in making pottery, an archeological dig or fashion metalware.

From here slot into '**La Via del Ferro**' (the iron route). Keep to the ensuing left fork for a climb over a modest crest, before passing a tomb and a remnant of old wall. The route joins a variant at a cluster of tombs and heads north through the ancient industrial zone. Here the remnant structures bear witness to the Etruscan's metal-working from late 6th to early 3rd century BC. Evidence of dwellings have also been discovered, along with necropolises. The path concludes at a small botanical garden near the **Visitor Centre**.

Populonia

A quiet shady 2.5km/1.6 miles road (with a number of steep short cuts for walkers) winds up to the promontory and Populonia, high above the gulf. The final stretch is lined with cypresses and several magnificent old umbrella pines, not to mention stretches of ancient Etruscan defensive walling. The village and its fortifications are eventually reached (181m). Below the tower, inviting benches are superbly placed for picnics and contemplation of the vast expanse of the Tyrrhenian Sea and distant headlands. The city occupied this elevated site in Etruscan times and ongoing excavations can be visited a short distance below the parking area. In the old walled township itself, the private museum is noteworthy, as is the climb to the lookout tower, belonging to the 14th-century castle, for even more stunning views over the Golfo di Baratti and out to sea to the island of Elba.

The 'Pineta'

It's a shame to leave the area without a stroll through the stunning pine wood and along the beautiful sweep of sand for a swim. The beach is opposite the Parco, and you can walk north toward the wood of umbrella pines that stand in swaying sculpted forms against the wind. Twenty minutes or so along are a couple of bars and restaurants, where a road leads up to the welcoming family-run hotel.

Accommodation
Baratti:
Pensione Alba
tel.0565/29521, open
March–October

ISOLA D'ELBA

Maps: Of the plentiful maps sold on the island, most useful for walkers are the Multigraphic 1:25,000 'Isola d'Elba', the E.R.A. 1:30,000 map including helpful symbols and notes on vegetation and wildlife, and also the Kompass 1:30,000 n.650 'Isola d'Elba'.

Access & Transport: Elba lies a mere 10km from the industrial port of Piombino on the mainland, or the continent as the islanders refer to it. Piombino in turn can be reached by train on the branch from Campiglia Marittima on the Livorno–Rome line. A continuous year-round series of hydrofoils, high-speed catamarans, car and passenger ferries ply the water between Piombino and Elba, taking anything from 15min to 1h. Most go to the island's main harbour Portoferraio, though several smaller ports on the east coast are also served. ➤

A popular legend recounts that as the Tyrrhenian Venus rose from the sea her girdle shattered into jewelled fragments, which became Elba and the neighbouring islands. Later mythological visitors were Jason and the Argonauts who dropped by during their quest for the Golden Fleece. The dark stains found on pebbles on the beaches there come from the sweat they scraped from their bodies with strigils, the curved blades used by the ancient Greeks.

Starting as far back as 3000BC a long string of colonisers – the Etruscans included – were attracted by the island's immense mineral wealth, as reflected in place names, notably Portoferraio, Iron Port and Monte Calamita, Mount Magnet. However, more often than not Elba is equated with Napoleon Bonaparte's brief period of enforced sojourn there in 1814–1815 as nominal emperor, prior to the final French defeat at Waterloo.

A walking guide to Etruscan Italy could hardly be considered complete without this splendid island, the third largest in Italy after Sicily and Sardinia. Shaped like a huge fish with oversized rounded fins, Elba is 27km long and 18km wide, and boasts some 147km of coastline surrounded by glorious aquamarine waters. It is one of the seven islands in the Tuscan Archipelago, which recently attained National Park status, in spite of heated local hostility, often in the form of deliberately lit forest and bush fires.

The island belongs to a submerged chain of granite mountains of volcanic ancestry. Its geological composition is complex, and includes sandstone and limestone, without neglecting the extensively mined iron-bearing deposits on the eastern coast. An estimated one thousand minerals have come to light and enthusiasts can visit the modest collection in the mineral museum at Rio Marina. The area has been proposed for inclusion in Unesco's World Heritage List of Geological Sites. For non-geologists, the volcanic origins mean fertile earth and lush vegetation, not to mention thriving agriculture which includes olives and grape vines, hence some memorable wines both red and white.

As far as the Etruscans were concerned, Elba meant iron. Smelting was carried out in furnaces on the island at first. An average of 10,000–12,000 tons per year are believed to have been extracted during the peak 7th–3rd century BC period. As well as looking to their own needs, the Etruscans exported supplies to Greek cities on the nearby Italian coast as well as the Aegean. The Greek historian Diodorus Siculus wrote of the island and its flourishing iron activities in 30BC. Diminishing timber supplies, lack of inland water and an increase in pirate attacks, however, caused work to be transferred to Populonia on the mainland (see Walk 19). Later on the Romans took it up again and it was mostly Elban iron that provided their armies with hardware.

Archeologically speaking there is very little to see, apart from the quintessential furnaces and the remains of a sanctuary to the Etruscan god Tinia (alias Jupiter) on Monte Serra in the northeast of the island. A couple of mid-4th century BC fortresses have also been identified above the Procchio gulf and Portoferraio. A modest Archaeological Museum in Portoferraio has odds and ends. The Etruscans were preceded by the Ligurians and Greeks, who knew it as Aithalia 'smoky', a reference to the iron smelting work, and followed by the Romans (who knew it as 'Ilva' as per iron), the Pisans, Medici and the Spanish, not to mention the French who annexed it.

There are then many worthwhile reasons to take the ferry over. Walkers can ramble to their heart's content in the rugged mountainous interior with vast wild areas of surviving bush honeycombed with paths and cart tracks. Age-old chestnut woods alternate with abandoned terracing where old vines are being outgrown by wild herbs, then there are paths high above the turquoise sea through terrain akin to that of a botanical garden in spring ablaze with the typical colours of the Mediterranean maquis – rock roses, broom, gorse, Italian everlasting flowers, orange lilies, camomile, flowering prickly pear, and myriad aromatic wild herbs. Wildlife is plentiful and you may glimpse the red-legged partridge, Sardinian

➤ Travellers with their own vehicle in the high season (especially August) are advised to arrange transport well ahead.

Though a car is undoubtedly the best way to visit the island, it is feasible by bus. The island's bus company ATL has a surprisingly extensive network reaching all over the island, though frequency is another matter.

Wind-sculpted granite boulders on the Chiessi–Marciana traverse

mouflon (shy wild sheep imported for hunting stock), or wild boar, who leave plentiful signs of their passage in the form of upturned stones and scratchings, particularly in thick chestnut woods. Vipers are not uncommon on sunny stony ground, though they will slither away if given sufficient warning. Long trousers are recommended, along with light walking boots as the terrain is uneven and rocky in parts. A dip off the rocks or from one of the pebble beaches into the glorious Tyrrhenian Sea is a perfect way to end the day.

The best times of year to walk on Elba are spring (up to mid-June – best time for wild flowers) and autumn (September onwards). Unless you have advanced bookings for both car ferries and accommodation and don't mind extortionate prices, blazing heat and traffic-choked roads, July–August are inadvisable. Autumn usually means perfect walking weather, good visibility and warmer sea for swimming, in compensation for drier vegetation and lack of flowers. The mean annual temperature is 15°C.

Isola d'Elba Tourist
Office Portoferraio
tel.0565/914671

Tourist Office Piombino
tel.0565/22085-63290

20: Isola d'Elba:
Oratorio di San Cerbone

Walking time:	1h30min
Distance:	4.3km/2.7 miles
Map:	on pp.154/155

The walk climbs to the site of the sanctuary – a pleasant stroll on well-graded paths through shady chestnut wood, well within everyone's range. Relaxing, cool and quiet best describe it. The woods provide shelter for Sardinian mouflon. There is also widespread evidence of the flourishing wild boar population who go on rummaging forays leaving a trail of uprooted shrubs and overturned rocks. The chances of actually seeing them are very slim. On the vegetation side, sweet edible wild strawberries can be counted on in summer, as well as purple orchids and reddish-violet cyclamens nestling beneath the trees.

Both Poggio and Marciana have accommodation and grocery shops.

THE WALK

Before starting out from **Poggio** (330m), fill your water bottle at the central fountain which spouts delicious spring water. Take the road southwest signposted for Marciana. A little way along, just after the small cemetery, is a turn-off for 'Oratorio S. Cerbone'. A wooden arrow and n.1 indicate the start of a path bordered by old stone walls, which heads into the cool chestnut woods. (There is also a wide track, barred to unauthorised traffic, a longer alternative.) You climb gradually, and as you near the wide track, keep right over a dry watercourse and continue upwards. A brief chaotic area of felled trees is soon clambered through, and near a bend of the track you pick up the old path once more. The church of **San Cerbone** (531m) is soon reached in its cool setting amidst abandoned terracing (45min from Poggio).

Access: the villages of Poggio and Marciana are served by the island's bus line, though only 3km of quiet tarmac separate them. Drivers should proceed southwest from Portoferraio via Procchio and Marciana Marina, before winding up to Poggio. There are limited parking areas at both Poggio and Marciana.

San Cerbone, 6th-century bishop from Populonia, attracted the ire of Totila the Hun for giving refuge to Christians on the run. As punishment he was thrown to a ferocious bear, but the animal turned docile and even started licking the bishop's feet. Later threats of persecution forced him to flee to the island of Elba, where he spent time in contemplation at the sanctuary that now bears his name. When he passed away, in accordance with his final wishes, faithful followers spirited the body back to Populonia for burial under the cover of a providential tempest which hid the boat from the Lombards who occupied the coastal region at that time.

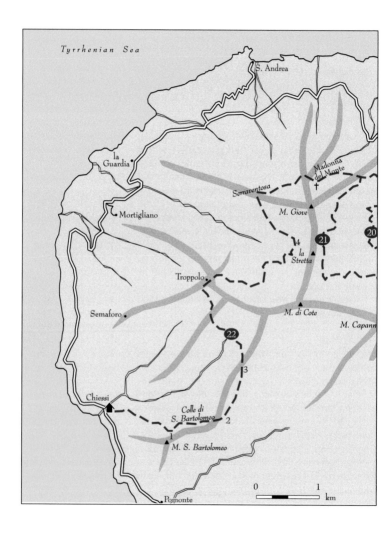

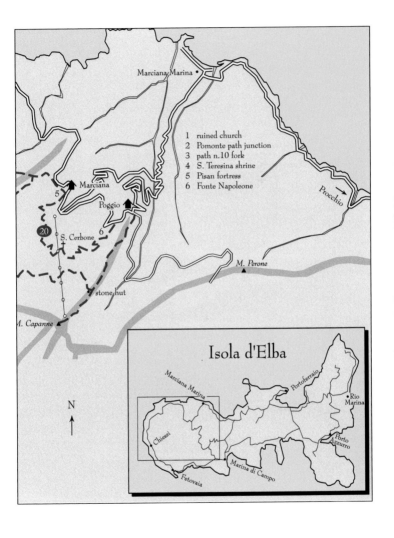

1 ruined church
2 Pomonte path junction
3 path n.10 fork
4 S. Teresina shrine
5 Pisan fortress
6 Fonte Napoleone

Isola d'Elba

Granite stepping stones below San Cerbone

After a contemplative rest in this peaceful spot, head west on the wide path (red and white waymarking – n.1 for Marciana). You pass under the open cabins of the humming cable-car for Monte Capanne. Ignore the unmarked turn-off right unless you need a steep exit route to the road below Marciana. Keep to the main track, in gradual descent now. The village of Marciana is glimpsed briefly through the trees to the north. You curve down to cross two moss-ridden watercourses via huge granite slabs, alias stepping stones, beneath magnificent specimens of ancient chestnut trees. The glittering sea also comes into sight from time to time.

A wooden bridge leads out of the wood beneath vegetable gardens to the edge of the village and fresh drinking water.

(For the fastest exit and return route to Poggio, turn right down the narrow road via the cable-car station to join the main road.)

The signs for *centro* lead along narrow alleys through a portal with a tiny church incorporated into the village wall. The main part of **Marciana** (408m, 1h30min total) is further along: you pass the main church then through the medieval gateway to a pleasant area of open air cafés. The bus stop is below on the road for the return to Poggio, however it's only a further 30min on the quiet road. At the last curve preceding Poggio is the well-reputed spring known, funnily enough, as Fonte Napoleone – the great man evidently came to partake of the water for health reasons. Locals queue to fill all manner of containers with this delicious fresh beverage, and the mineral water on sale all over Elba is bottled here. It's free of course at the roadside fountain.

Cerbone is said to have made his home here between 573 and 575 AD, but the actual building dates back to 1421 when San Bernardino of Siena suggested the Appiani family rebuild it. Much later on it fell into disuse, to be beautifully restored by an international group in 1993, with the inclusion of a full-length portrait of the bishop.

Accommodation
see Walk 21

21: Isola d'Elba: Monte Capanne Circuit

Access: Both Poggio and
Marciana are served by
the island's buses, but as
they are a mere 3km
apart, the return via the
shady road is not
unpleasant, should a bus
not be imminent.
Drivers take the road
southwest from
Portoferraio via Procchio
and Marciana Marina,
then the narrow winding
climb to Poggio.
Roadside parking is
possible here or further
around at Marciana.

Walking time:	5h15min
Distance:	8.3km/5.2 miles
Map:	on pp.154/155

At 1018m above sea level, Monte Capanne is the highest mountain on the island of Elba. Views from the top range in a vast sweep over the heterogeneous mass of Elba itself, along with a host of other islands dotted over the sparkling Tyrrhenian. But the best part is getting there – preferably on foot up the northeast ridge, where beautiful scenery can be admired from amidst blazes of early summer wild flowers. Furthermore encounters with the red-legged partridge and shy mouflon are not uncommon on open terrain, and the same is true of the omnipresent lizards. The starting point is the delightful village of Poggio, perched on the thickly wooded northeastern flank of Monte Capanne, overlooking Marciana Marina and its port. It offers accommodation, excellent restaurants, a grocery shop and fountain with fresh spring water, as well as the sum total of five piazzas which vie with each other for minimum dimensions. A perfect base for walkers.

After the visit to the top of the mountain, the itinerary cuts across the lower flanks of both Monte Capanne and Monte Giove and eventually approaches Marciana from the west. It can be modified and shortened in several manners by following appropriately signed paths encountered en route, for example a direct return to Marciana on path n.1 – allow 3h45min. Furthermore a small-scale cable-car (*cabinovia*) that departs a short distance south of Marciana, runs most of the way to the peak as an alternative.

Remember to carry plenty of drinking water on the walk as none is available en route. Light walking boots rather than running shoes are advisable to protect ankles and the soles of your feet on the stony terrain and provide

greater support on the steep stretches. Some 700m are climbed in ascent, and the final leg is somewhat steepish but nothing of consequence. The descent means a good but gradual 600m in addition to countless up and downs along the way. 'Average' on the difficulty scale.

Monte Capanne and its neighbours rise above thick chestnut and pine wood

THE WALK

From the centre of **Poggio** (330m), clear red and white waymarking for path n.2 directs you up through the shady premises of Hotel Monte Capanne. A brief stretch of wide track soon gives way to a good path that climbs decidedly southwards along the finger of crest that reaches down from the mountain. Granite steps lead through vegetation that is pure Mediterranean right from the word go. You rapidly lose count of the number of flowering shrubs – shoulder-high heather, perfumed broom and rock roses in mauve, yellow and white. Views back to the village of Poggio on its vantage point above the sea and Marciana Marina can be enjoyed at rest stops, while the modest rocky summit emerges ahead SSW out of the dark green swathe of wood. Once

The village of Poggio on the wooded flanks of Monte Capanne

past the junction with n.6 (628m), ground cover becomes lighter featuring cushions of miniature yellow broom spiked with dainty Elban violets in addition to camomile flowers.

At approx. 1h15min from Poggio is a junction at 750m (with n.1 from Marciana via San Cerbone), identifiable by its characteristic old stone goatherds' hut. Straight ahead, a little steeper now but problem-free, n.2 winds upward heading for a small building high ahead. (In the meantime path n.5 soon branches off east for Monte Perone and S. Ilario.) Some 2h from Poggio you reach the bar-restaurant and cable-car arrival. It's all very low-key really and doesn't get that crowded. Only a short climb away now, up amongst the TV transmitting towers is the actual 1018m top of **Monte Capanne** (total 2h15min). As well as views to the distant islands of Pianosa and Montecristo (south), Giglio (southeast), Capraia and Gorgona (northwest), Corsica (west) and the Tuscan coast (northeast), you get a good idea of the actual form of Elba itself, its varied coastline and vast mountainous interior.

(Path '00', a variant descent, forks off from here, but some experience and a head for heights are needed as several exposed points are touched on.)

Return the same way to the 750m path junction with the stone hut (30min). Now take path n.1 diagonally left to drop into Valle Grande and shady holm oak wood to a signposted junction – turn left on n.6 (or straight ahead to drop more directly via San Cerbone hence Poggio or Marciana, recommended on hot summer days as shade is a scarce commodity on the following stretch). The wide path heads westward through panoramic open terrain once more, orange lilies a possibility. Built up with dry stonework, it proceeds on a level, cutting across the vast smooth rock slabs of the northern flank of Monte Capanne, and passes beneath the cable-car. Back in conifer wood, another path junction is encountered – n.6 forks down right for a longish variant to Marciana.

Keep straight ahead (west) on the now unmarked path (numbered n.10a on maps). A gradual climb bearing north leads through scattered conifers recovering from a recent forest fire. At the next fork n.10a heads off left (SSW to La Stretta lookout point at 806m) whereas yours, now n.10, bears NNE, swinging high over the village of Marciana, with the sea glittering invitingly in the distance. The path descends easily through waist-high shrubs where curious rounded granite boulders dot the landscape. Tall conifers shelter the path as it crosses straight over a wider forestry track, to emerge onto the ancient paved access track (n.3) for the **Santuario Madonna del Monte**.

Turn right (east) downhill on it along with the Stations of the Cross. Cool chestnut wood characterises the final drop into the quiet village. You pass the 'Osteria al Noce' watering hole, then follow narrow alleyways through to the entrance piazza of **Marciana** (408m, 5h15min in all). The bus stop is below on the road.

Marciana also boasts a sizeable 12th-century Pisan fortress (closed to the public) and a modest archaeological museum with exhibits dating back to pre-Roman times.

Accommodation

Poggio: Albergo Monte Capanne
tel.0565/99083

Marciana: Private rooms c/o Birreria La Porta
tel.0565/901027 (shop hours) or
tel.0565/901149 (meal times)

22: Isola d'Elba: Chiessi–Marciana Traverse

Access: Chiessi is served by the bus line via Marciana to Pomonte, though several times a day runs connecting Marina di Campo with Fetovaia circle the entire western headland as well.

Without the bus, two cars are necessary – one to be left at the end point for the return trip.

Walking time:	4h30min
Distance:	10km/6.3 miles
Map:	on pp.154/155

This itinerary traverses Elba's vast scenic western headland, with astounding spring-flowering vegetation akin to a botanical garden. Due to its length it is not particularly popular, hence never crowded. Path maintenance is regular and no difficulties are involved. Those who make the effort are rewarded with some extraordinary undisturbed walking through a surprising variety of terrains. Midsummer is not advisable due to the heat on the long shadeless stretches.

While what has been described here from Chiessi to Marciana is in a northeasterly direction, hence with a total of almost 800m in ascent and 450m downhill, it is of course equally feasible in the opposite direction if you prefer more descent and less uphill. Timing is virtually identical. Don't be fooled, though, as there are plenty of ups and downs either way.

On the practical side, food shops and a range of accommodation are available at the low key coastal resort of Chiessi, while the possibilities at Marciana are limited to a few private rooms. The ideal way to tackle the walk would be as a 'transfer' with backpack, so that no bus times have to be respected at the end. It is usually possible to return to the starting point by mid-afternoon bus, but remember to check beforehand.

THE WALK

Leave quiet **Chiessi** (13m), its lovely rocky coast and clear water on path n.3, passing between Albergo dei Fiori and the church. Red and white waymarking soon appears to guide you up the bends of the narrow track. The few modest houses are quickly left behind and you zigzag through abandoned stone terracing where vines are smothered by masses of perfumed rosemary, fennel and bay laurel with its glossy aromatic leaves. Sweet yellow broom is of course plentiful. The vegetation is shoulder-high in places but the way is clear as you climb ESE towards Monte San Bartolomeo. Rest stops will give you the chance to admire views over the rugged coastline, and the flat island of Pianosa off to the south.

About 1h on is the signed turn-off to a lookout point and the ruins of a 12th-century church, although a single wall is all that's left standing. The path levels out now and traverses a wide shoulder, the Colle di San Bartolomeo (440m). You move east above the village of Pomonte and its valley, whose access path n.4 joins up, 1h30min from Chiessi. Monte Capanne is northeast now, crowned by antennas.

The path is much wider from here on, and heads in an essentially northerly direction, circling high above Chiessi. There is regular paving in the shape of large slabs of granite. (Path n.10 forks off soon northeast to Monte di Cote and an alternative link with Marciana.) A lovely area, wild flowers galore – broom, rock roses in mauve, pink, white and yellow, not to mention delicate hooded burgundy Serapias orchids in humid soil near trickling water. There is a long but gentle climb to a corner known as the **Troppolo**, the highest point on the walk at 692m (approx. 2h30min total). On clear days several islands are visible, starting with Corsica due east and Capraia to the northwest.

The area is like a well-kept and oversized botanical garden and you walk between masses of gaily coloured shrubs and cushion plants. In contrast, well below is fateful-sounding Uviale dell'Infernaccio, 'hell's water-course', which runs past the village of Mortigliano, the name a reference to death and terrible distant events perhaps. (Path n.25 turns down left WSW to the scenic point and signal station, Semaforo – an optional and worthwhile side trip, time and energy permitting.)

From this top spot, the path bears east and descends gradually into mixed wood with a couple of streams, weaving in and out of side valleys. Some 45min from the

Troppolo you move into an old chestnut wood and are greeted by a curious shrine to Santa Teresina carved into a tree trunk, and refreshed by cool spring water, the Sorgente del Bollero (560m, a short distance above the path). A welcome shady spot (3h15min total).

The last climb northwest along the flank of Monte Giove (Mount Jupiter) brings you out at another point with wide-ranging views and a signpost for another spring. If this Serraventosa point lives up to its name you'll at least get a breeze. The path coasts along east, high above the inviting turquoise cove of San Andrea. With luck, June walkers should find orange lilies along this stretch.

The final point to be rounded, as panoramic as ever, means weird wind-sculpted granite boulders, some like skulls. Pine trees reappear and shortly around right is the cool shade and peace of ancient chestnut trees at the Santuario **Madonna del Monte** (630m, 4h). The 16th-century exedra behind the church houses a fountain with delicious spring water, while the 11th-century frescoed church itself can probably trace its origins back to pagan times. It is, however, said to have been constructed to house a stone with a painting of the madonna, the work of an invisible hand. Most present-day visitors though are attracted by the fact that Napoleon spent twenty days of his exile here, causing great gratitude to be expressed by the local authorities who affixed large commemorative plaques to this effect.

The last half an hour is in easy descent on a paved Via Crucis track accompanied by modern Stations of the Cross. The final leg drops steeply through wood once more, and into the picturesque village of **Marciana**. You are guided past the interesting rustic restaurant Osteria al Noce, and after steep narrow streets you pass through the imposing medieval gateway and can collapse in one of the outdoor cafés in the small piazza at 408m, after a total of 4h30min walking.

The bus stop is below on the road.

Accommodation Chiessi:
Albergo dei Fiori
tel.0565/906013

Marciana:
see Walk 21

23: Parco della Maremma:
San Rabano Loop

Walking time:	3h15min + 45min beach detour
Distance:	7km/4.4 miles (detour 3km/1.9 miles)
Maps:	on p.166, also Multigraphic 1:25,000 'Parco dell'Uccellina. Monte Argentario'.

Bewitching red-haired beauty Margherita Marsilia was abducted from her father's castle high above the beautiful beach of Cala di Forno. Her captor was none other than the infamous 16th-century Turkish pirate Khair ad-Din, alias Barbarossa the Corsair. He sold her in Constantinople, where she wasted no time in becoming the favourite wife of the great Sultan Suleiman the Magnificent. A tower in the park is named after her.

An unusually happy ending for the best-known of the legends of pirates and brigands that abound in this vast wild stretch of inhospitable Tyrrhenian coastline between Southern Tuscany and Northern Latium, thus explaining the inordinate number of old watch towers scattered over the hills. Maremma, as the area is known, actually means 'maritime', though it is used more specifically to denote an unhealthy marshy area near the sea. Long, swampy, mosquito-ridden and malaria-prone – though some local people are reported to have developed resistence – it underwent large-scale land reclamation in the 18th century, hence the intensive agriculture practised nowadays. Drainage channels were dug and lines of maritime pines planted both to anchor the sand dunes and filter salt-saturated winds that would otherwise damage the graceful umbrella pines, important for their valuable crops of pine nuts.

Some wild wetland zones still survive intact in the proximity of the River Ombrone, providing the perfect habitat for a local variety of long-horned cattle as well as

Access: easiest by car – on the SS 1 (Aurelia) 16km south of Grosseto is the signposted turn-off for Alberese. It's a further 4km northwest in to the actual village and Park entrance. Leave your vehicle at the visitor centre.

By public transport the most straightforward system is to take the weekdays-only RAMA bus from Grosseto to Alberese. A July–August extension also serves the Marina di Alberese.

As far as trains go, only the very rare one stops at Alberese Scalo station, while bus connections for the remaining 4km to the actual village are a matter of luck.

As regards entry to the actual park, for a modest charge, hourly shuttle buses provide transport from the visitor centre the 5km along winding Via degli Olivi to Pratini, where the walk starts. Remember to check on return bus times before starting out as it's a long walk back if you miss the last one.

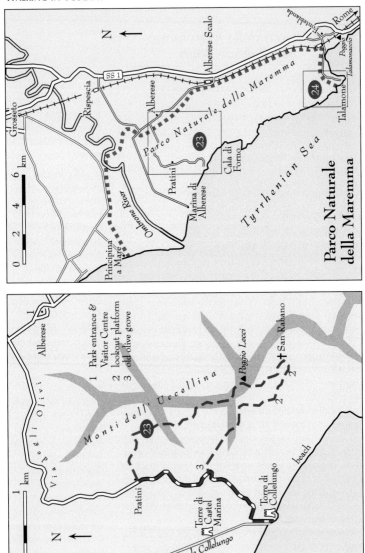

Parco Naturale della Maremma

N ←

6 km
4
2
0

Grosseto
Rispescia
SS 1
Alberese Scalo
Alberese
Fontebianda
Rome
Poggio Talamonaccio
Talamone
Talamone

Parco Naturale della Maremma

Pratini
Cala di Forno
Marina di Alberese
Ombrone River
Principina a Mare

Tyrrhenian Sea

24
23

(second map)

N ←

1 km
0

Alberese

1 Park entrance & Visitor Centre
2 lookout platform
3 old olive grove

Via degli Olivi

Monti dell' Uccellina

Poggio Lecci

San Rabano

2
2

23

3

Pratini
Torre di Castel Marina
Torre di Collelungo

beach

Canale Collelungo

wild horses which run free, unless commandeered by the *butteri* or cowboys. The latter give displays of their prowess in the local version of rodeos, and one good place to watch them at work is at Alberese on May 1st when 'La merca del bestiame' (the annual livestock fair) is held and colts and young bulls are branded.

Parallel to the coast and backing the stunning beaches and lowlands are the Monti dell'Uccellina, a low-lying range of limestone and siliceous rock which reaches a maximum height of 417m. The name means 'little bird' and comes from the multitudes of migratory birds which find refuge here as they pass through on their annual flights. Permanent inhabitants include wild boar, fallow and roe deer, porcupines, badgers, foxes and wildcats. These hills form the backbone of the Parco Regionale della Maremma, established by far-sighted nature lovers in 1975 on a unique unspoilt 100-sq km area, now open to the public. In addition to a modest visitor centre, a selection of marked itineraries, varying in length and difficulty, lead over the heavily wooded countryside through pristine maquis and along the stupendous beaches. Plenty to keep you busy for a good couple of days.

The walk described here gives the first-time visitor an excellent overall picture of the park area, as well as offering a rewarding walk in itself through some wild hills. Path A1 heads along the Monti dell'Uccellina ridge to the abandoned Romanesque abbey of San Rabano. A suprising variety of typical close-growing maquis vegetation accompanies the path, as do wide-ranging views over the magnificent spread of coastline. There is an optional but highly recommended detour to the beach.

This walk should, quite frankly, be considered compulsory.

Walkers must carry their day's supply of food and water as none can be found in the park, and swimming costumes are recommended. Remember there is no shelter from either sun or bad weather, so be suitably prepared. The hilly terrain involves a total height gain (and loss) of some 400m, but nothing steep or difficult. Moreover, while paths are generally clear, a good walking map is helpful.

Tourist Office Grosseto
tel.0564/462611

Parco Naturale della Maremma Alberese
tel.0564/407098

From Alberese entry is permitted for a maximum of 500 visitors per day to the central paths starting out at Pratini, year round from early morning to sundown. The entrance fee covers the shuttle bus.

Accommodation
nothing in the immediate vicinity.

Modern Grosseto offers a good range of hotels, otherwise see Walks 25 & 26 for Orbetello and the Argentario promontory. There's also a long line of camping grounds strung out along the SS 1 (Aurelia), southwards.

Lookout platform in the Parco della Maremma

Other worthwhile marked walks in the central Park area are A2 – Le Torri (the towers), 6km/4h; A3 – Le Grotte (the caves), 8km/4h; A4 – Cala di Forno, 12km/6h.

Further walks depart from Talamone in the Park's southern reaches (see Walk 24), as well as from Marina di Alberese on the northern edge – path n.2 in the vicinity of the mouth of the River Ombrone 5.5km/3h.

Note: June to September may mean restrictions due to fire danger hence accompanied walks only to set areas. Walkers are advised to phone beforehand to check on conditions.

THE WALK

From **Pratini** or 'little meadows', the clearing where the Park shuttle bus turns around, signposting for path A1 sends you off eastward to start the climb to the main ridge. You pass through thick vegetation, typical of the maquis. There are bushy holm oaks with their leathery oval leaves, which used to be a favourite with the charcoal burners, whose now-abandoned clearings you pass through along the way. As well you see the curious strawberry trees hung with clusters of orange-red fruit balls or delicate white blossoms. Spring brings the scented yellow display of flowering broom, along with rare wild orchids. Keep an eye open for the cork oaks with their unusually thick fissured grey bark, stripped every six or so years for commercial reasons, and once an important source of income here. The widespread scratchings and evidence of digging are the telltale signs left behind by wild boars, though close encounters can virtually be ruled out as the beasts are notoriously timid, as are the deer.

Some 1h30min of weaving your way SSE through undulating terrain, and you reach the highest point on the Monti dell'Uccellina – Poggio Lecci, 417m. A grassy clearing, perfect for picnics, enables you to admire a superb panorama which spaces over the rolling wooded terrain to the coast, beyond which the Isola del Giglio sprawls on the southeast horizon.

A gradual descent leads to the evocative ruins of the **Abbazia di San Rabano** (325m, total 2h), almost hidden amidst a wood of tall downy oak trees. This white stone Benedictine abbey was probably named after 8th-century Frankish scholar Rabanus Maurus. It dates back to the 10th century and was both active and influential through to the 16th century. Under the monks large areas of forest were cleared for agriculture and in all likelihood a settlement grew up nearby. The growing menace of pirate attacks in the early 1300s made it necessary for a group of knights had to be called in, and the fortifications and Torre dell'Uccellina were constructed under their direction.

This point is the furthest south on the walk and path A1 proceeds northwest, with ever-improving views over the coastline. Two wooden lookout platforms are placed along the way for this purpose. Downhill at a decent rhythm you drop to an olive grove with ancient gnarled trees, to emerge on narrow surfaced **Via degli Olivi** once more (66m, 3h).

To return to Pratini and the bus, turn up right for a final winding 15min on foot.•

• **Detour to the beach**
(45min return time)
A dip in the Tyrrhenian Sea from a perfect beach (a mere 20min away) is an appropriate reward for all the hard walking. From the olive grove, head left downhill on the road. It curves around beneath the tall graceful pines, on the edge of the 600-hectare forest planted in the 18th century. One of the old drainage channels is followed briefly, and you might catch sight of otters at play there. A passage through the dunes leads finally to the wide expanse of pale sand. In addition to an excellent swim, you also get a good look back up at the limestone cliffs and the nearby watch towers built by Duke Cosimo dei Medici in the mid 1500s. Return the same way to the Via degli Olivi hence Pratini.

24: Parco della Maremma: Punta del Corvo-Talamone

Walking time:	2h15min
Distance:	5.5km/3.4 miles
Maps:	on pp.166 & 171, also Multigraphic 1:25,000 'Parco dell'Uccellina. Monte Argentario'

Access: By car 24km south of Grosseto on the SS 1 (Aurelia), turn off west for Fonteblanda, then continue the 4.5km through to Talamone. The walk starts approx. 1km before you actually reach the township, and it is possible to drive in as far as the start of the path itself, though the track is rather rough.

As far as buses go, several services a day go as far as Talamone, with connections at Fonteblanda (on the well-served Grosseto–Orbetello line). Get off at the Camping Village Talamone stop, 1km before the township. The odd train also stops at Talamone station (located at Fonteblanda in actual fact!), but connecting ongoing buses for the remaining 4.5km are another matter.

The history of Talamone can be traced far back into mythical times as it is said to have been founded by Telamon, one of the Argonauts, and Jason himself is believed to have paid a visit. Under the Etruscans it was known as Tlamu, and most likely occupied a site, south across the gulf from the present township, on the prominent hill Poggio Talamonaccio. This sizeable settlement featured a temple dating back to the late 4th century BC, though not discovered until the late 1800s when the Italian government decided to construct a fort there. The impressive 2nd century BC pediment, the 'Frontone di Talamone', 14m long and 3.5m high, has been recomposed and will hopefully be on display locally, as plans were under way to transfer it from the Florence Archaeological Museum. It is decorated with richly modelled terracotta figures vividly depicting the myth recounted by Sophocles of the celebrated expedition of the 'Seven Against Thebes'. Other finds from the site include an interesting collection of votive objects, also on display in Florence. Both temple and town were devastated by fire in 82BC at the hands of the Roman general Sulla, in retaliation for the 6000 Etruscans enlisted by his arch enemy General Marius during the Roman civil war.

In the Middle Ages the Sienese purchased Talamone in what turned out to be a futile attempt to relaunch the port in order to compete with Pisa. Turkish pirates then wrought havoc with their frequent pillaging, until the Spanish took over and organised full-scale restoration. Later visitors were Garibaldi and the Thousand who

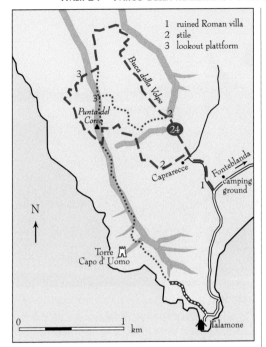

1 ruined Roman villa
2 stile
3 lookout plattform

Buca della Volpe

3

3
Punta del Corvo

2

24

2
Caprarecce

Fonteblanda
camping ground

1

N

Torre Capo d' Uomo

0   1   km

Talamone

This peaceful walk traverses the wild uninhabited southern reaches of the Parco Naturale della Maremma (see Walk 23 for the central area of the Park). An easy route (entry fee applicable) that promises expansive views of sea and unspoilt coastline below the Monti dell'Uccellina hills colonised by pristine maquis vegetation. A rewarding end to the day's efforts is a stroll around nearby Talamone. Massive ramparts guard a sleepy village and its 14th-century castle, poised dramatically on the cliffs, behind a small harbour crammed with yachts side by side with fishing boats whose day's catch is proudly displayed on the quayside.

called in en route to Sicily in 1860, to collect arms and supporters as part of the campaign to unify Italy.

While the route described is adequately marked, walkers must be equipped with food and water, not to mention suitable equipment for protection against the sun or bad weather, as there is no shelter along the way. Several shorter variants are given in the following description.

Note: From June to September the area may be subjected to restrictions due to fire danger. Walkers are advised to check beforehand by phoning the Visitor Centre at Alberese (see Walk 23).

In the southern reaches of the Parco della Maremma, with Poggio Talamonaccio in the background

Tourist Office Grosseto
tel.0564/462611

Tourist Office Orbetello
tel.0564/860447

Accommodation Talamone:

Hotel Capo D'Uomo
tel.0564/887077 (3-star)

Talamone International
Camping
tel.0564/887026

THE WALK

On the road about 1km east of **Talamone**, soon after the camping ground and paddocks, a rough lane turns off right (NNW). There are signs for 'Ippica le Cannelle' and the Parco Naturale della Maremma, all but hidden by shrubs. A short way up on the left are the overgrown ruins of several Roman cisterns and a villa. Ignore the turn-off right, and soon over the rise you reach the signposted entrance to the Park and T1/T2 itineraries in the vicinity of a Visitor Centre (entry tickets on sale) at **Caprarecce** (49m, 10min this far). Possible parking. The initial stretch of path northwest follows an old stone wall through an olive grove, which soon gives way to unbelievably dense thickets of evergreen rosemary bushes decorated year-round with clusters of pale blue flowers. Interspersed are pastel-coloured rock roses and goldy-locks, also known as 'stinking everlasting' as it emanates a curry-like smell when crushed. The clay and limestone-based path proceeds to the edge of a wood and a stile (total 20min). (T1, a shorter circuit, heads off left/west at this point and joins T2 on the ridge.) Stick to T2 which proceeds straight ahead (northwest) below the shady canopy of trees to follow the shallow valley called Buca della Volpe (the Fox's Hole). The damp sclerophyll wood is the perfect breeding ground for a multitude of mushrooms and toad-stools, in addition to the local variety of wild boar whose scratchings and digging are everywhere. You climb back out to dry scrubby vegetation once again, tall clumps of heather included. Back are clear views over the gulf, southeast.

It's a total of 45min to the crest. For a brief stretch the path leads left, then to a branch right (signposted) through to a wonderful **lookout** point complete with wooden platform, high above the rocky coast and blue sea. It takes in the Argentario promontory and the Isola del Giglio. A lengthy stop is in order.

T2 heads steeply downhill towards the sea now, necessitating some scrambling and a little extra care as it can be slippery if wet. 15min from the lookout a wider track is joined. Keep left (a sign says 'T1 lungo') for the gradual climb southeast below the Punta del Corvo amidst some marvellous panoramas of the Maremma coast – and numerous watch towers to boot.

Back on the ridge again (total of 1h30min), turn left at the intersection of paths (198m), as per T2.•

• Ridge alternative
(40min)
Should the steep drop from the lookout point not be to your liking, return to the ridge path and turning right, proceed south along it. You encounter a further marvellous panoramic platform with good views to Talamone and the castle, then two feasible paths present themselves for the return drop east to Caprarecce to complete the loop.

Variant exit to Talamone (40min)
From the 198m intersection, by taking the right branch, it is possible to reach Talamone without backtracking. The clear but unmarked path drops a little, and heads south towards an old 16th-century watch tower known as Torre Capo d'Uomo (on private property). The run-away wife of a sultan evidently took refuge here along with some wonderful treasure. Threatened by a raiding party led by the much-feared Barbarossa the Corsair, she fled by way of a web of mysterious passageways cut into the cliffs, and the search is still under way for the mysterious treasure.

Follow the wire fencing down left to a gate. Here it is possible to leave the realms of the Park and drop to Talamone via the residential area.

The main itinerary goes north now, and there are some lovely views southeast over the gulf to Talamonaccio, not to mention the vast hilly hinterland. Loaded strawberry trees under siege from huge butterflies line the way. Just a short distance along, T1/T2 leave the ridge to drop east through shady wood once more. Several clearings once used by charcoal burners are passed, then an old olive grove. A stile needs crossing, then a final sea of rosemary shrubs before a stone wall, where you go right for the exit and parking area (2h).

Back down at the road, it's a further 10min right past the cemetery for **Talamone** itself (2h15min total).

25: WWF Oasi Laguna di Orbetello

Walking time:	2–3h (guided visit)
Map:	on p.176

Another highly recommended visit for bird enthusiasts, in addition to the Lago di Burano Reserve (see Walk 28) is the 'Oasi di Protezione e Riserva di Orbetello'. This sizeable 850-hectare reserve occupies the ample northern corner of the Laguna di Ponente (western lagoon), north of Orbetello. It was established by Italy's World Wildlife Fund for Nature in 1971, and has been recognised as a wetland of international importance under the Ramsar Convention. It receives fresh water from the River Albegna and has two outlets to the sea. The lagoon boasts over 200 bird species, a combination of full-time residents and winter visitors. Actual numbers are up in the tens of thousands at peak times. The shallow water, with an average depth of 1m, is the perfect spring nesting ground for the star of the reserve, the elegant black-winged stilt, also known as the Knight of Italy. Unmistakable, it strides through the wetlands on oversized spindly red legs to lay its eggs amongst salicornia plants. A one-time visitor which now nests on a regular basis is the stunning flamingo, observable in noisy flocks along the lagoon edge. The other numerous clients of the fish-rich waters are spoon-bills, avocets and even storks. Foxes, badgers, porcupine and an unusual array of butterflies complete the wildlife picture. Here as at Burano the vegetation ranges from dune cover and maquis to thick woods made up of poplars, ash and elm, with notables such as rare orchids in spring.

As is the norm in the 'oases' run by the World Wildlife Fund for Nature, visitors are accompanied by wardens on an informative guided walk along the edge of the lagoon via several lookout posts. This is possible from autumn through to spring, after which time the birds are allowed some privacy for family matters.

Access: RAMA buses run between Grosseto and Orbetello (except for Sundays) and will drop you off at the entrance on the southern outskirts of Albinia. From the main road it's only a short walk to the entrance to the 'Oasi della Laguna di Orbetello'. Drivers on the SS 1 (Aurelia) will see the signposted turn-off about 2km east of Albinia, and 6km west of the turn-off for Orbetello.

Oasi della Laguna di Orbetello
tel.0564/820297. Open for visits Thursdays, Saturdays and Sundays at 10am and 2pm, September 1st – April 30th. Entrance fee.

Accommodation Orbetello:
see Walk 27

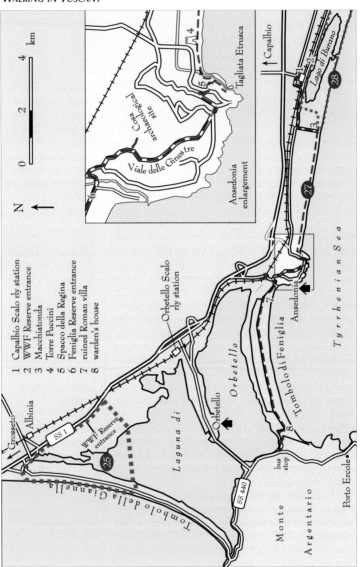

1 Capalbio Scalo rly station
2 WWF Reserve entrance
3 Macchiatonda
4 Torre Puccini
5 Spacco della Regina
6 Feniglia Reserve entrance
7 ruined Roman villa
8 warden's house

26: The Argentario Promontory

Walking time:	3h45min
Distance:	13km/8.2 miles
Map:	on p.179, also Multigraphic 1:25,000 'Parco dell'Uccellina. Monte Argentario'.

As the handsome, battle-weary knight crossed the threshold of the tower, the precious gold hen and chicks he had brought from the Orient miraculously came to life. It was as though life were compensating for the tragedies to come – the knight was to be smitten by grief on discovering that his beloved blue-eyed maiden with golden hair had fallen into a trance and since wasted away. A Tuscan Rapunzel, her residence was the Torre dell'Argentiera, an unusual tall tower on the Argentario promontory, built above Porto S. Stefano by the Sienese in 1442 as a lookout tower for marauding pirate ships from Turkey. It survives to this day, curiously devoid of windows and doors, with the exception of a single slit opening originally reached by ladder, and is the first stop on this circular walk.

George Dennis called Monte Argentario the 'natural Gibraltar of Italy'. Part of an immense submerged chain along with the islands of the Tuscan Archipelago, it has had a chequered past in terms of both nature and man. Jutting out well into the Tyrrhenian Sea from the coastline of southern Tuscany, it brings to mind an octopus with tentacles outstretched to the land, or, for Dennis 'a majestic vessel ... moored by its three ropes of sand'. It is easy to imagine the island it once was – 'Insula Matildiae' for the Romans, though partially joined to the mainland then, as testified by the Cosa-Porto Ercole road which ran along the Tombolo di Feniglia. The present name Argentario is probably a reference to the banking activities of the local Roman landowning family (*argentari* means bankers). Nowadays it has three links to the main

Access: RAMA buses from Grosseto serve Orbetello, from where there are frequent connecting runs to Porto S. Stefano. By train, you'll need the station of Orbetello Scalo, hence bus to nearby Orbetello and so on. NB. there are several daily through trains from Florence via Siena and Grosseto to Orbetello Scalo.

With your own transport, from the SS 1 (Aurelia) there are well-signed turn-offs for the Argentario and Porto S. Stefano from both Albinia and Orbetello Scalo via the SS 440.

coast, in the form of the Feniglia and Giannella *tomboli* or sand spits, then the causeway from Orbetello built in 1862 along the course of an ancient Roman aqueduct.

The Argentario promontory 'peaks' at 635m with antenna-ridden Monte Telegrafo. Despite the devastating forest fires which rage every summer and the rampant construction of holiday houses over the rapidly diminishing wooded hillsides, vast wild tracts of holm and downy oak and maquis vegetation continue to shelter wildlife and flora including rare specimens of wild orchid in spring.

Generally speaking, better walking is to be found in the wilder Parco della Maremma Park to the north. However the itinerary described here has been chosen for the stunning views it affords on the final stage embracing a host of islands belonging to the Tuscan Archipelago as well as Corsica. On the whole the walk is trouble-free, though several steepish stretches are involved. It follows a series of narrow roads and tracks as well as the occasional path through small properties, circling above the valley backing Porto S. Stefano, before culminating in the scenic tract. A total of 370m are involved in ascent/descent.

The lookout site (ex signal station) can also be reached more directly from Porto S. Stefano: you can actually drive as far as Fontana Carpina, though the road is particularly steep and narrow.

Avoid visiting during the July–August period if possible, as roads and beaches tend to be congested, and accommodation both costly and hard to find. Furthermore the summer heat can mean unpleasant conditions for walking in the innermost valleys, though sea breezes are a bonus on the coastal tracts.

THE WALK

From the large car park on the eastern edge of **Porto S. Stefano**, follow the main road uphill (east) above the port and turn right along Via delle Fornaci, keeping left at the first turn-off. Several bends in ascent and the houses are left behind in favour of quiet shrub cover and olives and a narrower road, southeast now. Up on the Costa delle

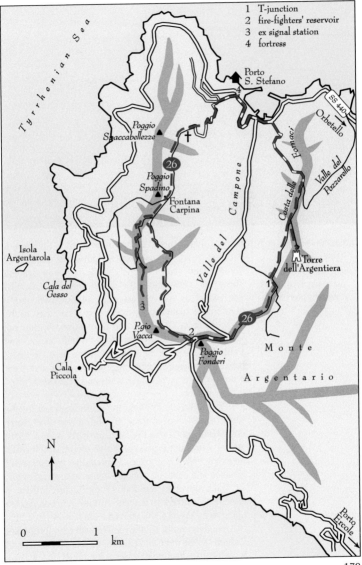

1 T-junction
2 fire-fighters' reservoir
3 ex signal station
4 fortress

Tyrrhenian Sea

Porto
S. Stefano

SS 440

Orbetello

Poggio
Spaccabellezze

Poggio
Spadino

Fontana
Carpina

Valle del Campone

Costa delle Fornaci

Valle del Pozzarello

Isola
Argentarola

Cala del
Gesso

Torre
dell'Argentiera

1

3

26

26

P.gio
Vacca

2

Cala
Piccola

Poggio
Fonderi

M o n t e

A r g e n t a r i o

N

0   1   km

Porto
Ercole

Both Isola del Giglio and Montecristo are visible from the old signal station lookout on the Argentario promontory

Fornaci ridge (150m, 25min from Porto S. Stefano), it becomes a dirt track and bears south in the direction of the tall slender tower, namely the Torre dell'Argentiera. There are views over the lovely nearby Valle del Pozzarello (an old military road winds down here – possible alternative exit), then beyond northeast to the Tombolo della Giannella and the lagoon. Further on, views in the other direction mean Porto S. Stefano and Valle del Campone, built-up to say the least. You pass between scattered smallholdings where grapes and olives grow enclosed by old stone walls and guarded by dogs, usually friendly.

At a fork (10min along the crest) keep left for the steep rough access track to the tower. The **Torre dell'Argentiera** (50min this far), 25m high, is set at 252m amidst a remnant cypress and pine wood, which while impeding views, guarantees an evocative atmosphere of isolation and calm, far from the frantic tourism below.

Back down at the fork (10min), turn left on a concrete-base track in descent. At the T-junction, go left uphill to a ridge (147m), then take the narrow track right between high walls, southwest. Through more properties it climbs a little more and emerges on the road from Porto S. Stefano. You continue in ascent for a brief stretch along the road to **Poggio Fonderi** (280m, 1h30min) and more wide-ranging views. Turn right at the junction (the road is signposted for Hotel Torre di Cala Piccola). There is a glimpse of the Isola del Giglio before you take the first turn off to the right, past a modest reservoir for fire-fighting purposes. A shady track leads west now through an oak wood dotted with cyclamens to pass below Poggio Vacca, before emerging to bear north beneath the rocky crest of Costa dei Ronconali. The terrain becomes wilder and more interesting with abandoned terracing invaded by blazes of multicoloured rock rose and broom in spring. The vineyards further ahead are in good hands, producing the fine local white wine Ansonico.

Half an hour from Poggio Fonderi will see you at a fork in the track (230m) and a marvellous outlook north to the seemingly never-ending coast of Tuscany. (For drinking water, Fontana Carpina is but a few minutes' dash along the track right.)

Go left here for the easy climb southwards on a narrow concrete and stone road, ignoring all turn-offs. The few huts and properties are soon left behind and you pass through wilder bush with plenty of flowering shrubs and herbs. However you will be kept occupied by the ever-widening panorama that opens up all around. Keep left on the upper track to the crest. As the track curves left to enter private property, leave it for the narrow path straight ahead. Overgrown in parts, it follows an old stone wall underfoot and a further 15min will see you at the **abandoned signal station** (2h30min). Set at 370m among limestone outcrops high above the coastline, it is an unbeatable picnic spot with a simply magnificent panorama worthy of lengthy contemplation: the triangular rocky island below is known as the Argentarola, while WSW of course is the Isola del Giglio with Montecristo to its right and on a clear day the distant hilly coast of Corsica west, and the spread-out mass of Elba northwest, without forgetting the extensive wild Maremma coast to the north, and back to the Orbetello lagoon. Monte Telegrafo and its antennas can also be seen southwest, and Giannutri around the corner south. Judging from the overgrown surrounds, and profusion of

View to the Tombolo della Giannella and Orbetello with its lagoon

fig trees, broom and rock roses, hardly anyone seems to come this far.

Return to the 230m fork, allowing a further 30min (3h total).

Keep left now, and a further intersection is reached, where you'll find **Fontana Carpina** and drinking water – the tap is in the welcome shade of trees on the left, with a couple of chairs! Continue on the quiet pleasant road in the same direction, skirting beneath modest Poggio Spadino, while there are lovely views of the Tombolo della Giannella and Orbetello jutting out into its lagoon. After a level stretch just after modest knoll Poggio Spaccabellezze, the road bears right to start its descent. A somewhat incongruous shrine crowned with a brick cross is passed. Below, where the road (asphalted now) curves to the right, a faint path cuts straight down into the residential area to rejoin Via della Grotta, on its rather steep descent. Keep straight on down to an intersection then keep right on the continuation of Via della Grotta. You soon join the wide panoramic road Via Baschieri Salvadori opposite **Porto S. Stefano's** historic 17th-century Spanish fortress. Keep right, and not far downhill is the port area once again (3h45min grand total).

Tourist Office Porto S. Stefano
tel.0564/814208

Accommodation Porto S. Stefano:
Hotel Alfiero
tel.0564/814067

27: Ancient Cosa and the Tombolo di Feniglia

Walking time:	4h30min + extra for visiting the ruins of Cosa
Distance:	17km/10.6 miles
Map:	on p.176, also Multigraphic 1:25,000 'Parco dell'Uccellina. Monte Argentario', except for the initial stretch to Macchiatonda.

On the wild southern coast of Tuscany are immense expanses of reclaimed swamps, work done over past centuries to combat the scourge of malaria, along with several remaining placid lagoons, havens for the multitude of birds seeking protection from hunters and rest during long migratory flights. Along the edges are long deserted beaches backed by thickly wooded dunes sheltering fallow deer, interrupted by picturesque bays and rocky promontories once belonging to Etruscan then Roman dominions, and now scattered with ruins of port structures, settlements and villas. This is the setting for a long but rewarding itinerary which encompasses a breathtaking range of natural and historical landscapes and offers treats for lovers of archaeology, ornithology and seashore habitats, as in beaches!

A convenient base is the small township of Orbetello, which occupies a unique position on a narrow isthmus in the middle of a lagoon, and well known for glorious sunsets. It is linked to both the mainland and the Argentario promontory by road. Though the town gained great importance in the mid 16th century under the Spanish, it was founded by the Etruscans in 4th century BC. A satellite city under Vulci, it became an essential port, with the lagoon at that time separated from the sea solely by the Feniglia sand spit. It was known as Cusi under the Etruscans and probably gave its name to the nearby later Roman colony of Cosa. The walls, made from massive polygonal sandstone blocks, survive to this day

Access: RAMA buses from Orbetello en route to the medieval hilltown of Capalbio drop in at Capalbio Scalo railway station, as does the rare slow train on the Grosseto–Rome line.

By car you'll need the turn-off for Capalbio Scalo on the SS 1 (Aurelia): those arriving from the west and Orbetello Scalo will find it after some 13km, whereas from the opposite direction, it's 22km northwest of Montalto di Castro.

At the end of the walk at the exit from the Feniglia Reserve, you can pick up one of the frequent year-round buses that connect Porto Ercole with Orbetello, where onward connections are possible.

The Feniglia Reserve itself is closed to traffic, while there are entrances for pedestrians and cyclists at either extremity.

and can be seen, partially submerged, on the western-most edge of town near the causeway. They were erected on foundations of oak and pine wood piles sunk deep into the mud.

Walkers are advised to carry their own food as no shops are passed, and the few bars and restaurants in Ansedonia can only be relied on during the summer months. Similarly, don't count on finding drinking water anywhere but Ansedonia. Swimming costumes are recommended June–September, as is insect repellent for the mosquitoes on the lagoon side of the Feniglia which seem to have a special liking for foreign skins.

The walk is feasible any time of the year, though July–August usually means congested roads and expensive if not fully booked accommodation. Bird lovers should make a point of waiting till midwinter for the migratory flocks.

The itinerary begins near the Burano WWF Reserve, which has been dealt with separately (see Walk 28) as time is too tight for a visit at this point in the proceedings.

While extremely rewarding, the walk in its entirety is rather long, not everyone's cup of tea. The first section along a beachfront is somewhat tiring, but can be eliminated by slotting directly into the walk at Ansedonia, preferably by car. Otherwise the Orbetello-Capalbio bus along the SS 1 (Aurelia) will drop you off at the first sign-posted exit for Ansedonia. It's then only 20min (1.5km) in to the Cosa site.

THE WALK

From **Capalbio Scalo** station, head west on the road parallel to the railway. Once over the level crossing, turn right, signposted for Macchiatonda (whereas the left branch leads to the Burano WWF Reserve). This quiet road runs between the railway line and the lake, lined by graceful eucalyptus trees, imported from Australia last century for the purposes of land reclamation. Egrets and birds of prey are a common sight in the surrounding fields and canals. The road bends a couple of times and eventually heads left towards the sea. Forty minutes will see you at a run-down building (**Macchiatonda**, 40min), near a low-key beach resort where a beachfront bar/restaurant operates in summer. The sand is very dark here, due to its high magnetite content. Head right along the beach for the trudge WNW towards the distant promontory of Ansedonia. The island of Giannutri lies southwest off the coast and the massive Argentario headland looms west-ward, with Porto Ercole clearly visible protected by its two dominating Spanish fortresses. Towers of a different type can be seen in the opposite direction, namely those belonging to the Montalto di Castro thermonuclear plant, never completed due to the 1987 referendum in which the Italians decided against nuclear energy.

The beach here, none too clean in parts but mostly deserted, widens somewhat and is backed by low dunes anchored by scrub cover. Allow 1h20min for the entire length, unless you stop off for a swim. The softish sand makes for tiring walking, but the coarse grains do wonders for rough feet – a natural pedicure!

After a total of 2h walking, just before you come to the cliffs is a tower known as the Torre della Tagliata or Torre Puccini, where the composer stayed during the final years of his life while working on his opera *Turandot*. Nearby are the meagre ruins of a Roman villa, a mere vestige of a series of impressive infrastructures.

In fact this corner was the site of the Roman port for Cosa. In order to drain the marshy hinterland and prevent silting in the harbour, an artificial outlet from Lago di Burano was diverted via a deep natural cleft in the rock face ahead known as the Spacco della Regina. George Dennis left this description from the early 1800s:

'You enter a long cleft in the rock, sixty or seventy feet deep, and on one side perceive a huge cave, within which is a second, still larger, apparently formed for baths; for there are seats cut out of the living rock – vivo sedilia saxo – but all now in utter ruin. The place, it has been remarked, recalls the grotto of the Nymphs, described by Virgil; but popular tradition has peopled it with demons...'.

In early Roman times when rockslides obstructed the flow, a series of cuts were made for an alternative, the intriguing **Tagliata Etrusca** (the Etruscan cutting). Follow the canal left past a low bridge to the deep-cut passage. Cavities along its sides were used for the sluice gates to keep the fish in at the turn of the tide. On the sea side are interesting ruins of Roman breakwaters in ancient concrete. Steps take you to the outermost sea entrance of the Tagliata Etrusca. The appellation – erroneous as it was actually a Roman project – is probably because the Cosa site and port were long believed to be Etruscan.

Backtrack briefly for the steps that lead upwards through scented flowering shrubs, and over the impressive karstic chasm of the Spacco della Regina, which runs a good distance through the promontory. The path soon comes onto a road in the discrete upmarket residential area of Ansedonia (10min from the beach).

Head up right to a junction and climb to a wide road, where you go left. Around the point is a three-way intersection and drinking water, where you take the middle road – Viale delle Ginestre (northwest). Coasting and climbing gradually it offers excellent sweeping views of the Feniglia dunes and beyond. Straight after the entrance to the Hermitage Residence is the signposted turn-off (right) for **Cosa** and car parking area (2h35min). A path leads quickly to the entrance to the spread-out site, and a map and board provide historic notes in various languages, English included.

The short-lived Roman colony of Cosa was founded following the defeat of Etruscan Vulci in 273BC, as part of the Roman push to take over this part of Etruria. Excavations have brought to light massive outer walls some 1.5km long, a forum, several villas complete with mosaic flooring, and a temple. A modest museum houses smaller finds and its courtyard contains several enormous terracotta jars found in the sea nearby. Following signs for 'Arx', don't neglect to climb to the highest point occupied by the towering remains of a Roman temple-cum-medieval castle, for the wonderful outlook onto the coast, east to the Burano lake, west onto the sweeping expanse of the Feniglia dunes, the Argentario promontory, Orbetello and the lagoon, as well as back to the hilly hinterland. 'Joyfully will the traveller hail the view from the ramparts of Cosa', wrote George Dennis.

The overgrown ruins are interspersed with olive trees, aromatic herbs and wild flowers, one of which, the beautiful yellow crocus-like sternbergia, is a treat for autumn visitors. Allow anything between 30min and 2h for a visit (not included in the total walk time).

Return to the road below the entrance to Cosa, and head downhill on the continuation of Viale delle Ginestre. Turn right at the intersection to drop to sea level. Go left at the next junction to loop back past tennis courts then a small restaurant before the bridge leading to the **Feniglia Reserve – 2h50min** to

The 'Etruscan cutting' at Ansedonia, with the Torre Puccini behind

here. (Left again here takes you straight to the stunning gold sand beach that runs the entire southern length of the Feniglia – an alternative.) A wide dirt track follows, closed to all but the vehicles of the Forestry Commission who supervise the area.

The Riserva Forestale Tombolo di Feniglia, as the name suggests, occupies a *tombolo* or sand spit which consists of a strip of land an average 1km in width and 6km in length. At the start of the century the area, then covered with a magnificent forest, was sold off and its trees cut down to make room for crops. No longer protected from the sea, the lagoon on its northern side underwent dramatic changes as it started filling with sand. This resulted in renewed outbreaks of malaria as well as great losses for the fishing industry. The trend was reversed in the 1930s when maritime pines were planted, the zone closed to traffic and the Reserve set up. Not only are the sturdy pines perfectly suited to the task of sand dune reclamation, but they can also be tapped for turpentine, while a similar species, the elegant umbrella pine, provides a harvest of nutritious pine nuts.

A short way in are Forestry Commission buildings flanked by the ruins of another Roman villa and a fish storage plant, probably located on the Roman road believed to have connected Cosa with Porto Ercole. A little further on you are faced with a terrible dilemma: whether to head straight down the middle track beneath the beautiful canopy of pines in the peace and quiet, uninterrupted but for the chirp of crickets or distant waves, take the right branch towards the lagoon, or make a beeline for the beach over left. A combination of visits to the different habitats is of course feasible, with zigzags back and forth across the wide strip. Either way it's hard to miss the placid fallow deer who thrive here and criss-cross the area with their tracks. They graze undisturbed but for the occasional walker or cyclist.

As concerns the lagoon, further along well past modern modest fish breeding enclosures, occasional paths lead through masses of pale lilac everlasting sea lavender to the lagoon edge and observation posts for the bird life. For the beach, on the other hand, several faint paths meander off to the left, but only trust the later vehicle-width tracks as false leads are blocked by a tall wire fence. The sand here is much firmer than the Macchiatonda section at the start of the itinerary, and walking along this immaculate beach is pure pleasure. Only the far western end has any resort-type organisation and car access, while the rest is reserved exclusively for walkers.

Back on the centre track, the end of the Reserve is marked by a warden's house, where you bear right along an avenue of pines to the official exit. Left then along a dirt road, then a right turn along a brief stretch of asphalt will bring you out on the Porto Ercole–Orbetello road, and the bus stop (total 4h30min).

Tourist Office Orbetello
tel.0564/860447

**Accommodation
Ansedonia:**
Locanda di Ansedonia
tel.0564/881317

Orbetello:
Pensione Toni & Judy
tel.0564/867109

28: WWF Oasi Lago di Burano

Walking time:	2–3h (guided visit)
Map:	on p.176

A must for bird lovers is this 1010-hectare wetland reserve and bird sanctuary on the southern coast of Tuscany. Set up in 1967, it was the very first of its kind to be run by the Italian World Wildlife Fund for Nature, and has since been recognised of international importance under the Ramsar Convention. A shallow coastal salt-water lake-cum-lagoon provides a safe winter stopover and rest area for tens of thousands of migratory birds. The best time to go is October to March when a 'full house' is virtually guaranteed. Wardens take visitors on an infor-mation-packed guided walk through the dunes bordering the Tyrrhenian Sea then to observation points over the lake itself where the multitude of birds amass to fish and breed. The tall close-growing giant reeds on the water's edge afford protection for darting kingfishers, melodious river nightingales and reed warblers, while regular resi-dents of the surface are a myriad ducks and coots, egrets, herons and cormorants, without forgetting winter visitors, the elegant flamingoes and wild geese whose numbers have been increasing steadily of late. The lake's abundant fish population of eels, sea bass and grey mullet together with crustaceans and insects, help feed the crowds, and are also preyed on by several types of falcon and hawk.

The Romans are believed to have used the lake for fish breeding, and were responsible for the long canal that runs west joining it to Ansedonia, where it was diverted into the sea via a cutting to prevent the port silting up (see Walk 27).

Additional interest is provided by the varied vegeta-tion. The light woodland is dominated by eucalyptus, imported last century from Australia for land reclamation due to their capacity for rapid growth and water reten-tion but now considered detrimental to native species as

Access: RAMA buses from Orbetello en route to the medieval village of Capalbio call in at the railway station of Capalbio Scalo. Trains that actually stop there are another matter (Rome–Grosseto line). On foot from the station, head west on the road parallel to the railway. Once over the level crossing, the signposts point you left (east) for 1km to the entrance to the Riserva Naturale Lago di Burano. 15min will do.

By car from the SS 1 (Aurelia) you'll need the turn-off for Capalbio Scalo, some 13km east of Orbetello Scalo, or from the opposite direc-tion, 22km northwest of Montalto di Castro. From the railway station follow directions as per the pedestrian route.

On the beach near Lago di Burano, looking towards the Argentario promontory

Riserva Naturale Lago di Burano
tel.0564/898829. Open for visits Sundays at 10am and 2.30pm, September 1st – April 30th. An entrance fee is charged and binoculars are available. Groups are admitted on other days with prior booking, and individual visitors can often tag along as well. Phone first. The commentary and brochure are in Italian at present.

rainfall is low in the area. The dunes have been colonised by scrubby species such as evergreen lentiscs, cork oaks, broom and a surprising number of flowers, including the woolly flowering goldy-locks, dubbed 'stinking everlasting' due to the curry smell it emanates when crushed. There is a relatively limited array of maquis types due to constraints imposed by the dark sand base, which has a high content of magnetite, meaning prohibitive constituents and temperatures of up to 60°C in summer. The dunes in turn provide refuge for hordes of hot-footed wild rabbits along with foxes, porcupines and tortoises, to name a few.

29: Sovana's Sunken Roadways and Necropolises

Walking time:	2h
Distance:	6km/3.8 miles
Map:	on p.192

Access: See Walk 30. A quiet road also connects Sovana with the renowned ancient spa resort of Saturnia in the west.

'It were vain to attempt a visit to these tombs unarmed with a hatchet, so dense are the tangled thickets; and all care must be had in crossing the yawning pits with which the slopes are furrowed; for the ground is kept moist and slippery by the overhanging foliage, and a false step on the brink would, in every sense, be a step into the grave.'

Thus did George Dennis caution his readers in the 1800s before they embarked on a visit of the wonderful necropolises on the outskirts of Sovana in south Tuscany. Access to the tombs scattered around the beautiful medieval village of Sovana is a trifle easier this century. The striking wild nature of the area is largely unchanged for the time being, though the area has become a 'Parco Archeologico'.

Information about Sovana's distant past is piecemeal. It may have been called Sveama in Etruscan times, and is believed to have been under the patronage of the powerful League city of Vulci. It flourished in waves, 7th–6th then 3rd–2nd century BC before falling to Rome when it was known as Suana. Roads connected it with settlements at Marsiliana (close to present-day Magliano) in the west, Lago di Bolsena to the east, in addition to Pitigliano and Sorano.

Later Sovana featured in early medieval times in a curious episode involving Charlemagne, who was encountering great difficulty in his attempt to overcome the fortified township and its fearless inhabitants. His nephew Orlando (Roland in English), the famous paladin immortalised in Ariosto's epic poem *Orlando Furioso* not to mention the earlier *Chanson de Roland*, was summoned. Initial failure led him to deep prayer and meditation in a field where he unwittingly lent on a tufa boulder. As he felt his legendary

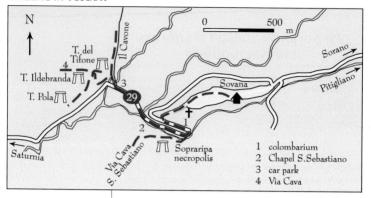

N

0   500
         m

T. del
Tifone
Il Cavone
Sorano
4
T. Ildebranda
Sovana
Pitigliano
3
T. Pola
29
†
1
Saturnia
2
Sopraripa
necropolis
Via Cava
S. Sebastiano

1 colombarium
2 Chapel S.Sebastiano
3 car park
4 Via Cava

might returning, his fingers gripped the rock and left an indelible mark – still visible today 2km east of Sovana close to the Pitigliano–Sorano intersection in the form of the curious rock 'Mano di Orlando'. What hope did Sovana have in the ensuing battle?

Sovana has several beautiful Romanesque churches facing onto its main street and central square where the original 16th-century brick paving, laid in an unusual fishbone pattern, has been restored. A stay at one of the small hotels, full of atmosphere, is warmly recommended, likewise the hearty local cuisine such as *buglione*, lamb stewed in a tomato sauce, and accompanied by the full-bodied red, Morellino di Scansano.

THE WALK

From the main square, Piazza del Pretorio in **Sovana** (291m), take either of the two traffic-free streets, both of which follow their original Etruscan route westwards, to the far end of the village and the 11th-century cathedral. Built on the site of a modest Etruscan temple, the present structure boasts a beautifully carved stone portal over the side door.

A lane below the *duomo* leads down and onto the asphalt, where you keep left and through a short road tunnel. There is an interesting columbarium above the tunnel exit. Soon off left after a curve is the signed path for the Sopraripa necropolis, datable back to 7th–6th and 3rd–2nd centuries BC (15min this far). The Fosso Folonia stream is crossed and you enter light wood where helle-bore, primroses and straggly wild asparagus make up the undergrowth in spring, along with a multitude of Etruscan tombs along the tufa rock face, which assumes yellowish or reddish hues depending on the time of day. The so-called Tomba della Sirena is one of the first, its façade somewhat eroded these days, though its trademark 'mermaid' still stands out clear on the carved pediment. An ensuing line-up of tombs consists of solid block-like excavated structures for ceremonial purposes and reached by flights of steps, the actual sepulchral chamber on a lower underground level.

Five minutes or so along the way, after a 'false' entrance, is a most spectacular ancient sunken road, the **Via Cava di San Sebastiano**. A good 15m deep and broad enough for the passage of a narrow cart, the moss-lined sheer-sided cleft penetrates the cliff of tufa. Inscriptions and tombs on a higher level clearly indicate the successive drops in level. The sky overhead is a mere strip and all but blocked off by overhanging foliage. The roadway rises very gradually on its climb to the level of the plain, however take the first exit up right, as the way ahead is blocked by debris. A clamber will bring you out at the remains of a cavernous rock church on the very dizzy edge of the cutting. Unique spot! (25min this far.) Return the same way out through the via cava.

Return the same way you came in. Once back at the road continue left some 600m to a car park and sign-posting for the Tomba Ildebranda, just after a watercourse (total 45min).

This easy itinerary guarantees a unique experience as you follow intriguing ancient roadways and explore a wide range of tombs in peaceful woods thick with wild flowers. Good walking shoes are recommended as there are occasional steep tracts which can be slippery, especially when covered by wet leaves. A torch is handy for exploring underground chambers and cavities.

The walk can be shortened if you drive out of Sovana along the road west for San Martino di Flora and Saturnia as per the map, and park at the turn-offs for the various tombs. **Note**: A Parco Archeologico has been established to protect the tombs and a small admission fee is sometimes applicable.

Vestiges of the temple-like Tomba Pola outside Sovana

Various routes branch off here. The **Tomba Ildebranda** makes a good start, left uphill. The erstwhile monumental construction dates back to 3rd–2nd century BC but has since been named after Hildebrand, also known as Pope Gregory VII (1073–1085), a native of Sovana. Wooden stairways have been fitted to reduce wear on the steps, the lower chamber wired for lighting and the area fenced off, though the structure can be seen clearly from the outside should the gate be locked. A total of 18 columns arranged in rows formed the uppermost structure, all richly ornamented with nature motifs and painted stucco.

Without returning to the road, continue along below the cliff southwest through holm oak and ferns for 5min to the **Tomba Pola**. An unusually narrow deep dromos, 18m long, leads to a vast rounded chamber where the members of a wealthy family were laid to rest on benches. In all likelihood wooden coffins were used, as nails were found around bodies in other burials. Above, however, are the remains of a magnificent temple-like structure, entirely carved out of the tufa. Of the original eight, a single fluted column now holds up the pediment, its sculpted capital once decorated with leaves and human figures. Traces of the painted stucco that covered the entire structure cling to the underside of the moulded ceiling. Return the same way past the entrance to the Tomba Ildebranda and take the lane up left, a modest via cava that continues to vineyards on Poggio Prisca. Back down where this roadway started, take the path off left through the trees under the cliff for the nearby Tomba del Tifone. The name was coined by George Dennis as he described the sculpted figure of a typhon – a monster in Greek mythology and one of the whirlwinds – on the roof, though this is now considered erroneous.

Return to the junction near the road (1h20min), and this time take the wide lane northeast, parallel to the watercourse. It quickly enters 'Il Cavone', a massive sunken road a good kilometre long and still used by farm vehicles. High on the flanks are inscriptions and tomb cavities that were cut through as the road was expanded.

Return to **Sovana** via the road, allowing about half an hour on foot, making a grand total of 2h.

Tourist Office Sovana
tel.0564/614074

Accommodation
Hotel Scilla
tel.0564/616531

Taverna Etrusca
tel.0564/616183 (3-star)

B&B tel.0564/614073 or
tel.0564/614120

30: Sovana to Pitigliano the Old Way

Walking time:	2h + extra for detours
Distance:	5.6km/3.5 miles
Map:	on p.198

'Nearly every rock here speaks Etruscan', George Dennis wrote in 1848 of the area. Surprise after delightful surprise is in store for those who venture along the ancient roadway that wends its way through astounding tufa landscapes between enigmatic Pitigliano and enchanting Sovana in the deep south of Tuscany. In use until the 18th century, the route was originally the work of the Etruscans to link trade centres en route from the Tyrrhenian coast and Vulci over east to the central artery, the Val di Chiana. Wild rambling landscapes are traversed, with pasture plains interrupted by abrupt ravines excavated by eroding watercourses. The Etruscan roadways followed the principal valleys then climbed escarpments to reach the settlements by way of passages cut into the tufa. Over time the passage of carts and chariots wore down the rock leaving ever-deepening ruts, which were evened out from time to time, the level becoming progressively lower. Over the ages they have witnessed the passage of traders, pilgrims, migrants, armies and peasants returning home from their fields. This is unquestionably 'via cava' country par excellence, and a good number can be visited around Pitigliano and Sovana in addition to those included in the walk.

Sovana, where the walk starts, is a laidback jewel of a village with several beautiful Romanesque churches, not to mention extensive necropolises, and is dealt with in greater detail in Walk 29.

Pitigliano, on the other hand, presents itself as an imposing and fascinating medieval stronghold, perched high on a reddish, steep-sided and eye-catching platform of tufa. Its outermost houses seem to grow out of the thick

Access: From the SS 1 (Aurelia) on the coast, some 6km north of Orbetello, turn eastwards inland at Albinia on the SS 74 for the 48km via Manciano to Pitigliano. It is also straightforward from the east and Lago di Bolsena and Orvieto. The quiet village of Sovana lies 8km northwest of Pitigliano, and is well signposted with yellow tourist signs.

By bus, RAMA coaches start out from Grosseto and head firstly south for Albinia, hence Manciano and Pitigliano. In addition there are links from Castell'Azzara and other localities on the southern reaches of Monte Amiata, as well as Acquapendente on the SS2.

Pitigliano and Sovana themselves are connected by a twice-daily service (except Sundays and holidays).

Descending a sunken Etruscan roadway, the Via Cava dell'Annunziata, not far from Pitigliano

rock base as a natural extension. Virtually nothing is left of Pitigliano's Etruscan past, the name included, though the present one is derived from the name of an important Roman family, the Petilias. It was probably a modest settlement under the political control of Vulci, and reached maximum development in 7th century BC, only to fall into decay and give no further signs of life until 1st century AD. Other landmarks in Pitigliano's history are the Middle Ages under the Aldobrandeshi and Orsini families who left a massive palace and fortress. The impressive landmark aqueduct also dates back to that time. An interesting episode belongs to the mid-1500s, when the township opened its gates to the many Jewish families expelled from the Papal States. Most have since left, and the synagogue, recently restored and open to visitors, remains the sole witness to their presence.

Any time of year is suitable for this wonderfully varied walk, with the exception perhaps of midwinter, when the odd snowfall can make for difficult driving on the winding narrow roads. Spring is the best time for wild flower enthusiasts, whereas even in the heat of midsummer, the shady glens and sunken roadways colonised by moss and ferns guarantee pleasantly cool conditions.

A profound sense of history pervades the area, and very little effort is needed to imagine all the feet, wheels and emotions that must have passed this way through the ages. A good many 'vie cave' have been cleared of brambles and debris, to the great advantage and enjoyment of walkers. Several steepish leaf-filled sections of these passages can be slippery after rain, though nothing particularly lengthy, if a little tiring. Walking boots with ankle support are recommended, as are picnic supplies and drinking water – no shops or bars are encountered en route.

THE WALK

Leave **Sovana** (291m) and the broad Piazza del Pretorio by way of the central road eastwards, out past the old Rocca belonging to the ubiquitous Aldobrandeschi clan. Out through the walls is the Saturnia–Pitigliano road, but you need the first turn-off down right, as per the waymarking (red and white paint stripes) used for long-distance paths in the Grosseto Province. The narrow surfaced road drops quickly to cross the Torrente Folonia, and a worthwhile detour off left for the signposted 3rd–2nd century BC necropolis and moss-covered sunken passage between tufa walls. Snowflake flowers thrive in these shady realms in spring (allow 15min or so – not included in total time).

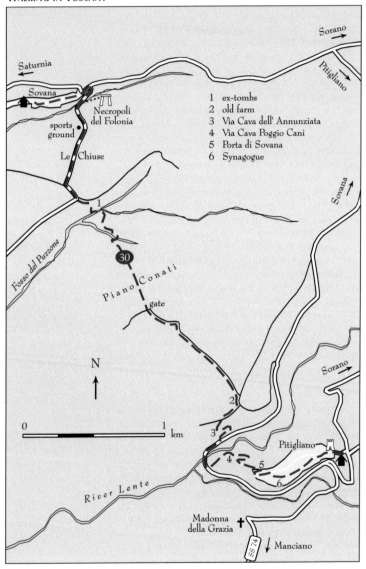

1 ex-tombs
2 old farm
3 Via Cava dell' Annunziata
4 Via Cava Poggio Cani
5 Porta di Sovana
6 Synagogue

The quiet road climbs past a sports ground and onto a broad plain which affords good views back onto Sovana and its cathedral. The road curves left, then as it veers right, leave it for the lane straight ahead, as indicated by the red and white waymarking (15min this far). You soon encounter an original stretch of emergent grooved roadway and the start of a modest 'via cava' (southeast). This winds quickly downwards sunk in the rock, and can make for slippery walking as fallen leaves are trapped here. The flanks are 'wallpapered' with moss, while around the edges oak trees provide shade for butcher's broom and violets. You emerge in a field, and up left are several ex-tombs converted into sheds for farm equipment. Keep right to cross the minor watercourse, Fosso del Puzzone, over a stone bridge, all but disguised by vegetation. A tract of thick perfumed broom leads around to a second stream and ruined miniature bridge (30min total).

Next is a steady ascent via a further intriguing sunken road which leads out to the peaceful panoramic **Piano Conati**, studded with crocuses among low bushes of broom and scattered oak trees, well away from it all. Make your way across the plain in essentially the same direction. The best rule is to follow the emergent stretches of old rutted roadway, marked sporadically by red and white stripes. A little further on a fence is followed through scrub cover to a higher area where a surprising series of parallel grooves and channelling from the old road cover the stone base (45min).

Through a gate, you join a wide farm track and continue in the same direction, past olive and wine properties for about 10min. Keep right at the T-junction with a wider dirt road, then right again past an old farm on the corner (309m, 1h total). Pitigliano seems but a stone's throw away now, however it lies beyond a deep gully. Soon a signpost announces the start of the **Via Cava dell'Annunziata** off left, and you are sent plunging down into the dark realms of moss and ferns. The turns in this extraordinary, almost underground track are akin to hairpin bends and divided only by a slender tufa wall. A collapsed section towards the end requires a brief clamber, but nothing of consequence.

It all comes to an end on the tarmac in the sunshine again at the foot of Pitigliano. Take the road a short way downhill and across the River Lente (250m), where several *vie cave* are signposted, an invitation for further exploration.

From the bridge across the River Lente, the road runs along the base of the tufa mass that supports Pitigliano, and which is clearly honeycombed with all manner of cavities, ex-tombs, stalls, and more excavated passages. Ignore the turning up left for the Via Cava della Tombolina, but take the next one, **Via Cava Poggio Cani**. The deep mossy passageway climbs past empty tombs, long employed for storing the local white wine in oak casks, to merge with a further laneway, and reaches a wide flight of stone steps for the final ascent into the township.

You climb beneath dramatic sheer cliffs, the most crazily-shaped dwellings above, half in and half out of the yellowish tufa flank, underground cellars omnipresent. Aptly, the township is entered via Porta di Sovana, where a careful look will reveal authentic Etruscan tufa blocks embedded in the medieval walls. Up at Via Aldobrandeschi, turn left and follow the narrow street between tall old buildings, keeping right at the church. Pop down any of the alleys on the right for the views from the breathtaking edge of town. The entrance to the Synagogue is passed and the street, now called Via Zuccarelli, eventually brings you out in Piazza della Repubblica. Here is the impressive Fortezza Orsini which houses the archaeological museum. The archway right and double gateway lead to the medieval aqueduct and past the hotel in Piazza Petruccioli. Around left is the bus stop (2h total time).

Tourist Office Sovana
tel.0564/614074

Accommodation
Pitigliano:
Hotel Guastini
tel.0564/61606

B&B Il Tufo Rosa
tel.0564/617019

Outside Pitigliano:
Hotel Corano, 3km along the Manciano road
tel.0564/616112 (swimming pool included)

Sovana:
see Walk 29

31: Poggio Buco

Walking time:	1h30min
Distance:	4.5km/2.7 miles
Map:	on p.202

Poggio Buco literally means 'perforated knoll', as the hill-side and plateau are riddled with a host of tomb caverns and channelling dating back to Etruscan times. Then it was another of the 7th century BC small-scale agricultural settlements under the powerful city of Vulci in the south of Tuscany. This walk is of minor interest from the points of view of nature and archaeology, overshadowed by those through the wild ravines and multitudinous necropolises around nearby Pitigliano. Notwithstanding, Etruscan enthusiasts will find stimulating food for thought here. Together with the foundations of a building, thought to be a palace, the principal attraction is the necropolis. It was extensively looted well before systematic excavation began, with only the odd unsaleable fragment of ceramic vase and terracotta roof decoration left. Quite a variety of structures is to be found, notably ditch graves and chamber tombs where rooms are decorated with sculpted columns and support beams. Unfortunately – though understandably – virtually all the tombs were converted into livestock pens and storage sheds by local peasants who have since abandoned the area themselves. There are also rare vestiges of the 3km circuit of walls that enclosed the 9-hectare settlement.

Roads once linked Poggio Buco with Marsiliana in the west, Pitigliano in the east, then south along the River Fiora to Vulci.

The dominating site was inhabited at length until recent times, and in fact farmhouses stand derelict atop the necropolis. In early spring magnificent flowering fruit trees burst into fresh blossom, and on a clear day views range all the way to the sea in the west and north inland to Monte Amiata. It is an easy, problem-free walk.

Access: Drivers will need the SS 74 (see Walk 30), as Poggio Buco lies approximately halfway between Pitigliano (10km) and Manciano (9km). A faded signpost on the western bank of the River Fiora indicates a lane off southwest, and you can park at the small abandoned quarry a little way up.

By bus on the RAMA Manciano–Pitigliano run, get off at the Trattoria on the eastern bank of the River Fiora, near the entrance to a quarry. Cross the bridge over the river for the lane off left signed for Poggio Buco, also marked with the red and white Grosseto Province waymarking.

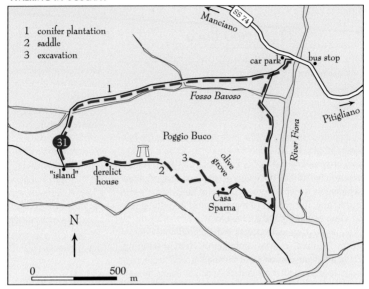

1 conifer plantation
2 saddle
3 excavation

Manciano
SS 74
car park
bus stop
Fosso Bavoso
Pitigliano
River Fiora
31
Poggio Buco
olive grove
3
"island"
derelict house
2
Casa Sparna
N
0   500 m

THE WALK

From the **River Fiora** (165m), the lane heads essentially southwest, and you keep right at two successive junctions, as per the red and white waymarking. Through fields where birds of prey are not uncommon, you climb gradually westwards towards lovely wild hills alongside a watercourse (Fosso Bavoso). After a conifer plantation a sidestream is crossed, and you stick to the main track even though the red and white marking cuts up left.

The first yawning cave tombs are soon passed, followed by an 'island' in the lane with a tree. Keep left (east) here for Poggio Buco (250m, 30min this far).

There is an interesting array of modest tombs cut into the tufa rock here, transformed into stalls for farm animals. This section of lane itself is a brief *tagliata*. Once through a gate, you pass a derelict house then proceed down the grooves of the evocative road to the most extensive and interesting part of the necropolis. Several spacious caverns feature sculpted columns, niches and evidence of timber beams, while the underground tomb chambers, accessible by way of a narrow corridor, are flooded more often than not. Periwinkles and speedwell flowers carpet the ground, while the fragrant blossoms from flowering fruit trees waft through the air. Other signs of the presence of man are the olive trees and houses dotted here and there.

Ten minutes from the 'island' a saddle is reached with an electricity pole and shed. Ignore the lane left and keeping to the right of a small cliff, take the old track up to the narrow plateau known as Le Sparne, originally occupied by the acropolis. Excavation work is continuing on a building at the far northwestern extremity – make your way left 5min along the edge of the splendid olive grove that thrives here. The raised man-made knoll consists of pieces of tufa and may date back to the late Bronze Age (12th–10th century BC). The foundations, on the other hand, are from 7th–6th century BC, and are believed to have belonged to an upper class residence.

From the excavations, proceed southeast back through the olives to another abandoned house, **Casa Sparna**, surrounded by rusting farm machinery (243m, total 50min to here). Ruins of an Etruscan temple were unearthed here, but absolutely nothing remains nowadays. It does make a good scenic picnic spot, though, with views north over the rolling hills towards Monte Amiata.

The acropolis once spread in a southeasterly direction along this upper section of the plateau through the present vineyard, and during medieval times the knights of the Order of Rhodes built a church here, all but disappeared and smothered by brambles and thick vegetation.

From Casa Sparna a wide track drops through sweet broom curving below the acropolis. It joins a wider lane parallel to the River Fiora, and you keep left. A further 15min of gentle ups and downs north through fields of wheat and sunflowers and you'll be back at the main road and the starting point after a total of 1h30min.

Tourist Office Manciano
tel.0564/629218

**Accommodation
Pitigliano:**
see Walk 30

32: Sorano to Vitozza
via the River Lente

Walking time:	2h20min + extra for exploring both Sorano and Vitozza
Distance:	7km/4.2 miles
Map:	on p.206

An exciting walk through wild areas steeped in history, this itinerary commences at the semi-deserted medieval township of Sorano which clings with varying degrees of success to a dramatic buttress over a gorge. Despite work to consoli-date the tufa rock base and foundations of the township, picturesque Sorano unfortunately continues to crumble and its outermost houses regularly slide valley-wards. Since 1929, when the town was all but evacuated due to major landslips, most of the inhabitants have moved over to safer ground in the new district off the Pitigliano road.

The sole traces of Sorano's presumed Etruscan past can be seen at San Rocco, the high outcrop which faces the township over a dramatic ravine on the opposite side of the river, and accessible from the Sovana road. There are scattered rock cavities and tombs believed to date from around 3rd century BC, the period of the Roman conquest, as well as a tiny church. A visit is warmly recommended for the spectacular views it affords onto Sorano. Several 'vie cave' sunken roadways also run through the cliffs, though they were in a bad state at the time of writing, obstructed by landslips. Definitely worth investigating.

In addition to the walk itself, do find time for a wander around Sorano's massive sprawling Fortezza which looms over the township any way you look at it. It was constructed in the 1500s by the Orsini clan and, now beautifully restored and in part occupied by a hotel, is a maze of ramps, moats, massive monumental doorways and internal squares. A later building is used by the school, and the town band can be heard tootling there of an evening.

The walk, on the other hand, follows a wooded river valley before climbing to Vitozza, a unique and evoca-tive series of cave dwellings now colonised by moss and ferns. The origins of the settlement can be traced back to the 1200s, and it developed into a fully-fledged town-ship complete with churches, fortress and defensive walls, not to mention the practical trappings such as water cisterns, dovecots, olive and wine presses, ovens, mills and the like. A good two hundred caves were in

Exploring the old paths between the rock dwellings of Vitozza

use. The inhabitants gradually moved along the broad outcrop to the extension of present-day San Quirico, though the last resident reportedly hung on until the 18th century. Vitozza is now totally abandoned, though some clearing has been carried out for the creation of a 'Parco Archeologico'.

As far as the walk itself goes, there is no difficulty involved, though there may be the occasional overgrown stretch should the present maintenance work cease. Several ascents and descents are encountered, but these are short and easily tackled. Food and water must be carried as none is found en route.

THE WALK

Starting out at the main car park at **Sorano** (385m), go downhill (north) past the spectacularly-placed bakery, fountains and arcades. Through the monumental gateway, proceed straight on, without descending, to the church. Follow the signs around right then left for the Masso Leopoldino. The laneway descends a little alongside a curious sheer wall topped with straggly TV aerials, the Masso (or Sasso) Leopoldino. This strange structure dates

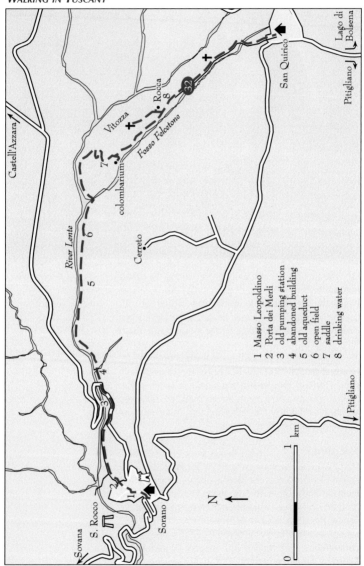

Castell'Azzara

Lago di
Bolsena

San Quirico

Pitigliano

Vitozza

Rocca

32

Fosso Felcetone

colombariūm

7

6

River Lente

5

Cerreto

4

3

Sovana

S. Rocco

Sorano

Pitigliano

Pitigliano

1 Masso Leopoldino
2 Porta dei Merli
3 old pumping station
4 abandoned building
5 old aqueduct
6 open field
7 saddle
8 drinking water

N

0   1 km

back to the 1700s and is a combination of masonry which encompasses a flat-topped tufa outcrop.

(It's worth detouring briefly ahead then up around left to panoramic Piazza del Poggio, its northernmost corner occupied by a 16th-century granary, and views down over to excavated tombs belonging to the San Rocco necropolis on the other side of the River Lente.)

From the base of the wall, turn right and follow the main picturesque lane winding downwards and out through the lower 16th-century gate, **Porta dei Merli**, complete with the slits for the drawbridge. Extensive and much-needed consolidation work was under way along these lower reaches of the township at the time of writing. A lane leads out of the gate and down eastwards towards the River Lente. Keep right at the junction (whereas left connects with San Rocco) and coast above the water-course, where well-kept vegetable gardens somehow survive the assault of crumbling rocks. Ignore turn-offs and follow the lane uphill and out to join the road from Sorano to Castell'Azzara. It drops past a cascade and an old water pumping station to a bridge over the River Lente (325m, 20min this far).

Don't cross the river, but stick to its right bank along a lane as far as abandoned buildings and a gate. Turn off left on the path which drops to cross a side stream. Through the undulating wood, it proceeds parallel to the river beneath beautiful chestnut trees, and occasional red paint stripes have now appeared. The undergrowth is a carpet of snowflakes, primroses, hellebore and dainty cyclamens in spring. Soon after a log bench, a number of interesting lengths of the old aqueduct are passed. Until very recently it channelled water from the spring at the source of the River Lente, a little further upstream, to Sorano and beyond.

About 50min from Sorano, keep straight ahead across an open field, and back into light wood (red paint marks on a tree). Thick vegetation may be encountered here. The narrow side stream (Fosso Felcetone) is close-by, and is easily traversed by way of stepping stones. The path emerges on the opposite bank at the northwestern base of the outcrop that houses Vitozza, though nothing

Access: See Walk 30 for access to the Pitigliano zone, then proceed the 9km northeast to Sorano. San Quirico and Vitozza are a further 6.5km to the southeast.

As far as public transport goes, Sorano is served by a decent RAMA daily bus service from Pitigliano, while links with San Quirico are slightly less frequent, though still useful.

The lower older nucleus of Sorano is only accessible to pedestrians. There is ample parking in the square in front of the Municipio (Council) building.

Medieval columbarium at Vitozza

is visible yet. Adventurous visitors can clamber straight up from here, but an easier and more evocative option is the route via the old medieval road. So keep left and follow the faint path close to the river for a good 5min, to where red stripes reappear for a path up right. It soon widens and the older rutted track becomes recognisable, climbing southeast at first, then south. The River Lente cascades away down below, and more old masonry structures from the water supply can be seen close to it. The lane makes its winding way up the northernmost flank of Vitozza, for some 15min in ascent. A delightful sunken mossy section leads to a saddle (approx. 400m, total 1h20min to here).

(Time permitting, follow the path right from here to the outermost extension of the old settlement with grottoes and the site of an old church.)

The main itinerary continues left to a clearing and section of wall with a collapsed gateway. Through it and down right on the dizzy edge of the cliff high above Fosso Felcetone now, is a fascinating series of authentic columbarium. Systematically scraped out of the rock face are niches where doves sheltered, serving a twofold purpose as their deposited excrement made excellent fertiliser and the birds themselves were within arm's reach for a delicious dinner.

Return through the open wall and the old sunken roadway which curves up rightish passing over a vast excavated room. A massive old wall marks an entrance to the high central part of **Vitozza** (425m, 1h30min total).

At this point, however, it is advisable to continue on the lane which skirts along right (southeast) on a level, as a host of unusual cave dwellings are encountered. For the most part the lower floor was used for storage purposes or as stalls for animals, while the upper storey, well positioned to catch the sun, acted as the main living quarters. Examples of basins for rainwater, grinding points and so on are clearly identifiable, and there is great potential for exploration in these mossy realms.

If you haven't already ended up on the actual upper platform by wandering through the caves, take the turn-off left signed for 'Rocca'. The lane climbs to enter the city proper through more tall walls, while a right turn will see you at the meagre ruins of the fortress amongst oaks and crocuses. Back on the lane, follow it in a northwesterly direction to the vestiges of a church and a panoramic clearing where the countryside for miles around spreads out.

Back down on the main track, proceed southeast again past a turn-off for a drinking fountain (*acqua potabile*) and a visitor centre complete with a toilet block (2h).

The last leg continues in the same direction past yet more caves, complete with multilingual explanatory signboards. Many of the final ones have been converted into garages and cellars. At a junction presided over by a rock shrine, keep right down over the watercourse and past the outlying houses belonging to the quiet village of **San Quirico** (506m, total 2h20min). The bus stop and modest hotel (with adjoining recommended restaurant) are in the main square, while a yellow sign for Vitozza aids those who come from the opposite direction.

Return to Sorano by bus or even on foot, the 5km northwest.

Tourist Office Sorano
tel.0564/633099

Accommodation
San Quirico:
Hotel Agnelli
tel.0564/619015

Sorano:
Hotel della Fortezza
tel.0564/632010 (3-star)

33: A Stroll around Velzna, Etruscan Orvieto

Access: Not all Rome–Florence trains stop at Orvieto Scalo station so remember to check. The ensuing trip uphill to Orvieto itself is best via the modern funicular to Piazza Cahen, the main bus terminal. Buses also cover the route and can be handy outside the funicular operating hours. Drivers should leave the A1 autostrada at the Orvieto exit. Other useful roads are the SS 71 from Chiusi, or its extension south to Montefiascone where it is joined by the SS 2. In the city centre, traffic is both restricted and confusing, so use one of the many car parks just outside the walls.

Walking time:	2h
Distance:	4km/2.5 miles
Map:	on p.212 + detailed city map from the tourist office.

The wealthy Etruscan city of Velzna, better known as Volsinii in Latin as per Roman sources, flourished here from 6th to 4th century BC, and was a member of the powerful confederation. It controlled a vast territory of fertile terrain that encompassed north–south trade routes along the Chiana and Tiber valleys, crucial for the whole of Etruria. Furthermore, its was a border position with the territory under the Umbrian tribes. The city itself occupied a total area of 80 hectares, and while very little is known about the buildings, an extensive system of extant underground passageways is gradually being emptied of the rubbish and detritus of ages and providing precious clues. The broad tufaceous outcrop is honeycombed with channelling and cisterns for drainage purposes and resulting subterranean premises are unusually dry and perfect for storage purposes. Larger rooms were feasibly workshops, as per the later medieval tradition. The city in fact produced a vast range of ceramics and bronze objects, largely for export. It also minted its own coins, and these have provided scholars with many answers such as the name Velzna, in a variety of spellings.

Clusters of tombs have come to light around the city. Richly decorated and stocked with luxurious personal objects, they confirm the existence of an aristocratic class. In fact in its later years, one of the most serious threats to prosperity was civil unrest – namely uprisings by the city's many slaves. In combination with long-running conflicts with Rome, this was to lead to its downfall. In 294BC Velzna suffered defeat in battle at the hands of the Romans and in return for a forty-year long truce, was forced to pay the outrageous sum of 500,000 'as' (an Etruscan coin later adopted by ancient Rome). However the Romans returned a little ahead of time – in 264BC – supposedly summoned by local aristocrats to put down a revolt by servants. They did a little more than that, sacking the city and completely razing it to the ground.

Survivors were sent to found the new colony of Volsinii Novi, now Bolsena, on the eastern shore of Lago di Bolsena (see Walk 34). In the meantime a good 2000 bronze statues were removed to Rome, booty from an important Etruscan sanctuary known as Fanum Voltumnae, possibly Civita di Bagnoregio (see Walk 35). The present name Orvieto comes from Urbs vetus, old city, as it came to be known after the sacking.

Several brief notes are in order for later events. As regards Orvieto's world-famous cathedral, 'extraordinary' comes to mind, though to some it is overwhelming and even gaudy. Façade notwithstanding, it is rare for the recently restored 15th-century fresco cycle *The Last Judgement* by Luca Signorelli not to draw gasps of admiration, as it did for Michelangelo whom it served as inspiration for his Sistine Chapel masterpiece. The actual building was erected to house the famous blood-stained altar cloth from Bolsena, which led to the proclamation of the Corpus Domini feast described in detail in Walk 34. For a great distance around, the womenfolk in every single town and village, no matter how small, decorate streets and alleyways with intricate designs of flowers and dried petals. It is known as the 'infiorata'. Orvieto is no exception, and there is the added attraction of a procession in historic costumes.

The walk itself is a matter of a fascinating stroll around the city and no difficulty is involved.

THE WALK

Start out on the eastern edge of Orvieto, at the upper station of the funicular in **Piazza Cahen**. Take the road briefly north, past the Pozzo di San Patrizio (St. Patrick's Well, with its famous double corkscrew ramps designed in the 16th century for donkeys to haul water up to the

Stately and mysterious **Orvieto**, in the southern reaches of Umbria, is spectacularly placed on a tufa platform over a wide valley. The site has been occupied in a continuous manner since prehistoric times, right through the intrigue-ridden Middle Ages and the Renaissance.

The majority of modern visitors who ride up the modern funicular railway are attracted by the glittering Gothic cathedral, however apart from its medieval delights, Orvieto has an Etruscan heart well hidden in its surprising underground realms. You literally step back through dense layers of its rich history in a matter of metres.

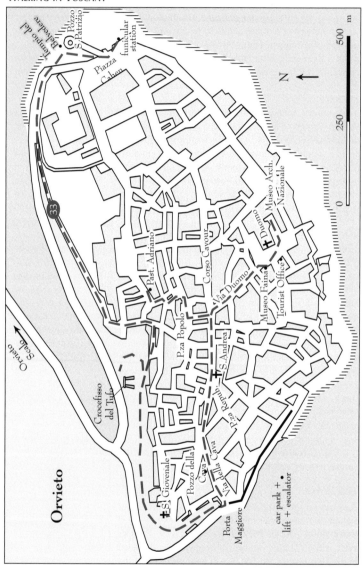

Orvieto

surface in case of siege). In the nearby panoramic public gardens is a modest podium reached by a wide flight of steps belonging to the Tempio del Belvedere (5min), but one of the eight temples of Etruscan Velzna. It once bore sculpted roof decorations in terracotta. Inscriptions and votive objects found there suggest it was a sanctuary dedicated to Tinia, the Etruscan Jupiter.

From the park, take the main road in the direction of Orvieto Scalo, but only for a matter of metres as a pedestrian-only promenade (Viale Carducci) soon branches off left. The lovely lane with sweeping views up the Val di Chiana leads west through parkland. At a playground it veers briefly left then first right to duck through a car park. On the cliff edge, an impressive raised walkway takes over in gentle descent to the foot of the sheer orange-red tufa drop.

A zigzag stepped way turns down right, leading to the **Crocefisso del Tufo** necropolis set in pleasant shady surrounds. After the visit, return to the path at the cliff base and proceed right (west) over the necropolis, to round the westernmost bastion of Orvieto with a tiny underground chapel and market gardens. The Madonna del Velo church precedes Porta Maggiore, where you turn left and enter the city precincts once again. In the vicinity of the massive Etruscan entrance, rare vestiges of the original wall are still in place. The ensuing street, narrow Via della Cava, is held to have been the principal access in Etruscan times to the higher central part of the city and in all probability was itself excavated into the tufa. It ran the full length of the tufa platform to terminate at the opposite gate in the proximity of the Tempio Belvedere.

The way climbs steeply to reach n.26, **Pozzo della Cava**. The keen owner of the craft shop/bar/restaurant has gradually been clearing out an astounding series of passageways beneath his property, and visitors are welcome (a small fee is charged). Spacious tunnels, cisterns clay-lined for waterproofing and masses of ceramic fragments from a nearby kiln have been unearthed. However the *pièce de résistance* is the huge Etruscan well (pozzo) the place is now named after. The yawning 36m deep shaft comes complete with footholds,

Crocefisso del Tufo

Brought to light in 1874, this unique and fascinating complex consists of a series of 'streets' facing onto which are square single-floor terrace 'houses', alias tombs, staggered up the hillside and set back-to-back. A necropolis in the true sense of the word: city of the dead. Weighty stone slabs served as doors, and on the lintel above was the occupants' family name, inscribed in the typical back-to-front characters adapted from the Greek alphabet. The interior features the stepped stone vaulting found in many Etruscan structures, the precursor of the arch. The joined roofs, now grassed over, originally bore large round stone stelae or markers. Over 300 burials have been found here altogether. A half hour or so should suffice for the visit (not included in the total).

and a lower tunnel leads off from the very bottom level. Helpful multilingual signs are dotted around. As is common practice in the city, the maze of underground tunnels has long been used for storing the excellent local dry white wines, the older version of which verges on golden nectar. An excellent way to conclude the visit is a drink or recommended meal in the adjacent premises. Ask to be seated directly over the second well, covered by a reassuring sturdy glass slab.

Via della Cava continues its ascent to become Via Filippeschi before emerging in Piazza della Repubblica (45min), the site of the ancient forum. Its farthest side, alongside Corso Cavour, is taken up by the Chiesa di Sant'Andrea, where evidence of an Etruscan temple and roadway have been identified in the crypt. However excavation/restoration work was underway at the time of writing, to the exclusion of visits.

Proceed east along pedestrian-only Corso Cavour past several side streets, and after about 5min opt for the narrow way left, Via della Costituente, on the corner of the Torre del Moro (well worth climbing for its brilliant 360° views). Bear right through the Piazza del Popolo, skirting the magnificent Romanesque-Gothic Palazzo del Popolo, deep beneath which a building dating back to Etruscan times has been discovered, ostensibly to have served religious purposes. At the rear, in the far right hand (northeastern) extremity of the narrowing square is Via della Pace. At n.26 is the cake shop and wine bar **Pasticceria Adriano**. Work permitting, the affable staff will accompany visitors downstairs through an amazing succession of passageways, cisterns and grain stores, which now double as well-stocked cellars. About 600m^2 have been cleared out exposing intriguing multi-coloured layers of rock and soil such as solidified lava and marine sands, and incorporating carbonised petrified roots and branches. (As no entrance fee is charged, you'll be expected to sample Adriano's delicious freshly baked wares afterwards, an extremely enjoyable experience.)

Return to Corso Cavour the same way, but proceed straight ahead on Via Duomo. It is lined with shops illustrating the city's age-old pottery tradition – there's everything from Etruscan *buccheri* made in accordance with the original techniques, through to myriad medieval pieces and modern ceramic styles. This will bring you out in spacious Piazza del Duomo where an Etruscan temple once stood, but now home to the city's masterpiece.

Facing the cathedral on your right is the **Museo Claudio Faina**. Its core comprises a renowned historic collection of Etruscan finds from a range of sites as well as coins and ornate imported Greek vases. The ceramic roof decorations from the Tempio Belvedere are also here, not to mention the famous marble Venus figure Venere della Cannicella from the necropolis of the same name on the crumbling south side of town, unfortunately long closed to visitors.

On the opposite side of the square, flanking the cathedral, is the **Museo Archeologico Nazionale**, housed in the cavernous former stables of the Papal Palace. Here pride of place goes undoubtedly to the painted wall decorations from the two 4th century BC tombs named after Golini who discovered and excavated them in the late 1800s near Settecamini, briefly south of Orvieto. To protect them from further deterioration, the frescoes were removed from the site in 1950 and are now on display in a special room in reconstructed 'life-size' tombs. Bright active figures at banquet scenes and involved in games in honour of the deceased have survived for something like 2500 years. Other displays include more examples of intricate *buccheri* vases, the unusual black pottery found at the Crocefisso del Tufo necropolis.

Tourist Office Orvieto
tel.0763/341772

Accommodation
B&B Scaletta al Duomo
tel.0763/375009

Villa Mercede
tel.0763/341766
spotless, centrally
located and run by
monks

Hotel Posta
tel.0763/341909

34: Orvieto to Bolsena by the Corpus Domini Procession route

Access: For Orvieto, see
Walk 33. Bolsena, on the
other hand, is on the SS
2, also known as the
Cassia, the nearest
sizeable towns being
Acquapendente in the
northwest and
Montefiascone to the
south. Otherwise from
Orvieto take the SS 71
and branch off on the
signposted minor road.

Bolsena is served by
COTRAL bus from
Viterbo as well as the
ATC line from Orvieto.
The latter allows you to
return to Orvieto at the
end of the walk and at
the time of walking there
was a perfectly-timed
late afternoon run
(except Sundays and
holidays).

To avoid the short stretch
of asphalt at the start of
the walk, orange city bus
n.3 is handy. It departs
from Piazza della
Repubblica and will drop
you off at the cemetery
(*cimitero*).

Walking time:	4h
Distance:	15.6km/7.7 miles
Map:	on p.219, also Istituto Geografico Adriatico 1:50,000 'Orvietano e Trasimeno' (available at the Orvieto Tourist Office)

Orvieto, a proud medieval township whose landmark is a glittering cathedral, and the village of Bolsena in a quiet backwater on a placid lake some 13km away as the crow flies. What could the two possibly have in common? An incredible series of inextricable bonds bequeathed them by history, as it turns out: the earliest dates back to Etruscan times, 264BC to be precise, when the powerful city of Velzna – alias modern-day Orvieto – was sacked by Rome and the survivors deported to found Volsinii Novi, now Bolsena. This young lakeside settlement which flourished with the construction of the Via Cassia, was soon to witness the miracle of the early Christian martyr Santa Cristina. Condemned to death by her father the Roman prefect, she was subjected to terrible tortures and even cast into the waters lashed to a boulder which floated miraculously back to the surface, bearing both the young girl and her footprints. The complete epic is replayed each summer in a colourful pageant on July 24th, her feast day. Many centuries later in 1263, it was at a chapel dedicated to Santa Cristina in Bolsena that a Bohemian priest, assailed by terrible doubts concerning transubstantiation, stopped to say mass en route to Rome in pilgrimage. As he raised the host, blood began to drip onto the corporale, the white linen altar cloth, staining it. The event was proclaimed a miracle by the Pope from his palace in Orvieto, and the Catholic Feast of Corpus Domini established. The precious relic, the corporale in question, was borne in procession to Orvieto in 1293. Both an elaborate reliquary and the

famous cathedral were consequently constructed to hold it. The event is celebrated faithfully in Bolsena in June with a procession through streets covered with magnificent carpets of flowers.

During the Orvieto–Bolsena traverse

Fire-breathing lions, vengeful witches and a lame devil are but some of the mythical creatures that populate the other stories recounted around the Lago di Bolsena, a legend in itself. Its very waters are said to have turned to blood once as a harbinger of pestilence. The body of water formed in ancient times in the crater of an extinct volcano, ringed by the Monti Volsini. It is Italy's largest volcanic lake with a vast shimmering surface area of 144sq km. Of its two islands, Bisentina boasts seven Baroque churches and a 16th-century palace. The lake waters plunge to a surprising maximum depth of 146m and swarm with tasty fish such as perch, freshwater houting known locally as *coregone*, and eels, which rated a mention by both Dante and Petrarch. Thanks to the volcanic heritage the surrounding hilly countryside is fertile, to say the least. Its rich soil supports cereal crops and fruit such as figs and sweet grapes for the famous Aleatico dessert wine produced at Gradoli, on the north-western shore, without forgetting the excellent white wine known as 'Est! Est! Est!' from Montefiascone in the southern reaches.

The walk described here follows the original medieval route over the hills, touching on a group of modest Etruscan tombs and terminating at Bolsena and its splendid lake. An astounding variety of beautiful natural landscapes is encountered along the way. Wandering through vast swathes of wood and open scenic countryside is a lovely way to spend a day.

Waymarking is patchy, so directions need to be followed carefully. Some 430m in height gain is involved, and a little less in descent, but it's all very gradual. Walking in the opposite direction from Bolsena is feasible if not straightforward, and the ATC bus could always be used as far as the turn-off for 'Azienda Agricola del Grillo'.

No shops, bars or restaurants are encountered so carry all picnic supplies and drink. A torch is handy for the Etruscan tombs, as is a swimming costume for a rewarding swim in the lake, though it is a trifle shallow on the edges.

THE WALK

To leave **Orvieto** (260m), follow Via della Cava down to the southwest gate, Porta Maggiore, and out through the massive walls. Turn right then first left (Strada Dritta del Marchigiano), where you'll see red/white waymarking. Downhill it leads to a wider road (the SS 71), where you turn right. Stick to this for some 10min, as per road signs for 'Lago di Bolsena'. At the end of stone bridge **Ponte del Sole** (184m, 20min), a shrine on the left commemorates the 1293 meeting with Pope Urban IV who came to welcome the arrival of the procession from Bolsena.

Now leave the main road which bears right and up past the cypress-ringed cemetery with its yellow octagonal dome, and continue straight ahead (southwest) through Tamburino on a minor road climbing steadily through peaceful countryside where olives and grapes flourish. You pass the church of S. Spirito, Romanesque in appearance. In places the road reverts to the original dark basalt cobble stones. Where you intersect the surfaced road (45min from Orvieto), don't neglect to look

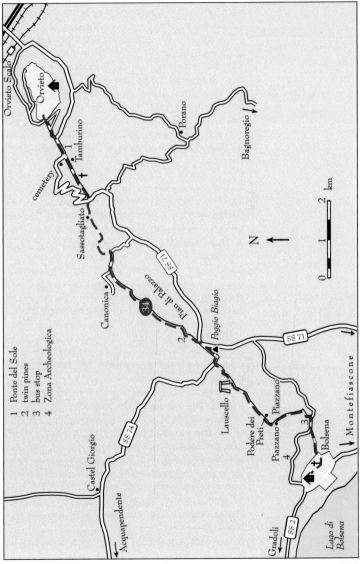

1 Ponte del Sole
2 twin pines
3 bus stop
4 Zona Archeologica

back for the lovely profile of the city and its landmark cathedral.

A signed path proceeds through shady woods to a curious passage known as the **Sassotagliato** ('cut stone', 424m) ostensibly because the rock spontaneously split open to allow for the passage of the procession bearing the miraculous altar cloth. An old bridge is passed amongst beech trees, then several caves. The route (marked as 4f in places) maintains its southwest direction and, flanking a watercourse and fields, follows a beautiful deep lane overhung with sweet chestnut trees then oak.

After about 1h10min, the lane takes a sharp right to leave the wood and embark on a short westward loop (to avoid private property). As per red/white stripes, stay on the lane over a rise. After farms and a minor watercourse turn left for a lane (4f) which soon leads to tarmac.

Follow the road right past houses and through rolling farming countryside for 5min to where a signposted lane branches off left (1h20min total). Heading southwest again, accompanied by thick hedgerows you pass rural properties, while across to the right (west) the picturesque hamlet of Canonica is visible. Don't be tempted by the numerous turn-offs, but stick to the main track. After a climb bordered by grape vines, woodland takes over, followed by a beautiful longish stretch through open fields, almost English countryside. This area is known as the **Pian di Palazzo** (approx. 550m).

Some 2h will see you at prominent **twin pines** for a marked curve left (south). The track soon brings you out on main road SS 71 once more. Keep right on a parallel minor road for about 1km past Poggio Biagio (591m). After the broad curve downhill protected by a guard rail, take the first track off left (signposted) between fields crammed with sunflowers. Be sure to leave this track the moment it curves left, for the rougher lane straight ahead in light woods. A brief climb away is a series of modest **Etruscan tombs** not far from **Lauscello** (2h30min). Under protective roofing are modest underground chambers accessible by way of steep crumbly steps and a corridor. A torch is handy.

After the necropolis you soon join a wider track on the edge of open fields planted with maize then hedgerows, maintaining a constant southwesterly direction. From a crest (approx. 620m) Lago di Bolsena comes into sight in all its glittering glory. An immense expanse of water backed by the Monti Volsini and watched over by the township of Capodimonte on the opposite shore, southwest. Its two islands seem to brood or float, depending on light and weather conditions. Overlooking the valley of Fosso del Ponticello the lane soon veers down right, ignoring a ruined house (Podere dei Preti). Keep left then a short way uphill left again, branching southwards off the main route (until rights-of-way issues are cleared up, the original medieval route must be left here, detouring south). At a house a wider track is joined for a pleasant stretch uphill past a property (Piazzano, 583m, 3h10min). With the lake on your far right now, follow a stately tree-lined avenue as it winds to the road and a bus stop (502m, 3h25min).

Not far downhill turn left on a steep narrow road, which forbids transit to all 'escluso residenti'. This handy short cut saves you the long winds of the main road, and drops quickly past a church, on the lower flanks of the

Well-earned picnic on the shores of Lago di Bolsena

221

ancient crater now. A curious crag of rock, honeycombed with caves and tunnels used as storage and hutches, precedes the town proper. You finally arrive, right in Piazza S. Cristina, **Bolsena** (347m, 4h total).

Once you've recovered from the exertions of the walk, cross the square, alias the ertswhile Roman forum, and pop into the 12th-century church with the Cappella del Miracolo and the miraculous stone imprinted by Santa Cristina's feet. And don't miss a visit to the 4th century early Christian catacombs adjoining the church. While modest in comparison to those in Rome, they are unusual as the burial recesses are arranged in a multi-storey sense, instead of extending lengthways, so that the deceased could rest in peace as close as possible to the body of their beloved saint.

A short distance stroll away to the right, is the main square where the Orvieto buses terminate, below the grey stone buildings of the old quarter. Not far away on the lakeside, lined with rushes, are diminutive beaches, perfect for enjoying a picnic, a cool off and a legendary sunset.

Other Etruscan sites around Lago di Bolsena
The southwestern shore of Lago di Bolsena was once occupied by Etruscan **Bisenzio**, a site dating back to 9th century BC and the earlier Bronze age. Vestiges of buildings have come to light at Monte Bisenzio, northwest of present-day Capodimonte as have several necropolises in the surroundings. It also produced some exquisite bronze work, which can be seen in the Villa Giulia musem in Rome along with an unusual pair of wooden sandals.

Zona Archeologica (1km from Bolsena on the Orvieto road). Ruins of the Roman city Volsinii Novi including several buildings and an amphitheatre.

Accommodation
Bolsena:
Hotel Italia
tel.0761/799193

Hotel Nazionale
tel.0761/799006

Orvieto:
see Walk 33

35: Civita di Bagnoregio and the 'Calanchi'

Walking time:	2h + 30min if on foot from Bagnoregio
Distance:	3.9km/2.4 miles
Map:	on p.225

Possibly the most extraordinary itinerary in this guide for the combination of the three distinct worlds it encompasses – a picturesque crumbling medieval hill town, a unique Etruscan tunnel and the 'calanchi'. The latter refers to extensively eroded clayey terrain where, over time, razor-narrow ridges as high as 50m and separated by yawning chasms have formed, giving rise to bizarre forms in a dramatic landscape, lunar in some ways. The area has several tiny cluster villages still miraculously balancing on crests and cliff edges, kept

The Torrione aka Montiglione on the edge of the 'calanchi' from Bagnoregio

apart by deep gullies. The slow bus between Viterbo and Bagnoregio makes a series of excursions down and back up such side ridges to service the hamlets and prolong their precarious state of survival just a little longer. It makes for a fascinating trip and a good introduction to the walk.

One of the most intriguing 'survivors' is the township of Civita di Bagnoregio, 'la città che muore' (the dying city), which perches forlorn (and traffic-free) on a crumbling crag akin to a castle. It would be isolated from the surrounding countryside were it not for a pedestrian bridge constructed in the 1960s to replace the previous one which was partially demolished at the end of the Second World War. The unstable nature of the terrain at Civita has long been known and the first recorded collapse was probably that of a monastery well back in 1450, while an entire 'contrada' (district) collapsed during a later earthquake in 1695. Luckily the main square and a good few buildings have survived, including a Romanesque church and tower dating back to the 1500s. The inhabitants in the meantime moved to the sleepy neighbouring township of Bagnoregio, named in all likelihood after Roman baths in the area. It was however better known as the birthplace of San Bonaventura, the 13th-century Franciscan monk and mystic entrusted with the task of writing the official life of Saint Francis, which inspired Giotto's famous paintings in Assisi.

Civita's Etruscan past is confirmed by its unique tunnel together with the scattered tombs, each inscribed with family names, though most have been swallowed up in the landslips. A couple of remnants along with columbaria are visible in the cliffs just before Mercatello. Some scholars have even equated Civita with Fanum Voltumna, one of the most important sanctuaries to the goddess Voltumna known to have existed in the Volsinii/Orvieto area. In addition to religious functions, it was believed to be the site of annual festivities which brought together representatives from different cities and tribes, as well as for meetings of a political nature.

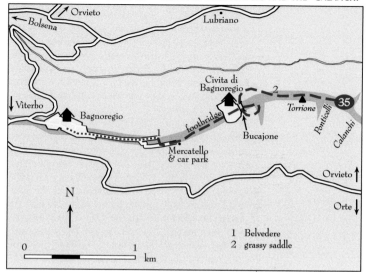

These days Civita is experiencing a low-key revival and boasts a snack bar and restaurant which doubles as B&B, along with craft boutiques.

As for the walk itself, there are no difficulties as far as the Etruscan tunnel, apart from the usual up and downs, but nothing in excess of 100m. From there on, however the countryside becomes wilder and paths are notoriously overgrown, so long trousers are a good idea for the final stretch. Should you prefer not to continue, there are good views of the 'calanchi' even as you descend from Civita to the tunnel. Any time of year is feasible, however slippery muddy conditions are to be expected after wet weather, so take special care.

THE WALK

From what's left of **Mercatello** (395m), namely a cluster of houses and recommended restaurant Hostaria del Ponte, take the somewhat aerial bridge. You climb to the gracious 15th-century entrance portal of **Civita di Bagnoregio** (443m) and through to the square with the church of San Donato. It's worth setting aside time to

➤ **Bagnoregio to Mercatello on foot** (30min)
Should there not be a bus handy, take Via Roma through the town of Bagnoregio, then follow signs for the Belvedere. Steps then lead down to the road and nearby Mercatello.

225

wander the quiet streets as well as to fill your water bottle at the fountain. From the square, keep straight on past a 16th-century olive press on the left. Soon the way narrows and leaves upper Civita by way of a low cutting, curving right on recently restored steps bordered by scented broom. At this point the Torrione, a reddish castle-like rock formation, comes into view with the 'calanchi' further back to its right.

Not far down and dug into the soft tufaceous rock is the modest chapel known as S. Maria del Carcere, once an Etruscan burial site. The cliff is dotted with stalls for chickens and donkeys, probably all tomb sites once upon a time. At the bottom of the descent on the right is the yawning opening to the so-called 'Bucajone', the 50m-long Etruscan tunnel which burrows beneath the very outcrop on which Civita stands. Quite extraordinary. A torch is not necessary as sufficient light enters from each end. Several narrow slit-tunnels can be found along the sides, probably for Etruscan drainage purposes.

Out on the other side is a magnificent chestnut wood, and the path drops left (north) to a bench and info board. Ignore the route left for Lubriano, and go right through a gate. Further down through broom is a **grassy saddle** (327m) on the edge of the wood. Following a wire fence, take the path along the ridge in front of you (east), taking care at the ever-narrower tracts caused by landslides. Further up brambles and thorny scrub are encountered as you climb to the left of the rocky crest, where black and white porcupine quills are scattered in the light wood. Immediately after the **Torrione** aka Montiglione the path drops past a razor-thin crest running due south: known as Ponticelli, it was once part of a route to the Tiber valley, and planks still hang precariously from the clay terrain. Keeping well away from the crumbling edges, proceed down to a signer pole in a grassed clearing (340m) to enjoy stunning views onto other 'calanchi'. (This far takes about 1h, as does the return on the same path).

Accommodation
Bagnoregio:
Hotel Fidanza
tel.0761/793444

Civita: B&B c/o Trattoria
Antico Forno
tel.0761/760016

36: WWF Oasi di Alviano

Walking time:	1–2h (guided visit)
Map:	on p.228

Squeezed in between the Florence–Rome motorway and the main north–south railway lines – an unlikely site for a bird and wildlife reserve, the World Wildlife Fund for Nature's 'Oasi di Alviano' encompasses a surprising 900 hectares. A shallow lake is edged by the appropriate marshy terrain and bordered by light wood then fields of corn and sunflowers, perfect for a long list of wetland wingers. The lake itself was formed when this stretch of the River Tiber on the Latium–Umbria border was partially dammed by the Electricity Commission back in the 1960s.

The purpose of the reserve is to protect birds during their long migration flights in addition to their summer nesting period. Only since 1990 has it been under WWF

Access: more straightforward with your own transport – from the A1 autostrada, it's equidistant between the exit at Orvieto (for those coming from the north – head for Baschi and Madonna del Porto) and Attigliano (if you're driving up from the south – hence Alviano Scalo and Madonna del Porto). From the chapel overlooking the lake, a lane heads downhill under the railway line to the Oasi parking area.➤

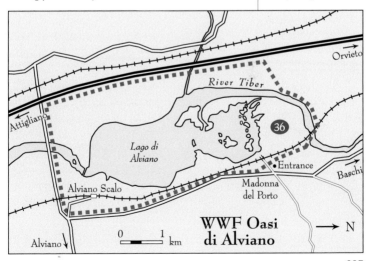

➤ By public transport, namely rail, it is theoretically possible to reach the area via the station at Alviano Scalo (4km from the entrance), but unfortunately very few useful trains stop there.

Oasi WWF di Alviano
tel.0744/903715. Open for visits Saturday, Sunday and bank holidays at 10am from September through to May. Entrance fee. Group visits on other days, subject to advance booking – individuals can sometimes join in as well.

Accommodation
Alviano Scalo:
Hotel Alviano
tel.0744/904625-6

management, and visits are now possible with the aid of a marvellous series of fenced-in walkways that run through the forest of towering grasses and rushes along the water's edge to numerous observation points and a lookout tower.

Long-term residents include a wide range of wild ducks such as the mallard and European teal, along with coots, the spoonbill, wild goose and the white and purple heron. Of the more unusual migratory species that call in at the lake are the marsh-harrier, osprey and even the black-winged stilt.

37: Vulci and the River Fiora

Walking time:	2h15min + heaps of extra time for the museum, old city and tomb visits
Distance:	6km/3.7 miles
Map:	on p.230

On the approach to former Etruscan Vulci in the Maremma hinterland, visitors cross a bare plain, windswept in winter and sun-scorched midsummer. This monotonous landscape is broken by a single structure – the modest dark stone castle, alias museum. Closer up, however, are a string of surprises in the shape of an exquisite Roman bridge, a beautiful hidden river gorge and some intriguing ruins of the ancient city, without forgetting the tombs. A powerful Etruscan city once dominated the vast territory that spread from Talamone on the coast, to the lower slopes of Monte Amiata in the north then Lago di Bolsena. Meagre scattered vestiges greet today's visitors, and even the name remains a mystery though the root Velch has been identified.

Vulci was inhabited from early 9th century BC and reached its zenith of prosperity 7th–6th century BC, sending out emissaries and nobles who founded smaller settlements such as Poggio Buco and Sovana in the environs. A member of the influential twelve-state Etruscan Confederation, it eventually came under Roman control in 280BC, thereafter marked by gradual decline, though a settlement persisted as late as medieval times.

The Etruscans, expert hydraulic engineers, implemented full-scale irrigation schemes and transformed the plain into a sea of wheat, though it was later allowed to revert to its wild state. It was not until the 18th century that serious attempts were made anew to tame the area and eradicate the malaria which had since taken hold.

Under the Etruscans an extensive network of trade relationships operated via the port of Regae, near

This marvellous circuit takes in all the key archaeological points and the river gorge, with several variants. It is problem-free with very brief climbs and drops, the only possible difficulty being at the crossing of the River Fiora for the detour to the necropolis and the Tomba François. The stepping stones may be submerged in winter and spring, and the only choice is to wade across. However you can always drive or walk there from the museum.

Summer walkers will need hats for the initial section as there is no shade until the river. Winter walkers should be prepared for the bitter winds that sweep the plain. Before starting out, remember to enquire at the museum for the opening times of the Tomba François and whether any others are accessible.

There are no shops at Vulci, though the Osteria bar/restaurant on the way to the old city is a good bet for meals and refreshments.

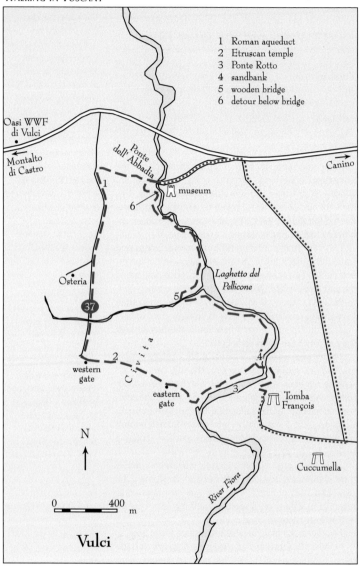

1 Roman aqueduct
2 Etruscan temple
3 Ponte Rotto
4 sandbank
5 wooden bridge
6 detour below bridge

Oasi WWF
di Vulci

← Montalto
di Castro

Canino →

Ponte
dell' Abbadia

museum

Osteria

Laghetto del
Pellicone

37

western
gate

C i v i t a

eastern
gate

Tomba
François

Cuccumella

N

River Fiora

0   400
          m

Vulci

present-day Montalto di Castro. This is illustrated by the fascinating range of imported burial goods that Vulci's tombs have yielded: there are bronze statuettes from Sardinia, scarabs and ostrich eggs from Egypt traded through the Phoenicians, then last but not least ceramics from Greece – this site is said to have produced more Greek vases than Athens! Vulci itself manufactured high level artistic bronze and ceramic objects. The close nature of the trade ties was further confirmed by the discovery of the cremated remains of an 8th-century BC woman from Sardinia.

The first actual discoveries of the ancient settlement date back to 1828. A peasant ploughing a field with oxen saw the ground give way to reveal an underground tomb chamber which held broken vases. The proprietor at the time, the Prince of Canino namely Lucien Bonaparte, Napoleon's brother, embarked on an ambitious and lengthy excavation campaign followed by a stream of others. The museums of all Europe, particularly the British and those at Munich and Berlin, not to mention Rome's Villa Giulia, acquired rich collections from these lucrative campaigns, though techniques reportedly left a lot to be desired. Workmen broke open tombs with pick-axes, and any objects not deemed marketable were trampled underfoot, while an armed overseer made sure nothing left the site. Of the 30,000 burials excavated and emptied, covering a vast range of architectural types and social classes, very few tombs can be visited, though one of great interest is included.

The impressive 4th century BC Tomba François was named after the archaeologist who discovered it in 1857, deep underground. It is one of the few painted tombs at Vulci that belonged to the aristocratic classes, however the bulk of the frescoes were quickly removed to a private collection in Rome. One surviving section remains today of the once extensive scenes of Greek mythology and Etruscan history. A curse of sorts akin to those of ancient Egyptian tombs is in the air here. A tale is told of a young *buttero* cowboy mysteriously attracted to a ruined tomb one night where he witnessed the apparition of a gracious Etruscan maiden. Alas, on attempting to join her, he met

Access: The Vulci archaeological site lies 12km inland from the Tyrrhenian Sea, about halfway between Rome and Grosseto. From the coast, leave the SS 1 (Aurelia) near Montalto di Castro on the Canino road. Follow the yellow signs for the museum alias castle, clearly visible across the fields, and park there. Road access from inland is straightforward from Tuscania and the Viterbo region, and there is also the SS 312 from Lago di Bolsena.

By public transport the closest useful service is the daily COTRAL bus that connects Canino with Montalto di Castro, Tuscania and Tarquinia. However after being let off on the SS 312, it means an 8km hike along a minor road. Hitchhiking is worth a try though traffic is usually light as there are no villages in the immediate Vulci area.➤

➤ To drive to the Tomba
François, leave the
museum and proceed
east on the road for
Canino. Go right at the
first intersection – signposted for both Montalto
and the tomb. A little
way along, an unsur-
faced track (signpost)
turns off west towards
the river again, and you
park at the end. The
tomb is a short distance
downhill.

his end by drowning as water unexpectedly gushed in.
His death was later 'explained' by the discovery of the
figure of Vanth, the female demon of death in Etruscan
mythology, in the frescoes of the Tomba François. The
curse is said to have continued as François himself
succumbed to malaria before completing work.

A further noteworthy burial site is the remarkable
Cuccumella tumulus. Its labyrinth of internal passageways
that reportedly total 700m in length, made it a candidate
for the legendary tomb of Lars Porsenna, King of Chiusi
(see Walk 14). Standing 18m high with a 65m diameter, it
was originally girthed by a ring of masonry and was richly
decorated with all manner of unusual carved animals.
Unfortunately it is not open to visitors at present, though
it can be seen from the outside. Otherwise on a slightly
less monumental scale, there is the Cuccumelletta
tumulus, a short distance to its south.

The 'Vulci Parco Archeologico Naturalistico' has
recently been instituted, to the great advantage of
walkers as there are helpful maps and bilingual
(Italian–English) information panels in key points, paths
have been cleared of debris and brambles and the banks
of the beautiful River Fiora have been made accessible.
As well, a number of toilet sheds have been discretely
placed along the paths. A nearby World Wildlife Fund
Oasis which provides refuge for otters and water fowl
can also be visited, as can Castro, another Etruscan site.
Details are given at the end of the walk.

THE WALK

The museum at **Vulci** (71m) stands on the verge of a
plunging gorge where a wonderful ancient stone bridge,
the **Ponte dell'Abbadia** (abbey bridge) spans the River
Fiora at a height of 32m. Originally triple-arched, it was
constructed in reddish tufa together with the dark
volcanic rock 'nenfro' and travertine. The lower part of
the piers dates back to Etruscan times, the upper arch is
mostly Roman, whereas the aqueduct along the parapet
is medieval. Centuries-long water leakage accounts for
the curious calcareous formation that droops, beard-like,
below the bridge's main arch.

After crossing the bridge, continue straight ahead (east) past a private fenced-in garden featuring several stunning wattle trees not to mention yapping dogs. Ignore the branch down left for the bridge (covered on the return

Ponte dell'Abbadia and the castle at Vulci

233

route), and go on to join an unsurfaced road (5min). Turn left here past the interesting raised stretches of Roman aqueduct. Then, unless you feel ready for a delicious country-style lunch in a shady garden, in the vicinity of tomb clusters from different periods, ignore the turn-off right for the **Osteria**. Proceed uphill to the parking area and western gate for the '**Civita**' (20min total).

The flourishing city spread over this dominating 100-hectare site, though the ruins visible nowadays are a mix of Etruscan and later Roman constructions, each presented by helpful bilingual explanatory signs. The most important is the sizeable (24 x 36m) temple from 4th century BC. A little further down are remains of a pagan temple where Mithra, a Persian divinity, was worshipped. The cult was probably spread by Roman soldiers (see Walk 47 for further details).

There is a stunning stretch of original dark basalt paving laid by the Romans presumably over the earlier Etruscan route. Running east–west, this main axis leads all the way downhill and out the eastern gate to the meadow where herds of horses and long-horned Maremma cattle graze. Keep right around the enclosure through a sequence of humans-only openings and light wood, beneath dark cliffs. At the river's edge is the site of the 'Ponte Rotto' – broken bridge, where the road once crossed the Fiora to the necropolises on the opposite bank.

Follow the river and its poplars along to the left, and a little further on is a delightful picnic area close to a sandbank (40min total this far). For the 20min extension to the Tomba François, the Fiora is usually passable on stepping stones in summer from the sandbank at the bend in the river. On the opposite bank, follow the faint path right through brambles then brief steep climb which takes you through light wood. Numerous entrances to rock tombs are passed, but all are fenced off and out of bounds unfortunately. A dirt track is soon reached hence the entrance to the **Tomba François**. •

A 27m long dromos corridor penetrates deep into the travertine hillside, and the custodians provide visitors with strong flashlights. Flanked by cells for minor burials, the tomb is made up of an antechamber and a central room

• The description of the opening of the **Tomba François** left by François's partner Adolf Noël des Vergers makes for curious reading:

'Everything was just as it had been the day the entrance was sealed, and ancient Etruria appeared in all its former splendour. There were warriors covered with their armour on their funeral beds, apparently resting after combating the Romans or our Gallic ancestors. Shapes, garments, fabrics and colours appeared for a minute or so, then it all faded as the outside air penetrated the crypt where, a moment before, our flickering torches almost died out. This plunge into the past did not even last as long as a dream and the scene vanished as though to punish us for our indiscrete curiosity.'

with seven openings. On the right as you enter are traces of the original painted decorations depicting the founder of the tomb, Vel Saties, and his wife Tanchvil Verati.

Afterwards, either return back across the river to pick up the main itinerary (1h total to here), or return to the museum as follows, without recrossing the river.

Alternative return to the museum (40min)

From the Tomba François, continue south up the lane past yet more tomb entrances and up to the flowered fields on the plain once more. The tumulus shape of the Cuccumella is recognisable over right. This massive untidy grassy mound in the middle of a field was closed to visitors at the time of writing. Take the wide vehicle track eastwards a short way through the olive groves, then left at the first intersection. North now past scattered properties where sheep graze and along old stone walls, the track soon becomes rutted and muddy, but problem-free for walkers. On the left of this track several important necropolises were explored last century. Thick broom, wild roses and wild flowers amongst the wheat fields keep you company 20min or so to the asphalt. Then it's down left and straight ahead for the final stretch back to the museum.

From the picnic area near the sandbank, proceed northwards a little way back from the river. More fenced enclosures are traversed then the path climbs via wooden steps. You are actually skirting the outer limits of the Etruscan city. Now follows a delightful section high above the river with beautiful views down into the stunning gorge. Signboards in shelters provide information on local fauna such as porcupines, who drop their grey-brown and white quills along the pathway. A brief descent follows through wood to a side valley and board map (total 1h20min).

Cross the wooden bridge northwards, keeping right along a lane which leads to the river's edge. The flow is forced to cascade through a narrow gap between sheer cliffs and here the river widens out into the **Laghetto del Pellicone**. This magnificent quiet shady spot lends itself perfectly to picnics and even a dip.

Oasi WWF di Vulci
tel.0766/897015. Open for guided visits Sunday at 10am & 3pm, from August through to April. Entrance fee. 340 hectares of riverside (Fiume Fiora) host both rare otters and coypu, a beaver-like rodent from South America originally imported into Europe for fur-breeding. The numerous waterfowl include cranes and the dipper, whose presence, along with a sort of freshwater crayfish, is indicative of clean water. The reserve, set up in 1982, is situated about 1km west of the museum, only 15min on foot.

A further Etruscan site, Castro, lies some 20km further inland from Vulci, on the road that joins Pitigliano and Farnese. From Vulci take the road for Ischia di Castro, and follow the yellow sign-posting. There are scattered remains of a sanctuary, rock tombs and vestiges of the city that was settled in 9th century BC. The beautiful Etruscan chariot of bronze-plated oak with iron wheels on ➤

➤ display at Rome's Villa
Giulia museum with a
pair of horses, came from
here during a Belgian
excavation campaign in
the 1960s.

Backtrack briefly to a further flight of wooden steps up through a wood of glossy dark green holm oak, and keep right at the top along the cliff edge. More picnic spots with benches and sign boards are passed, before a final stretch along the edge of fields of wheat and oats – take care not to trample or damage crops. A stone's throw from the photogenic castle and bridge now, just before the cyclone fencing, a path drops to the water once more for an interesting angle on the bridge (extra 10min detour). Follow the hedge and fence left around private property to rejoin the path and return right across the wonderful bridge to visit the **museum** (grand total of 2h15min).

The building started out as a medieval abbey, and went on to play a strategic role in the 18th century when Vulci stood on the border between Tuscany and Papal States, and heavy tolls were exacted of passers-by. Just inside the courtyard is a series of long metal rods confiscated from tomb looters who used them to sound out the ground for likely burial cavities. Below are examples of the massive carved nenfro stone sculptures of sphinxes, bull's heads, lions and griffons, grotesque at times, that once guarded the burial sites. Some seem straight out of a medieval bestiary. The museum also has an extraordinary selection of bronze and ceramic objects such as curious hut-shaped urns, some beautiful samples of black *bucchero* ware, mirrors, anatomical ex voto objects, and intricately decorated ostrich eggs.

**Accommodation
Canino:**
Hotel Guglielmi
tel.0761/437177

Montalto Marina:
Hotel Maremma sul
Mare
tel.0766/820070

Numerous camping
grounds on the coast.

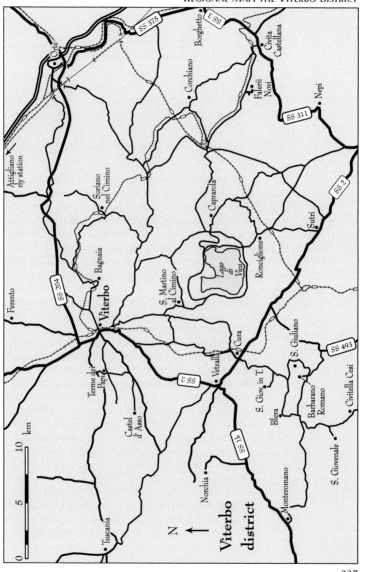

SS 375

• Borghetto

SS 3

• Civita Castellana

• Corchiano

† Falerii Novi

• Nepi

SS 311

Orte

Attigliano rly station

Soriano nel Cimino

Capraola

SS 2

• Sutri

Bagnaia

Lago di Vico

Ronciglione

S. Martino al Cimino

• Ferento

SS 204

• Viterbo

Cura

SS 493

S. Giuliano

Vetralla

SS 2

S. Giov. in T.

Barbarano Romano

• Civitella Cesi

Terme dei Papi

Blera

Castel d'Asso

SS 1b

N

Norchia •

S. Giovenale •

• Monteromano

Viterbo district

• Tuscania

km

0 5 10

237

38: Tuscania: Romanesque Churches and Etruscan Tombs

Access: See Viterbo district map on p.237. Tuscania is situated about halfway between Viterbo and the coast, and drivers have a multitude of roads and directions to choose from. COTRAL coaches, on the other hand, provide frequent daily links with Viterbo and Tarquinia (except Sundays), as well as smaller centres such as Canino.

Walking time:	2h30min not counting visits + 45min extension
Distance:	6.9km/4.3 miles + 3.2km/2 miles extension
Map:	on p.241

The graceful silhouette of San Pietro is visible for miles around. This proud monumental Romanesque church is the landmark of Tuscania and stands apart from the medieval township. Its hill site once hosted the Etruscan acropolis which came to light in the aftermath of an earthquake which caused widespread damage here in 1971.

The town's origins are, however, said to go back much much further. The mythical founder was none other than Tusco, offspring of a queen from ancient Scythia (Asia Minor) and Hercules, who determined that Mount Olympus was no place for a son of his and thus sent him to live amongst the mortals.

Tuscania's location at the confluence of two watercourses together with its key position at the crossroads for numerous former Etruscan settlements between the inland Viterbo area and the coast, made it a strategic trading centre. Very little is known about the town itself though the widely scattered necropolises and heterogeneous nature of the burials suggest it may have been a series of connected village-type settlements. Judging by the impressive burials of wealthy families an aristocratic class had emerged. However Tuscania appears to have become a virtual colony of Tarquinia from 5th century until 282BC, when control fell to the Romans, who consolidated its position on the Via Clodia. This ancient road from Rome to Saturnia was the work of the Etruscans, though the Romans were responsible for paving it. The town's most glorious period was undoubtedly the Middle Ages when it was a bishopric. The

The magnificent Romanesque façade of San Pietro at Tuscania

magnificent churches, town layout and defensive walling with the odd extant tower survive to this day. Lovely cobbled streets and inviting squares of what is now a quiet country backwater, make for a delightful wander.

As regards the walking itinerary, despite the initial and final stretches on surfaced roads, this varied circuit traverses some lovely countryside and leads to several interesting Etruscan tombs, not to mention Romanesque churches and the town itself with the museum. The easy paths, cleared and in good condition at the time of writing, make it feasible for all walkers, however stick to coolish weather as there is little shade along the way. Nothing monumental or even particularly extensive should be expected in terms of the tombs, not comparable with those in the immediate Viterbo area or Tarquinia or Vulci near the coast. Of the high number of necropolises dotted through the countryside around Tuscania, only a fraction can be visited, and, apart from the interesting underground Madonna dell'Olivo complex covered in the extension, are of modest dimensions though in attractive countryside settings.

THE WALK

Start out from **Tuscania's** (180m) Piazza Italia, where the buses pull in. Follow broad tree-lined avenue Viale Trieste, keeping straight on where the town walls veer to the right. Very soon on the right is the access ramp to the church and ex convent of Santa Maria del Riposo, and the **Museo Nazionale Archeologico**. Half an hour usually suffices for a visit here (not included in the total walk time). There are enormous stately sarcophaguses belonging to the aristocratic Curunus and Vipinana families, along with a painted exemplary depicting the Amazons at battle, from the Tomba della Regina hypogeum.

After the museum, return to the town walls and follow them around left (Via Fontana Nuova). It's a matter of minutes to the left turn along Via Nazario Sauro, signposted for Marta.

Alternative:
An alternative this far bypasses the museum but traverses the old town instead. You'll need to navigate the labyrinth of streets and lanes inside the walls, and exit via Largo XII Settembre.

Head north uphill and soon after the cemetery take the narrow road right, with a faded yellow sign for the Necropoli. After a downhill stretch enclosed by hedgerows, the road curves left. A short distance along on the right is a rusty gate, and despite signs such as 'Proprietà Privata', this is the way to go as the ample openings in the fence suggest. The ensuing path was long infamous for its thick tangles of brambles, but a local cooperative now clears the way regularly. A short way downhill is a fork where you keep left for the detour to the nearby **Tomba del Dado** (40min this far). Set in a rock outcrop, this unusual massive tomb construction, dating back to 6th century BC, resembles a long house with a sloping roof. It has been partially restored, but continues to be invaded by vegetation such as colourful rock roses. Though isolated now, it once belonged to an extensive necropolis, since all but levelled to make way for the

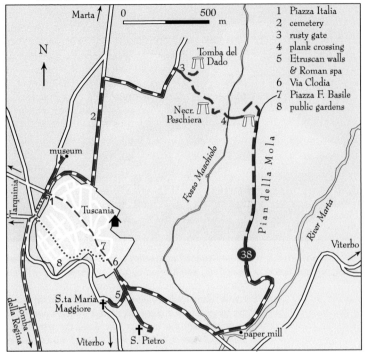

1 Piazza Italia
2 cemetery
3 rusty gate
4 plank crossing
5 Etruscan walls
   & Roman spa
6 Via Clodia
7 Piazza F. Basile
8 public gardens

olive grove. It overlooks a thickly flowered meadow sloping down to the watercourse, and several of the Pian di Mola tombs are visible on the opposite bank.

Return to the fork and go left for the **Necropoli della Peschiera**, right on the edge of the cliff at 180m in a pretty wooded setting (10min from Tomba del Dado). A series of metal ladders and railings lead through various cavities alias ex tomb chambers, making for an evocative visit. Afterwards, you'll need the decent path, recently cleared, that starts from the southernmost reaches of the necropolis and winds its way down to the Fosso Maschiolo and a plank crossing (approx. 125m). From here it's a matter of an easy climb in a couple of minutes straight up to the **Pian della Mola** necropolis set among oaks (1h15min total). There's virtually a row of 'terraced

Etruscan sarcophagi portraying female figures, Tuscania

houses' entered via a series of moulded doorways, some sealed off, and flanked by stairways to an upper level. Stumps of columns suggest an original grandiose effect. A rough lane leads left through a wire gate and up out of the trees to join a quiet dirt road. Turn right and head south through the olive groves along the panoramic plateau of Pian della Mola, with views of the Dado and Peschiera rock tombs, in addition to the township and churches. About 15min along past the odd house, road surfacing starts, then you drop quickly past a small recycled paper mill (*cartiera*) and cross the Fosso Maschiolo once more (total 1h45min). Keep right at the ensuing intersection for the short climb up the narrow road northwest beneath the site of Tuscania's ancient acropolis. Go left at the saddle and straight up for the final stretch to San Pietro. The church is preceded on the left by ruins of the ancient Etruscan acropolis which encompassed the religious-administrative centre. Evidence unearthed here suggests it was settled back as far as the Bronze Age.

The magnificent church of **San Pietro** (182m, total 2h this far) was constructed in the 11th century, though on the foundations of earlier religious structures. The building and the entire hill site were abandoned in the

15th century, and this ensured the church did not undergo modifications, leaving its marble bestiary figures and intricate frontal columns in their Romanesque simplicity. Numerous Etruscan sarcophaguses removed from various necropolises occupy the grounds.

Walk back a short distance down to a 3-way inter-section, opposite which are remnants of Etruscan walls and a Roman spa. Take the second turning on the left in descent for the church of Santa Maria Maggiore, hidden away at the foot of the hill. It is similar in construction to San Pietro, while the interior retains rich decorations in the shape of 13th-century frescoes – allow 10min for this detour – total 2h15min in all this far.

Back at the 3-way intersection, turn left now back towards the town, past a stretch of the paved Via Clodia. The most direct route back to the starting point involves keeping straight on uphill and into Piazza F. Basile. Both sides of the square are lined with lids from Etruscan sarcophaguses, bearing stately female figures with sophis-ticated coiffured heads, the stone now brightened by a host of colourful lichen. Proceed straight ahead through Piazza Matteotti and its art deco café, then Corso Cavour and eventually out through the walls close to **Piazza Italia** (total 2h30min).

Alternative return:
More interesting and only slightly longer, this route entails a first left after the Via Clodia, then left again past the elegant medieval seven-spouted Fontana Sette Cannella. The narrow walled curve of Via della Lupa (the she-wolf) leads up to a tower and the public gardens, a perfect place for admiring San Pietro yet again. The street near the tower, Via Torre del Lavello, which later becomes Via Roma, leads back to the northwestern edge of town, not far from Piazza Italia.

Tomba della Regina extension (45min return time on foot)
Before setting out, ask at the museum for a custodian to unlock the Tomba della Regina. It's well worth making the effort to visit this unusual necropolis, famous for its

Graceful Romanesque San Pietro on the site of the Etruscan acropolis in Tuscania

Tourist Office Tuscania
tel.0761/436371

Accommodation
Affittacamere Carla
tel.0761/435021

Locanda Mirandolina
tel.0761/436595

labyrinth of underground passageways and columns. It was named after a painted female figure that once adorned the walls but that now has all but disappeared. Go by car if possible, otherwise plan for a stroll along a quiet country road. From the westernmost entrance to Tuscania, Porta di Poggio, cross over to the minor road Via dell'Olivo, signposted for the tomb. Twenty minutes on foot south past the sports ground you reach the tiny church of the Madonna dell'Olivo, to the left of which a dirt lane leads to the necropolis. Via the steps deep down inside the cliffside you enter an extraordinary series of underground chambers and passageways now, reinforced with concrete and ceiling girders. A total of 22 'cunicoli' have been discovered burrowing down into the bedrock, presumably for drainage purposes. There are three distinct levels, and the visit continues outside with lower chambers that feature sculpted relief beams and carved benches with double pillow headrests. The interesting view from here takes in a Roman arch on the Via Clodia below San Pietro.

Return to town the same way.

39: The Castel d'Asso Necropolis

Walking time:	1h30min + 1h if on foot from Terme dei Papi
Distance:	6km/3.7 miles
Map:	on p.246

Although Castel d'Asso alias Etruscan Axia is considered a minor site in archaeological terms, it is a magical spot for walkers. A short distance west of Viterbo, several quiet narrow valleys beneath the cliffs of tufa plateaux are lined with unusual multi-storeyed tombs that were excavated directly in the rock face. Seventy or so have come to light, decorated with relief carvings and inscribed with the family names of the ancient occupants. The settlement spanned the 6th to 2nd centuries BC. Located at the meeting point of two watercourses, not to mention the junction of several important roads, it was in all probability very extensive. Traces of an ancient gate and wall, along with several deep ditches for defence purposes, suggest that the town itself occupied the plateau adjoining the ruined medieval castle opposite the necropolis. Further clues have come to light in the form of an evocative stretch of ancient roadway, canals for drainage and sewerage, and a well in the residential zone.

This is a delightful and easy walk along country lanes amidst fields ablaze in summer with all manner of wild flowers and aromatic herbs and escorted by cheerful bird song. Height gain and loss are negligible and visitors are few and far between.

Of additional interest is the hot sulphureous spring known as the Bullicame, of Dantesque fame, but a short detour off the road leading to the site. It lies halfway between the extinct volcanoes whose craters are now occupied by Lago di Vico and Lago di Bolsena, and supplies the Viterbo area with its hot (60°C) spa waters long renowned for doing wonders for a wide range of ghastly ailments. Legend has it that, in bygone times,

Access: See map of Viterbo district on p.237. The Castel d'Asso site lies 9km west of Viterbo, which in turn can easily be reached by all manner of transport. By car you'll most likely arrive on the SS 2 (Cassia), unless you've left the A1 *autostrada* at Orte and opted for the link road SS 204 which heads west for Viterbo.

Train travellers coming south on the main Florence–Rome line will need to change at Attigliano-Bomarzo (slow trains only stop here – a change at Orte is sometimes more convenient) for the Viterbo branch line. A secondary line also comes from the Rome direction via the route of the old Cassia way.

Furthermore the private company COTRAL manages a historic line known as the 'Ferrovia Roma Nord', which still employs wooden carriages from the 1930s, and is a must for railway enthusiasts. Starting out at the Roma Porta Flaminia station, its single line meanders through the scenic countryside via Civita Castellana all the way to Viterbo. ➤

➤ The same company also runs faster direct coaches from Rome and connects with all the towns in the province, for those with limited time. Viterbo's bus terminal is located in the suburb of Riello, served by local bus.

To reach the start of the actual walk, by car from Viterbo follow signposting to the Terme dei Papi then the yellow signposts for the necropolis as far as the parking area. There are also indications along the Viterbo–Tuscania road. Don't, however, be tempted by signs for the ruined castle of Castel d'Asso – the site provides interesting views of the necropolis but difficult access as a watercourse needs to be forded.

For those without a car, catch local bus n.2 from Viterbo to the top class Terme dei Papi spa and hotel complex, and proceed as follows.

Terme dei Papi to the start of the walk on foot (1h)
From here on foot take the pretty narrow country road west signposted for 'Castel d'Asso, Necropoli ➤

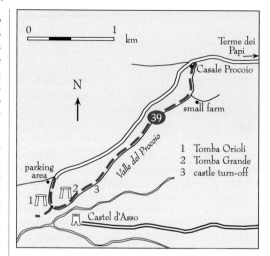

when the volcano Volta erupted and the Lago di Bolsena formed in its crater, the resident devils were forced to flee, taking refuge in these boiling waters. Though the odorous bubbling spring is fenced in nowadays, it is only a short distance from the Terme dei Papi, and in all likelihood you will be led straight there by your nose. The historic spa complex itself, though named after the Popes, was in use well before their time, as testified by the ruins of extensive Roman buildings in the area.

The provincial capital Viterbo, an excellent base, was once an Etruscan settlement called Surrina. It now boasts two reasonable archaeological museums along with an extensive medieval quarter, where sightseeing cannot be considered complete without the 13th-century Palazzo Papale with its graceful loggia. Lastly, garden enthusiasts will appreciate the manicured gardens and water-works from the 1500s of the Villa Lante at nearby Bagnaia.

THE WALK

After perusal of the helpful information board at the **parking area**, round the bar blocking the way to traffic and take the wide lane downhill. It drops into the shady valley and reaches the first tombs in a matter of minutes. Once monumental structures with magnificent façades hewn out of the steep volcanic tufa walls, they are overgrown nowadays but retain an indisputable charm. These multi-storeyed tombs typically had a broad platform on the upper part, believed to have been used for sacrifices in the name of the deceased. Below is a false moulded door to suggest the idea of passage into another world at death. On the next layer down is a room for holding the ritual meal, while the body was carried down the long dromos corridor to the underground burial chamber.

On the right soon is the imposing structure of the **Tomba Orioli**, which bears the name of its discoverer after the 19th-century custom. Its curious rounded chamber is low-roofed but spacious and measures 17m in length. On either side of a central passage are 62 individual

➤ Etrusche'. Half an hour along, keep left on the asphalted road at the fork with unsurfaced Strada Camorelle. Continue a further 30min to the parking area and signboard for the necropolis.

A glimpse of the old castle, Castel d'Asso

Original Etruscan roadway to cliff tombs at the Castel d'Asso necropolis outside Viterbo

body-length cavities that were chipped out from the solid base. Tiles probably covered each body.

Nearby outside is a tract of original road with wide grooves left by the passage of ancient vehicles. Where the lane curves left, take the path instead that continues right around the cliff edge for a worthwhile 10min detour. You are led through perfumed broom up to several more tomb fronts and good lookouts, while interesting remnants of channelling can be found on the lower levels. In thick wood west across the valley from here are the ruined towers of medieval Castel d'Asso, on the southernmost edge of the original town site. The broad valley watered by a watercourse is thick with golden wheat in the summer.

Return to the lane and follow it in gradual descent (northeast) past more overgrown tombs with a variety of decorated façades. Narrow paths can be taken to continue exploration from closer quarters, though many entrances are obstructed. Another impressive structure, the **Tomba Grande**, is soon reached. Its long access corridor leads to several subterranean chambers where over 40 sarcophaguses once rested. According to experts, the building was originally protected by a carved roof with engraved tiles to imitate a real house.

A little further along, the track is barred to vehicles (30min to here), and walkers keep straight ahead.

(The turn-off right eventually leads to the ruined castle: after an abandoned house you have to make your way across a field and ford the stream for the ensuing climb – exclusively for the adventurous.)

A pleasant stroll is next along this lovely valley, Valle del Procoio. It is flooded with yellow corn, the inevitable poppies and full-bodied birdsong, occasionally drowned out by the passage of helicopters from the military training bases nearby. At the end of the valley, leave the track as it curves right to a small farm, where livestock pens are caves. Instead keep straight up and over a low wire fence onto a disused and overgrown track, possibly one of the original Etruscan routes. You soon climb out onto the road, to the left of house n.8 known as **Casale Procoio** (235m, 1h to here).

Those on foot turn right here to return to the bus stop at the spa area (30min). Whereas to pick up your car, turn left to return to the parking area where the walk started, a further pleasant half an hour through open countryside.

Tourist Office Viterbo
tel.0761/304795

Terme dei Papi spa complex (tel.0761/350555) incorporates a pricey hotel but a hot water open-air pool and other facilities are open to visitors year-round.

Accommodation
Viterbo: Hotel Roma, Via della Cava 26
tel.0761/226474

40: The 'Island' of Norchia and its Multi-Storeyed Tombs

Access: See the map of the Viterbo district, p.237.
Norchia is south-west of Viterbo. From the SS 2 at Vetralla, take the road (SS 1bis) westish in the direction of Monteromano. Some 9km along is the sign-posted turn-off right for Norchia (or 8km from Monteromano). Follow the quiet narrow road north, ignoring side lanes. At a T-junction, keep left and continue right to the end, where you park.

As concerns public transport, COTRAL buses from Viterbo en route to Monteromano will take you as far as the sign-posted turn-off for Norchia mentioned above. However it's then a further 6km on foot to the actual site, meaning an extra 2h30min return time to be added to the total.

Walking time:	1h20min not counting visits + 30min extension
Distance:	2.2km/1.4 miles
Map:	on p.251

Deserted by all but shepherds and flourishing jungle-like vegetation since 1435, the erstwhile Etruscan settlement has retained its medieval name of Norchia. It first prospered under the hand of nearby princely Tarquinia starting around 6th century BC, but when the latter submitted to Rome, Orcla, as it was then called, began its gradual decline. The town was later revived by the Lombards, and developed in the medieval period when it boasted a sturdy castle and graceful church.

The Etruscan acropolis, of which virtually nothing has survived, occupied a central tufa 'island' ringed and protected by watercourses, while the inevitable extensive necropolises took up the steep flanks of the surrounding streams. Very few visitors come to these wild and unspoilt valleys, and a wander through the area is a guaranteed delight.

The site is always open and the walk is both rewarding and easy, with several short climbs and descents up and down the gullies, but nothing difficult. With additional exploration, there is plenty to keep you busy for a good few hours, so it's a good idea to be equipped with food and drink.

Unfortunately the itinerary is not feasible unless you have your own transport.

THE WALK

From the **parking area** (160m), take the unsigned but obvious path through fields of grain carpeted with brilliant cornflowers and poppies, and understandably alive with full-bodied birdsong. The towering ruins of medieval

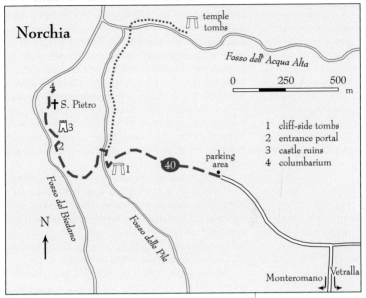

Norchia are visible over northwest right from the start. Five minutes on is the edge of the gorge where the path heads down left with some railings. Very promising. Visitors find themselves literally plunged into an Etruscan cemetery (4th–3rd century BC) which boasts fascinating cube-square tomb structures with majestic façades and false moulded doorways. The bare stone is a reddish-grey hue, but all was originally coated with coloured stucco. Terraces of monumental multi-storeyed sepulchres were painstakingly etched out of the solid tufa cliff face, and flights of stone steps connect different levels. It is believed that the upper platforms served as sacrificial and ritual areas, whereas the deceased and his family were laid to rest in the lower burial chamber, following a solemn procession. There are clear similarities with the necropolis at Castel d'Asso close to Viterbo.

Ten minutes or so in descent is sufficient to the bottom of the broad valley shaded by a variety of oaks. Turn right along the wide path to a branch off left with a

• **Extension to the Temple-tombs** (30min return time) (see p.252) Visitors equipped with long trousers and a sense of adventure can proceed north along the right bank of the watercourse, the path almost totally submerged in vegetation at points. After crossing another stream, the Fosso dell'Acqua Alta, make your way right (east) into this side valley. A little way up high on the left flank are several 3rd century BC temple-tombs ➤

251

➤ with impressive pediments and even fragments of the original Greek-style painted friezes. The most impressive is known as the Tomba Lattanzi. Reaching any of them involves a great deal of scrambling, and their present crumbling and neglected state makes a visit a little difficult. However George Dennis, visiting last century, was nothing short of ecstatic: 'At length we turned a corner in the glen, and lo! a grand range of monuments burst upon us. There they were – a line of sepulchres, high in the face of the cliff which forms the right-hand barrier of the glen, some two hundred feet above the stream – an amphitheatre of tombs! for the glen here swells into something not unlike that form. This singular glen is perhaps the most imposing spot in the whole compass of Etruscan cemeteries.'

bridge over the Fosso delle Pile. This narrower path ascends gradually to the evocative ruins. There are a couple of possible ways up, but stick to the 'main' route, and it will soon bear rightish over a rock base and pass through the tunnel-like entrance portal. The fortified medieval stronghold is a jungle nowadays and visitors are dwarfed by unusually high grasses interspersed with thistles and purple vetch. Several manmade structures emerge, namely stretches of ivy-covered defensive wall, fragments of the 12th-century castle, as well as the shell of the church of San Pietro in warm orange-coloured tufa blocks (155m, 30min to here).

A little further past the church to the left is a decent-sized columbarium in a small cave, partially hidden by a ledge. Then, vegetation permitting, there are views over the Fosso del Biedano to the neighbouring plateaus and even south as far as the Monti della Tolfa. On its way between Blera and Tuscania the Etruscan-Roman way, the Via Clodia, ran the entire length of Norchia.

Several paths branch off into the tangled undergrowth and it's worth wandering around to explore as much of the platform as you can reach. Two other gateways have been identified at the northernmost and eastern side of the town, and several man-made moats cross the site.

Return to the valley floor the same way, and either climb back to the parking area or embark on the detour to the Temple-tombs (see p.251).•

41: Lago di Vico

Walking time:	5h15min – 1h less with a car
Distance:	17km/10.6 miles
Map:	on p.256

A jewel of a lake sheltering out of the sight of main roads, in the crater of an extinct volcano. 'Who that has seen has not hailed with delight the exquisite little lake of Vico, which lies in the lap of the Ciminian Mount and, just above Ronciglione?' mused George Dennis in the mid 1800s. But for its southern edge, Lago di Vico or 'Ciminus lacus' is completely ringed by delightful woods of oak, chestnut and beech on the slopes of the Monti Cimini, and thick with all manner of flowering shrubs and wild flowers. Hazelnut plantations, lush pastures then an extensive reedy marsh on the water's edge account for the lower reaches. Luckily the zone is now a nature reserve of over 3000 hectares, incorporating a good percentage of the lake's 12sq km surface area. Its maximum depth is 50m and the waters are swarming with eels, pike and perch, trout and freshwater houting, known locally as *coregone*. Some fishing is permitted in the southern section, apparently without interfering with the multitudes of voracious resident and migratory water-fowl that rely on the supplies. The great crested grebe can often be seen at the lake, its nest hidden on a floating platform among the reeds, then there are mallard, pochard, herons and even kingfishers. Birds of prey are not unknown despite the thick forest, which in turn provides refuge for wild animals, reportedly foxes, beech martens, weasels, hares and wild cats.

According to legend, Hercules was responsible for creating the lake. When asked by insistent locals to give proof of his strength, he thrust his club into the ground. When none of the onlookers could budge it, the hero wrenched it out himself and water welled up to fill the entire valley. Science instead tells of an ancient volcano

Access: see Walk 39 for Viterbo itself, and map of Viterbo district, p.237. San Martino al Cimino can be reached by Viterbo city bus n.11 via the hospital. Once the bus has miraculously squeezed its way into the town centre, stay on board as it navigates the steep streets and get off at the highest stop.

By car, follow signs from Viterbo for San Martino then Lago di Vico. Limited parking is possible at the start of the walk, near Poggio della Croce, other-wise park down on the lakeside near the bird observation posts, for instance, and join the walk there.

Other useful towns for access to the lake and reserve are Caprarola and Ronciglione in the east and south respectively. Both are served by frequent COTRAL buses from Viterbo, though are only really suitable as bases for the walk if you have your own transport. Furthermore, a branch of the state-run Rome–Viterbo train line passes a short distance south of the two towns, but runs are a very rare occurrence.

Shepherd and flock on the shores of Lago di Vico

whose collapse left a basin soon occupied by a vast lake. Monte Venere, a later volcanic formation, was an island.

Such a beautiful and fertile area did not escape the attention of the enterprising Etruscans, already well established in the neighbourhood. They are believed to have lowered the level of the lake by way of drainage channels, to create extra land for crops which flourished in the rich volcanic soil. Writing at the turn of the millennium, Greek geographer Strabo cited the Lago di Vico among others, for its important contribution to the prosperity of the Etruscan realms. In addition to lake fish and marsh birds, material such as rushes and papyrus were transported to Rome via the River Tiber. A manmade subterranean outlet on the southern side has in fact been located; it joins the Torrente Treia to run east to the Tiber.

But rather than the lake, it was the Ciminian forest, the 'Cimina Silva', that made the area infamous in late Etruscan times. Long dreaded for its treacherous and impenetrable nature, it represented a formidable barrier to Rome in its advance northwards. Even after the Etruscans had been routed at Sutri in the 4th century BC, the consul Fabius Rulliano was ordered by the Senate not to enter the wood. Not only did he disobey, much to the horror of all Rome, but descended with his company to carry out raids in the great Etruscan plain. That was in 309BC, and in retaliation, allied Etruscan and Gallic forces gave battle at Lago Vadimone near Orte in 283BC. The victory for Rome spelt the beginning of the end for the Etruscans.

This walking itinerary commences at the fascinating township of San Martino al Cimino, 5km south out of the former papal city of Viterbo. Built on a surprisingly steep hillside it is elliptical in layout, and its outer walls are comprised of staggered terraced houses. A proud Cistercian cathedral is one of the highlights.

Any time of year is suitable for the walk, apart from midwinter, and the shady woods provide welcome cool in the summer. With the exception of an overgrown stretch near the start, the walk follows clear lanes and is both trouble-free and extremely rewarding for all ranges of walkers. Several climbs and subsequent descents are necessary, 300m at the most in one go.

The route covers a wide range of unspoilt landscapes and terrains along this northern edge of the lake. Numerous picnic spots can be found all along the way, several with drinking water, but nothing in the way of food available.

Close to the lake's eastern shore is the Renaissance township of Caprarola, worth a visit for both its position and layout along a narrow ridge as well. It is dominated by pentagonal baroque century Palazzo Farnese with frescoed rooms and monumental gardens.

THE WALK

Leave the township of **San Martino al Cimino** (567m) by way of the highest gateway, and continue straight ahead uphill, past a large signboard for the 'Riserva Naturale Lago di Vico'. The narrow road winds and climbs stiffly through a lovely chestnut wood to the shrine of **Poggio della Croce** (748m) on the northernmost lip of the ancient crater housing the Lago di Vico. Cross over the road which goes on to skirt the entire rim, and take the wide lane down into the beautiful wood (30min on foot from San Martino, parking possible here).

255

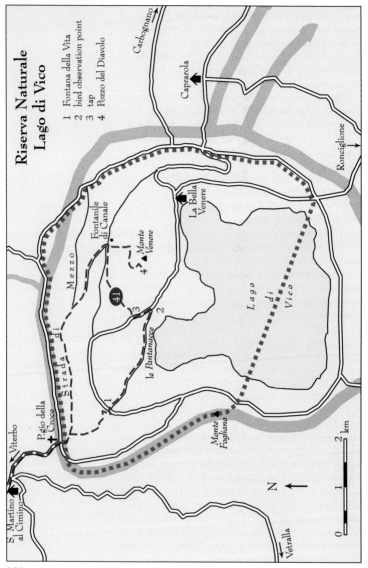

Riserva Naturale
Lago di Vico

1 Fontana della Vita
2 bird observation point
3 tap
4 Pozzo del Diavolo

Five minutes downhill a decent path breaks off right. Steep at times, it heads south in the shade of towering trees. After about 20min, as it reaches cultivated fields, you'll need the overgrown path that turns off sharp left to run between stone walls. Insidious brambles and nettles do their best to bar your way, but only for 5min or so, until a wide farm track is reached. Go right and follow it twisting and turning past fields and farms, hopefully ending up on the tarmac road that circles the lake. Across the road a handy landmark is the Fontana della Vita (523m), though despite the name the water is not drinkable (total 1h this far).

Follow the lane that runs alongside the fountain, heading towards the lakeside. The vegetation is scrubbier now with a range of wild grasses, good fodder for sheep. At this low level you get a good idea of the surrounding remnant crater with prominent Monte Fogliano southwest and rounded Monte Venere eastwards, though the highest peak in the Cimini range is actually some distance to the north, 1053m Monte Cimino. Be warned that you are walking on the verge of a low-lying area known under the sinister name of '**le Pantanacce**', the wretched bogs, thick with rushes and often submerged in winter.

25min from the fountain you join the road briefly, close to a bird observation point amidst reeds on the lakeside (510m, 1h25min total). Turn left along the tarmac and continue alongside the fields for 5min, then at a brick wall and tap, take the narrow lane right. It climbs between plantations of hazelnuts and quickly reaches the edges of another dense wood where you fork left (northeast). This is a wood and a half. A concentration of magnificent beech trees accompanies you around the base of Monte Venere. Many are huge stately specimens, their bark a nursery for bizarre fungi. A wider track completes the stretch eastwards to the parking and picnic area of **Fontanile di Canale** (578m, drinking water, 2h to here).

In case you hadn't noticed, the park information boards inform visitors that this beautiful beech wood is 'depressed'. The 'faggeta depressa' is a rare phenomenon. Eighteen thousand years back, temperatures plunged and

Lago di Vico and Monte Fogliano

plants and animals were forced to descend to lower altitudes. Later on when things warmed up again, most forms of life re-ascended to their previous positions, except for here. Although beech usually grows over 1000m above sea level, as in the Apennines, this particular wood stayed put, its lower limit 500m, the level of the lake.

The ensuing climb up Monte Venere requires 1h15min return time. Don't expect any views from the top of this 839m peak as the vegetation is too dense. It is however a pleasant and trouble-free climb through more beautiful beeches with the added attraction at the top of the Pozzo del Diavolo, the 'Devil's Pit'.

The 'summit route' is the popular 'Sentiero Natura – Pozzo del Diavolo' climbing southwards from the fountain. There is occasional red and white waymarking, but the path is clear and alternates steep stretches with more restful ones. Butcher's broom and its scarlet berries flourish in patches amongst the undergrowth, intertwined with spindly wild asparagus on the upper reaches. Anemones and cyclamen appear in spring and autumn. A flat saddle is reached after a good 40min. In the vicinity are heaps of stone blocks, some fenced in. Evidence perhaps of the ancient temple to Venus that once stood on Monte Venere and which gave the mount its name? The path descends a little through scrubby oaks to a wire fence around a huge hole, alias the **Pozzo del Diavolo** (810m). This large natural cavity was in actual fact one of the extinct volcano's mouths. Home to bats and owls these days, it used to be the refuge of medieval brigands according to local lore.

Despite the tempting rope, exploration is not recommended for non-experts. Return to the fountain the same way (grand total 3h15min).

From the fountain take the lane (second from the left) heading northwest. More hazelnut groves are passed then it begins a steady climb bordered by overgrown stone walls then chestnut and oak trees. Ignore a turn-off right, but continue uphill, curving left, to a bar blocking vehicle access where both crops and lane come to an end (20min from the fountain). A clear path climbs diagonally northwest through the wood for a further 20min to the track known as the **Strada di Mezzo** at 750m, an old medieval way. Left now, it proceeds with gentle ups and downs around the wooded crater rim once more, narrowing at times. The path cuts through thick banks of broom and ferns, and the spectacular views over the lake and surrounding countryside improve with every step you take.

4h45min total time should see you back at the road near **Poggio della Croce**. Those on foot return to San Martino in 30min via the road as per the start (5h15min in all).

Tourist Office Ronciglione
tel.0761/625460

Accommodation Viterbo:
see Walk 39

San Martino:
Hotel Doria
tel.0761/379924

Caprarola:
Il Farnese
tel.0761/646029

Below Caprarola on the northern shore:
La Bella Venere
tel.0761/612342 (3-star)

42: Blera: Ancient Roadways and Bridges

Access: See map of
Viterbo district, p.237.
Blera lies some 25km
southwest of Viterbo, and
plenty of daily COTRAL
buses connect the two
via Vetralla. Don't be
deceived by the train line
shown on maps as
passing close to Blera.
An old line was to be
restructured, but money
apparently ran out and
work was abandoned. By
car you'll need the SS 2.
Three kilometres south-
east from Vetralla is the
Blera turn-off at Cura.

Walking time:	1h45min + variants
Distance:	5.8km/3.6 miles
Map:	on p.263

Worlds away from classical Tuscan scenery, the area around Blera in northern Latium is wild and rambling as well as being crammed with Etruscan remains. There are vast tomb complexes as well as a lengthy stretch of the ancient Via Clodia, featuring bridges and intriguing sunken sections. Modern-day scenes of everyday village life in low key Blera have that timeless quality common in the south of Italy. At the crack of dawn stout women clad in black return home from the communal wash house, bundles of immaculate laundry set firmly on their heads. Their menfolk have long been out in the olive groves or tending sheep and goats. Tourism is very low key, and as an example, postcards are unheard of.

As concerns the countryside, on the other hand, little seems to have changed since the 1840s when indefatigable George Dennis explored the district, leaving an enthusiastic description: 'The scenery here was very romantic. The height of Bieda was lofty and precipitous, and as usual was a tongue of rock at the junction of two glens, which separated it from corresponding heights of equal abruptness. These glens, or ravines, were well clothed with wood, rich with the tints of autumn. Wood also climbed the steep cliffs, struggled for a footing among the wild masses of tufa split from their brow, and crowned in triumph the surface of the platform above.'

Evidence from the Iron Age has been found in the whereabouts, though permanent settlement is believed to date back to 9th century BC. It flourished right through Etruscan times under the influence of both Tarquinia and Cerveteri, before the Romans inevitably took over.

Around 5th century AD the townsfolk were subjected to a reign of terror inflicted by a bloodthirsty flame-spitting dragon. Luckily the resident hermit-saint Sensia was on hand to deal with the crisis. Having tamed the beast, he led it away and persuaded it to cast itself into a nearby river. Later catastrophes were caused by the Lombards who destroyed the township though it developed again in the Middle Ages as a powerful farming centre and a seat for bishops, and even boasted two popes.

As far as the name goes, Bleva is quoted as one of the earliest, though Blera is generally accepted for the Etruscan then Roman town. This was successively modified to Bleda hence Bieda in medieval times, in use right up until 1952, when the inhabitants decided to revert to Blera. As far as the etymology goes, the experts cannot quite seem to agree: it has been traced to the ancient Greek for 'fortified site', Phoenician for 'keeper', Hebrew for 'well' and Latin for 'flow'.

The walk described here is suitable for all walkers, only has a couple of brief ups and downs, and can easily be shortened if desired at several points. Long trousers are a good idea for the Ponte del Diavolo extension as well as the overgrown area around the Fosso Biedano. Here, in rare cases of very heavy rain, it might mean actually fording the stream. Picnic supplies and water are essential on the walk, and a torch can be handy though not essential, for exploring tomb interiors.

There are several helpful information boards at relevant points explaining the history and architecture, in both Italian and English. The bulk of Blera's sepulchral finds are in the archaeological museum at Viterbo, though a local display is in the making.

Visitors who make an early start on Easter Monday or in early May will find themselves part of the San Vivenzio pilgrimage. Cheered on by the town band, the processsion, bearing the holy relic of the saint's arm, leaves Blera around 7 o'clock in the morning and heads west along the Via Clodia and the Torrente Biedano to the saint's grotto and chapel, close to the archaeological site in Norchia – some 10km in all.

Variant to La Fontanella (45min):

From the necropolis, continue west to a gate and take the clear path left, downhill. As the rock flank opposite comes into view make your way down to the Fosso Biedano watercourse, which may entail splashing over after heavy rain. Then dense undergrowth awaits en route to the base of the cliff where you head up diagonally right. An ancient path quickly becomes obvious and twists and turns its sunken way to the top. Keep left along the ensuing track to join a motorable lane at S. Barbara, a vast plain honeycombed with tombs, all long explored, raided and buried beneath fields. Enclosed by low stone walls, continue east to a surfaced road and the church of **Madonna della Selva** (244m). Soon take the lane in descent through wood, to a medieval bridge and watch tower, directly below Blera, at **La Fontanella**.

THE WALK

From the bus stop or car park in Piazza Papa Giovanni XXIII at **Blera** (261m), take Via Roma northwest. It runs the entire length of the medieval-Renaissance township, the rock base of which is honeycombed with Etruscan-age channels and passageways. Once out of the far gateway, turn right past a signboard, proceeding west along a lane through market gardens. A dogleg path right leads into the archaeological area, inclusive of benches and a fine **lookout** at its extremity. The narrowing promontory squeezed between two watercourses hosted the ancient city, also referred to as Petrolo. Backtrack briefly for a path that drops left down the northern flank, emerging on the valley floor. Close-by, right, is the single-arch bridge **Ponte della Rocca** (45min, 200m), which dates back to 3rd–2nd century BC.

In front of you, framed by flowering shrubs, is the sprawling **Pian del Vescovo** necropolis used 7th–3rd century BC. All manner of sepulchres linked by a labyrinth of deep passageways, drainage channels and flights of rock steps have been burrowed out of the hillside. Some tomb interiors have a rock bench and 'pillows' for the occupants, in addition to relief decorations such as imitation columns and scrolls. Plenty of scrambling and exploring is to be done on the upper reaches of this delightful spot as well. High up in the far left corner is the sizeable 6th century BC Tomba della Sfinge, so called as parts of an interesting sphinx statue were found there.

Head back towards Blera, along a longish sunken section of the ancient Via Clodia. As a consular road under the Romans it conformed to the constant width of 14 Roman feet, that is 4.1m. It cuts along the midriff of the hillside above the valley and is lined with the odd fragment of ancient tufa wall block as well as elongated rock recesses for burials. The grooves to divert rainwater are still clearly visible, though many cavities have since been recycled as sheds for livestock or farming tools. All very rural and peaceful. At an information board on the lower edge of the village, turn right for the ramp beneath wonderful lichen-coloured rock flanks to an old bridge leading across to **La Fontanella** (30min).

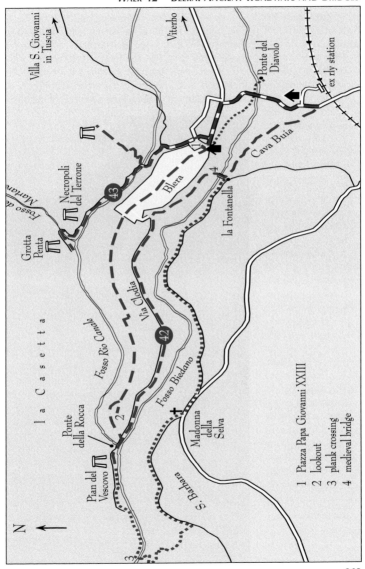

Villa S. Giovanni in Tuscia

Viterbo

Ponte del Diavolo

ex rly station

Cava Buia

Necropoli del Terrone

43

Blera

4

la Fontanella

Fosso della Martana

Grotta Penta

la Casetta

Fosso Rio Canale

Via Clodia

42

Fosso Biedano

Ponte della Rocca

Madonna della Selva

Pian del Vescovo

S. Barbara

N

1 Piazza Papa Giovanni XXIII
2 lookout
3 plank crossing
4 medieval bridge

• **Extension to the Ponte del Diavolo (45min return)**

This branch of the Via Clodia leads to the triple-arched Roman bridge which has miraculously survived to this day. Vegetation tends to take over in the lower reaches, so be prepared with long trousers and don't be put off.

From the southern edge of Blera's main square overlooking the river, take the signed route below the old communal laundry troughs. It is lined with stables and kennels nowadays in place of ancient monuments and burial chambers. Dropping gradually it passes under the road bridge, and quickly narrows. Ferns, moss and huge broad-leaved plants flourish down in these damp but wonderfully peaceful depths, and do their utmost to conceal the **Ponte del Diavolo** (the devil's bridge), constructed in blocks of tufa.

Return the same way.

Ahead on the left, follow signposting for the 'Cava Buia', virtually parallel to the stream. The lane is quickly immersed in thick wood and becomes a fascinating tunnel sunk deep into the mossy rock, draped with creepers and ferns. The move from the sunny countryside to this sort of dank underworld is quite extraordinary. A large circular tomb can be seen overhead on the right

The Ponte del Diavolo

soon, while unusually narrow but high passageways lead off left. Rockfalls ('caduta massi') mean occasional detours to an open path with inspiring views to Blera. The way climbs steadily to the top of the plateau, where you keep left to emerge on the road. Turn downhill past Via Marconi (and the hotel) and continue north via a cutting to the airy single-span road bridge constructed in 1937, high over the three-arched Roman bridge Ponte del Diavolo, all but submerged in a thick sea of greenery.

(The lane off right just before the bridge leads to a curiously shaped boulder, fountain and cave, the site of San Sensia's feats). A final uphill stretch then a left turn along Via Umberto I will bring you back into **Blera** and its square once more (30min). •

Tourist Office Viterbo
tel.0761/304795

Accommodation
Da Beccone
tel.0761/479210 (3-star, with swimming pool).
10min on foot over the road bridge.

Rooms c/o Bar-Trattoria La Torretta
tel.0761/479189

43: Blera: More Necropolises

Access: see Walk 42

Walking time:	1h + extra time for exploration
Distance:	2.7km/1.7 miles
Map:	on p.263

Another itinerary through more intriguing Etruscan cemeteries of Blera. These complexes are located to the north
of the township, and their size and complexity testify to
the varied and stratified nature of the population of
Etruscan Blera. There are several modest monumental-
type structures on various levels with sculpted façades
and frescoed chambers for the aristocratic burials, close
to simple rock recesses for the lower classes. Generally
speaking, the area is in a state of abandon and, while the
access tracks are clear and problem-free, visits often
mean wandering through the under-growth in search of
hidden monuments – a thoroughly romantic endeavour.

As can be said for the area as a whole, the surroundings themselves make the trip worthwhile. Rolling fertile
countryside, wheat fields bright with poppies and other
wild flowers in summer, then there are deep gullies
eroded by streams that separate lofty platforms of volcani-
cally formed tufa. The site in fact is but 10km from the
once highly active volcanic group of the Ciminian
Mounts to the northeast.

The walk is straightforward and here too a torch is
useful for examining the tomb interiors.

See Walk 42 for the history and other information
regarding Blera.

THE WALK

From the central square in **Blera**, namely Piazza Papa
Giovanni XXIII, round the corner south and turn left along
the alley Vicolo del Suffragio, opposite the old washing
area. It is signposted for 'Necropoli etrusche'. Heading
north, the way leads under a road then becomes a steep
concrete ramp shaded by fig and elder trees. Ignore the

lane off right unless you feel like a pleasant 40min walk north to the village of Villa San Giovanni in Tuscia, with Etruscan remains dotted along the way.

Go all the way down to the bottom of the valley and over the watercourse. Immediately after the concrete causeway, turn sharp right for a climb northeast. The steep flanks host numerous tall crumbling tombs hewn out of the rock face, some with grooved decorations. A flight of steps sometimes leads to an upper platform. Up on the top of the plateau itself you'll find quite an assortment of abandoned tombs, many with numerous windows then interior chambers with a sloping ceiling as though in a house, instead of the usual level or rounded one. The necropolis competes with thick broom and beautiful wild flowers, not to mention the artichokes from the market gardens. There is plenty of exploring to be done, though remember that the land is mostly private property.

Return the same way to the valley bottom and junction, and turn right parallel to the watercourse Fosso Rio Canale. The vehicle-width track bears northwest at the base of cliffs pockmarked with a surprising variety of sepulchres excavated into their face. This is known

Rock tombs in the Grotta Penta complex at Blera

Accommodation
see Walk 42

collectively as the **Necropoli del Terrone**, the name a corruption of *torrione* or tower, after the modest cylindrical Roman mausoleum it encompasses.

After a picnic area, the track curves right and crosses a stream known as the Fosso del Martarello to the **Grotta Penta** complex in shady light wood. The 'painted' chamber in the gaping cavern on ground level is usually locked, though one of the local guides will hopefully be around with the key. The 4th century BC decoration has suffered centuries of neglect, and the cave (alias stable) is blackened with the soot from fires. A central column and red-black painted bands are however still discernible on the walls.

Plenty of other tombs and cavities wait to be explored further along the lane, in addition to those on the edge of the Casetta plateau above. The necropolis actually extends over a kilometre and eventually joins up with the Pian del Vescovo complex to the west.

Wildflowers smother Etruscan tombs outside Blera

When you've had your fill of cemeteries, return to Blera along the main track.

44: Barbarano Romano: San Giuliano and the Marturanum Park

Walking time:	2h30min + 1h if on foot to & from Barbarano Romano
Distance:	4.5km/2.8 miles
Map:	on p.271

This stunning area well off the beaten tourist track encompasses an extraordinary series of Etruscan necropolises set along the wooded flanks of tufaceous plateaux and plunging ravines. In addition to the natural and Etruscan marvels, surprises come in the form of a Roman bath house hewn into a cliff side and a picturesque though ruined medieval church. Walkers will find themselves strolling through sunny fields marvelling at the wild orchids one minute, before dropping unexpectedly to follow a moss-ridden stream through the likes of the underworld. A true feast for the senses. On the fauna side there are joyous song birds, silent birds of prey, elusive porcupines, several harmless snakes and even the odd viper, though they will slither home if given the time.

Thus are the realms of the 'Parco Regionale Marturanum' created in 1984 to safeguard 1450 hectares of beautiful countryside in northern Latium. The core of the Park is the San Giuliano plateau, inhabited from around 8th century BC by the Etruscans, thanks to its natural defences. It is believed to have gone under the name of Cortuosa and to have belonged to the vast territory controlled by the powerful confederation city of Tarquinia. Another theory attributes it with the name of Marturanum, after a vase fragment bearing an inscription reading 'donated by Laro of Marturanum'. One date is certain – 388BC when the city was sacked by the Romans during their expansion northwards. Settlement possibly continued through to the Middle Ages when the population moved

Access: See map of Viterbo district, p. 237. From the SS 2 (Cassia), turn off via the SS 493 approx. 21km south of Viterbo. Seven kilometres along is the fork for Barbarano Romano. Prior to the township take the road right (north) opposite the cemetery. A couple of kilometres along is a signposted entrance to the Park (handy for those on foot from Barbarano Romano – see below). However as roadside parking is limited here, continue on to the northern entrance for the sizeable car park and even bbq facilities.

Daily COTRAL buses running between Viterbo and Rome will deposit walkers at the Barbarano Romano cemetery junction mentioned above for the quiet ensuing 30min surfaced stretch. From rickety wooden gate at the signed park entrance, take the shady path left in to nearby Tomba Cima, where you slot into the walk.

to the present site of Barbarano Romano, itself a quiet medieval-style village.

As well as being fascinating and wonderfully varied, the route is straightforward with the sole exception of the later section that circles west below San Giuliano. Overgrown stretches are inevitable and long trousers recommended. However this can easily be avoided – see the map. Edibles and drinks must be carried as nothing in the way of refreshment stops is encountered. Furthermore, a torch is handy for exploring the interiors of the numerous tombs.

The township of Barbarano Romano has a museum which houses precious sepulchral items such as statues and sarcophaguses in dark volcanic 'nenfro' stone, in addition to curious obelisk grave markers from the San Giuliano necropolis. An Etruscan chariot unearthed of late is currently undergoing restoration at the Villa Giulia museum in Rome, but will hopefully be on display here in the future.

Entrance to the Marturanum Park outside Barbarano Romano

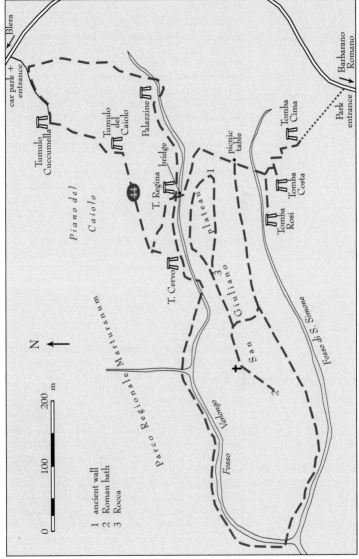

N ←

0   100   200 m

1 ancient wall
2 Roman bath
3 Rocca

Blera
car park + entrance
Tumulo Cuccumella
Tumulo del Caiolo
Palazzine
T. Regina bridge
44
T. Cervo
Piano del Caiolo
Parco Regionale Marturanum
Fosso Verlongo
San Giuliano
plateau
picnic table
Tomba Cima
Tomba Costa
Tomba Rosi
Fosso di S. Simone
Barbarano Romano
Park entrance

THE WALK

The **car park** doubles as the entrance to the magical realms of the Parco Suburbano Marturanum (355m). Take the clear path southwest cutting across the Piano del Caiolo alias flowered meadow towards the large stone blocks around an enclosure, all that remains of the reconstructed chambers of Tumulo Cuccumella. Then veer left (south) for the metallic roofing protecting the important **Tumulo del Caiolo** from early 6th century BC. Entrances to its intriguing inner realms can be found below left, and it is complete with columns and sepulchral beds.

Afterwards head westwards along the edge of the plateau traversing a fragrant sea of camomile and oregano. Keep your eyes peeled for a faded yellow/black signpost for the 'Percorso etrusco' that drops sharp left. Detour via the first fork right to reach the uppermost platform of the multi-storeyed 4th–3rd century BC Tomba del Cervo (Tomb of the Deer) where funereal sacrifices and rites were held. If the precarious wooden ladder has been replaced you'll be able to descend a little further to admire the elegant relief sculpture of a deer struggling with a wolf or dog, the emblem of the Park. In any case return to the fork and continue down diagonally right to the monumental bulk of the 5th century BC **Tomba della Regina** (Tomb of the Queen, 20min), its spacious façade decorated with unusually large false twin doorways.

A right turn now leads along the valley floor and past the base of the Tomba del Cervo. Though narrow, the path is clear and follows the right bank (and the left for a short stretch) of the trickling stream Fosso Verlongo, mostly west. The atmosphere of shade and silence is magical. Cliffs tower on either side, and the jungle-like vegetation with trees draped with trailing ivy lets in very little sunlight. Hazel, flowering ash and alder scrub contribute to the dense foliage cover, while the undergrowth is mostly made up of ferns with the occasional bulrush on the water's edge. About 10min from the Tomba del Cervo a side stream is crossed, then ups and downs follow past several crumbling 4th century BC tombs. Rounding the

corner in the shade of the imposing tufa cliffs beneath the San Giuliano plateau, close to the confluence of another stream, the path crosses to the left bank and swings east, climbing and weaving between mysterious moss-covered cavities. You enter a new valley, Fosso di San Simone. A gradual diagonal ascent away from the watercourse and a little bush-bashing, and you'll hopefully emerge on the access track to the acropolis zone and erstwhile medieval stronghold on the **San Giuliano** plateau. Follow this up (left) to the meadow, bearing left (west) for the ruined 15th-century **church** (347m, 40min), which incorporated recycled Roman columns in its construction. Patches of frescoes are still visible inside below graceful arches.

A further delight awaits, as a short distance away on the southern edge of the plateau are the remains of Roman bath house ('*bagno romano*'). Steps lead below the field level and you enter a wonderful room that looks out over the Fosso di San Simone and the wood beyond. Back at the **church,** thread your way east through the oak trees and broom for the meagre vestiges

A fascinating assortment of rock tombs in glens hung with drooping ivy in the Marturanum Park, Barbarano Romano

of the medieval Rocca, without neglecting the northern fringe for wonderful views onto the necropolises and Piano di Caiolo.

Then take the access track back to the Fosso di S. Simone, keeping left (east) to a path junction and **picnic table** at the foot of ancient walling.

Turn right (south) now for a stream crossing and access to further fascinating necropolises. First off right is the **Tomba Rosi**. Grouped with other sepulchres, it occupies a cool clearing and is the roomy third construction, featuring internal chambers fitted with windows.

Back on the main path it's not far to the detour for a fascinating assortment of rock wall cavity tombs in glens hung with drooping ivy. First on the left is the 6th century BC **Tomba Costa**, which totals 8m in height and 13m in length. A deep dromos leads to intercommunicating burial chambers.

Lastly, a short climb away is **Tomba Cima**, an impressive large round tumulus that incorporates a dromos access and internal sculpted false beams. It was used over an extended period of time as from 7th century BC, and its shape, unusual for this area, shows the strong influences of the city of Cerveteri to the

The massive Tomba della Regina in the Marturanum Park, Barbarano Romano

south. It is not a construction in the true sense, but rather a sort of sculpture as it was entirely hewn out of the tufa. The unusual forecourt was used for holding sacrifices and funeral rituals, and entrance is via a double row of marker stones.

Return across the stream to the **picnic table**. Not far ahead, bear left for the bridge across the delightful moss-ridden watercourse surrounded by alder trees, elder and hornbeam. Take a right past Tomba Regina once more, then right again via the porticoed tombs of the Palazzine complex. A gradual climb north takes a small sunken 'via cava' to emerge at the **car park** once more.

Below the San Giuliano plateau

Accommodation Barbarano Romano:
Hotel Marturanum
tel.0761/414368

45: Barbarano Romano: the Via Clodia

Walking time:	1h + 30min to and from Barbarano Romano on foot
Distance:	3.3km/2.1 miles
Map:	on p.277

Access: see Walk 44 for Barbarano Romano.

The daily COTRAL bus service between Blera and Barbarano Romano transits via the ex railway station, near the start of the walk.

By car or on foot from the southern edge of Barbarano Romano, take the road west via an airy bridge across the Fosso Biedano. Curving north it proceeds as Viale S. Barbara, passes the ex railway station (a good place to park) and reaches a level crossing (15min on foot). The railway line has long been abandoned despite futile attempts at recon-struction.

A short way south of the township of Barbarano Romano, a paved stretch of the ancient Etruscan way, the Via Clodia, runs through a beautiful swathe of wood of the Bosco della Bandita. It then proceeds across open rolling hills with marvellous views. While modest in comparison to the lengthy tracts at nearby Blera, it is definitely worth a look if only for the marvellous natural surroundings. The area is protected, incorporated into the central realm of the Parco Regionale Marturanum. The thick wood provides refuge for woodpeckers, cuckoos, porcupines and wild boar, whereas the open limestone hillsides to the south are employed as pasture for horses and cattle, though they were also the nesting and hunting grounds of the Egyptian vulture until very recently. A drop in prey as well as poisoning through fertilisers absorbed through its food have contributed to its disappearance, though of late there has been talk of reintroducing it in Latium.

As regards the Via Clodia, while its Etruscan origin is hazy, we are told it underwent adaptation and restoration at the hands of the Romans, who even equipped it with a full-scale 'service station'.

The short route described here, marked by short poles topped with yellow, is a delightful combination of nature and history, suitable for all walkers. Very little climbing and descent is involved. Long trousers are advisable as there are several overgrown thorny sections.

THE WALK

From the **level crossing** (335m), take the lane which turns up left, then leave it almost immediately for the fainter track parallel to the rail-less line. Past a picnic area you'll need to drop briefly onto the 'railway', then the track reappears with its yellow markers. It begins to climb gradually right (south) into the thicker wood of hawthorn, Turkey and hairy oak. Scratchings left by wild boar and quills discarded by porcupine are common. A good 20min from the start will see you at a couple of Park signboards with information about the **Via Clodia**, a decent paved stretch of which has been unearthed nearby. The remains of a modest tower, originally clad in marble and believed to have been a funeral monument, are in the vicinity.

Backtrack a little to the yellow markers and start climbing gradually northwest along the old Roman way. Though it often narrows to a path, the way is clear and the wood a delight with huge wild orchids in the undergrowth. Another quarter of an hour or so and a gate opens onto a startling change of landscape.

Open rocky hills of limestone are dotted with vestiges of an ancient past amidst straggly wild fruit trees,

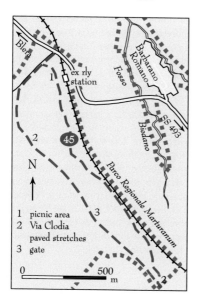

1 picnic area
2 Via Clodia
  paved stretches
3 gate

Roman mausoleum on the way to San Giovenale

perfumed broom, the spiny shrub known as Christ's thorn, and even the hardy Judas tree which produces beautiful purplish-pink flowers in the spring. Some effort is needed to imagine the heaps of stones as the busy 'Via Clodia service station' alias Roman 'mansiones' that once existed here. It incorporated lodgings, snack bars, stables complete with blacksmith and vet, market places, cisterns and even a temple for passing sacrifices. While examining the ruins, you may find yourself competing with the free-running horses and long-horned Maremma cattle that graze on these slopes.

Wander over the hill in a northwesterly direction to reach several evocative fenced-in stretches of excavated road discovered beneath layers of clay. A little further across the hillside the Via Clodia is left behind, and you turn right onto a wide track. This leads over the hill past some sheep pens, before dropping to the starting point near the **level crossing** (1h total).

46: San Giovenale and Civitella Cesi

Walking time:	1h50min + extra for detour and visits
Distance:	6.1km/3.8 miles
Map:	p.281

At a first glance San Giovenale is a mere overgrown heap of stones lying isolated in the rural landscape of Latium, south of Viterbo. However a closer look and a moderate degree of imagination will help visitors picture the fortified Etruscan town of Contenebra it once was. The site is located on a tufaceous tongue of land between two watercourses, and evidence of Iron and Bronze Age huts showed it was inhabited about 3500 years ago. The ensuing Etruscan settlement grew under Tarquinia from 7th century until 338BC when it inevitably fell to Rome.

A group of Swedish archaeologists were responsible for the 1950s–1960s excavation campaign which brought to light significant discoveries in terms of town layout and architecture of dwellings. There are also a number of necropolises dotted around, however the all but impenetrable vegetation makes the majority difficult to visit.

Archaeology apart, the countryside alone merits a visit. Late spring walkers can expect a veritable riot of wild flowers. The fields of ripening wheat and oats are a guarantee of poppies and corn marigolds like yellow daisies, while the waysides host pyramidal orchids, dog roses and vermilion gladiolus which vie with each other for brilliance. Hazelnut trees seem to be at their greenest here. Animal life includes porcupines, while graceful birds of prey are not unusual overhead scanning the open fields. Human visitors on the other hand are rare.

No difficulty is involved in the walk, though after especially heavy rain, be prepared to remove your foot gear to cross Torrente Vesca.

Access: See Viterbo district map on p.237. Two kilometres south from Blera on the Monteromano road is the junction for Civitella Cesi, where you should keep a look out for the curious circular Roman stone mausoleum in the wheat fields up right. Some 4km along is the San Giovenale turn-off, then a final 1km to a parking area. On the other hand the end point of the walk, Civitella Cesi, lies 2km further southeast.

For those without wheels, there are several daily COTRAL buses from Viterbo to Civitella Cesi (apart from Sundays and public holidays). They run late morning till mid afternoon and usually pass through Blera, which makes a good base. Ask to be let off at the San Giovenale junction. Hitchhiking is feasible though traffic is light.

THE WALK

From the bus stop at the **San Giovenale** turn-off it's about 1km southwest along the narrow access road. It runs between wheat fields bordered by hedgerows sheltering pretty purple orchids and dog roses, not to mention melodious song birds. After the rough **parking area** (150m, 15min), keep left at the signs and down the lane to high cyclone fencing and an information board. Keep right for the brief ascent.•

From the main lane uphill, you'll need the path on the left which leads into the fenced area and the first interesting excavations. Broad roofing protects foundations of houses, fire places and wells. Beyond the roofing are other remains, notably a well-preserved stretch of grooved road worn into the rock base.

Return back west now to enter the area housing what's left of the 13th-century castle. Its walls were built directly on top of the Etruscan fortifications as was the entrance portal. A little further across the plateau are more covered excavations of house foundations and the like. Mind your step as the invasive vegetation conceals holes and ditches. The site is neglected to say the least.

Return to the information board at the base of the acropolis (40min total so far), and take the shady lane on your right now. The road, sunk into the tufa, soon becomes the Tagliata delle Poggette, part of the original Etruscan access in the late period. There are several tombs to be visited off left. Low entrances give onto sculpted interiors and rock benches where the deceased were laid to rest. Unfortunately the complex has been systematically emptied of its contents by tomb robbers. The old road continues in gradual descent southwest as a long muddy lane beneath the castle and acropolis to cross the trickle that goes under the name of Torrente Vesca.

You climb past side paths leading to yet more modest tombs before the lane narrows to a path between the fields and reaches a junction (about 1h total). Turn left here onto the wide track SSE and continue past several houses. The view back to San Giovenale from here is lovely. Some 10mins on is **Fontanile Cammerata** (164m), followed by a sign for a further necropolis, Castellina in

• Detour to the Porzarago tombs
(20min extra)
Exclusively for the adventurous: a very faint path soon heads off right through jungle-like undergrowth. You make your way down northish to cross the small watercourse Fosso del Pitale, then scramble up the other side to an interesting group of tombs known as Porzarago. The grandest, the 'della Regina' – 'the Queen's', has a narrow dromos and double chambers. 20min or so extra time should suffice for this detour, though it will really depend on your abilities as an explorer.

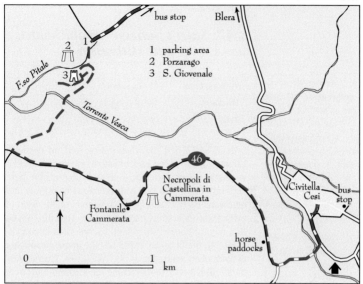

1 parking area
2 Porzarago
3 S. Giovenale

Cammerata, and a locked gate. But you'd have to be very lucky to find anything vaguely resembling a tomb.

The track goes up and down, and Civitella Cesi is now ahead on its tufa outcrop. Soon after horse paddocks, the track drops to join a surfaced road (almost 1h from San Giovenale). Follow it down left across the bridge, then left again beneath the village (whereas the longer right branch also climbs to the village via accommodation). A steep concrete ramp soon forks off and takes you quickly up to **Civitella Cesi** itself (190m, grand total of 1h50min).

The bus stop is a mere matter of minutes away around to the right, but it's worth finding time for a wander around this rambling though somewhat derelict medieval village. Among other things it features a modest castle, bar and food shop.

In the absence of a bus, for the return to the starting point on foot, allow a further half an hour or so for the 3km of quiet asphalt.

Accommodation
Civitella Cesi:
La Dimora degli Etruschi
(hostel) tel.0761/415031

281

47: Sutri's Sunken Amphitheatre and Mithraism

Walking time:	45min + ample time for visits
Distance:	1km/0.6 miles
Map:	on p.283

Access: See Viterbo district map p.237. Sutri lies on the SS 2 (Cassia), so is easily reached from either Viterbo in the northwest or Rome in the southeast. A useful minor road also connects Sutri with Ronciglione, 6km to its north, hence Lago di Vico.

Numerous COTRAL buses on the Rome–Viterbo line run via Sutri along the SS 2. The sites covered by the walk lie on the opposite side of the road to the township. Follow the signs for the 'Anfiteatro' to ample parking well off the main road.

Legend has it that the founding of Sutri, in northern Latium, can be traced back to Saturn, the Roman god for vegetation and agriculture. The fertile terrain here certainly bears that out with delicious hazelnuts and renowned beans, thanks to the proximity of the chain of extinct volcanoes, the Ciminian Mounts. They also served as a natural barrier which held back Roman encroachment into the Etruscan heartland. The ancient township of Sutri, often referred to as the 'Gateway to Etruria', was in all likelihood the outcome of a combination of Etruscan and contemporary neighbouring Faliscan cultures. Following the fall of Veio, it was quickly colonised by Rome around 383BC, and Sutrium, as it was then called, gained in importance as did the Via Cassia.

The curious sunken amphitheatre included in the itinerary belongs to the early Roman period, around 1st century BC. Around the same time a new cult known as Mithraism caught on. This ancient religion from Persia spread widely throughout the Roman Empire in its early years and was long a rival of Christianity, until out-lawed by Emperor Constantine. Mythical Mithra, the god of light alias the sun, slew a primordial bull (which represented creation), symbolising the conquest of evil and death. The world was fertilised with its blood, and initiates likewise during the re-enactment ritual. The main feast day to celebrate his birth was, significantly, December 25th. In Sutrium a suitable sanctuary was fashioned out of an underground Etruscan tomb, though a successive wave of worshippers turned it into a church. The Madonna del Parto, dating back to 13th–14th century, was dedicated to childless women who prayed

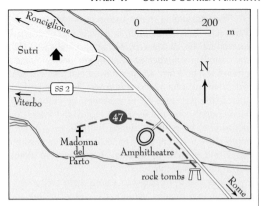

there for divine intervention. The birth of a baby was consequently the occasion for a column to be decorated.

Through the ages Sutri continued to be a religious centre and has its own bishop's palace in the town proper, the tufaceous platform on the opposite side of the Via Cassia to the walk described here. A further claim to fame is as the birthplace of Pontius Pilate.

It is a modest sleepy place nowadays, but offers visitors a series of unique sights that are intriguing to say the least. Namely the underground church/pagan sanctuary/Etruscan tomb, and the unusual amphitheatre followed by a series of rock cavity tombs. A hotchpotch of sights in actual fact, but ones that make for a captivating stroll that covers an astonishing sequence of events and beliefs in a very short distance.

THE WALK

From the parking area, ignore the amphitheatre of **Sutri** (291m) for the time being and turn right past the custodian's hut. A little way uphill, sheltered by a wood of holm oak, is a glen surrounded by towering cliffs of tufa riddled with manmade cavities on all levels. Many were tombs during Etruscan and Roman times, and now serve as storage spaces. One sizeable sealed cavity is crammed with jumbled bones removed from the various burial sites here – a hole provides a 'window' for the curious.

The unassuming church known as the **Madonna del Parto** (Our Lady of the Birth) is actually part of the rock face on the left. Access is by way of a locked gate which the custodian will open on request. You enter an underground vestibule first, where plenty of columns still bear extensive colourful medieval frescoes. The main body of the church has three naves separated by colonnades. Floor outlets are visible where blood and water are believed to have flowed during Mithraic rites. What's more, there is said to be a connecting series of passageways and catacombs leading all the way to Rome according to local lore.

Once you've managed to absorb these centuries of rites and myriad faiths, return to the custodian's hut and proceed right past willow trees for the **amphitheatre**. It is modest compared to an average Roman exemplary – a mere 55 x 45m along its axes – but is well worth a visit, first and foremost for its unique 'construction' technique – entirely hewn out of a brownish tufa rock promontory. From inside the actual arena it is easy to imagine the shape of the original rock mass before work began. Numerous long flights of rock stairs climb to the circular rows of benches where some 4000 spectators were once seated. There are a number of tall niches for statues such as those of the gods in whose honour the games were being held.

Back outside the amphitheatre, turn right and follow the lane parallel to the main road for 5min or so, over a minor watercourse. Light wood forms a canopy over a varied series of rock cavity **tombs** on several levels. The oldest are believed to date back to 5th century BC, though many were undoubtedly re-adapted for use during Roman times when more were added. A total of 60 niches can be inspected with a variety of forms and ornamentation such as overhangs and columns. Cremation was evidently the rule.

Return to your car or Sutri the same way.

Accommodation
Hotel Sutrium
tel.0761/600468

48: Falerii Novi and the Via Amerina

Walking time:	2h15min return + plenty of extra time for exploring
Distance:	9.4km/5.8 miles
Map:	below

Like the ancient Etruscan city at Orvieto, Falerii alias modern day Civita Castellana was sacked by Rome and its inhabitants sent to found a new colony. Situated in what is now central Latium on a high tufaceous plateau perched amid deep ravines, the original Falerii long served

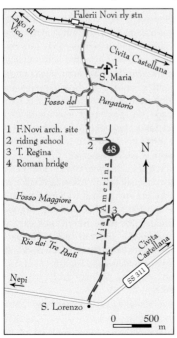

Laso di Vico

Falerii Novi rly stn

Civita Castellana

S. Maria

Fosso del   Purgatorio

1 F.Novi arch. site
2 riding school
3 T. Regina
4 Roman bridge

2 **48**

N

Via Amerina

Fosso Maggiore

3

Rio dei Tre Ponti

4

Civita Castellana

Nepi

SS 311

S. Lorenzo

0   500
          m

Access: See the Viterbo district map on p.237. The start of the walk, Falerii Novi, lies 6km west of Civita Castellana. The occasional COTRAL bus stops there but the best bet is the single track railway known as the 'Ferrovia Roma Nord' that slowly winds through the hills from Viterbo via Soriano and Civita Castellana, eventually terminating in Rome. As the station at Falerii Novi is unmanned, passengers wishing to alight must ring the bell on board to give the driver due warning to stop. In order to get on, you'll need to flag down the train. Tickets can be purchased on board. See Walk 39 for further notes.

Civita Castellana, on the other hand is only 8km south from the Tiber valley, so is handy for the A1 autostrada (nearest exit Magliano Sabino). Numerous roads also reach it from the west. The town is on the above train line and is also served by buses. ➤

➤ Those with a car can cut half an hour off the walk time by driving to the Falerii Novi ruins then to the start of the Via Amerina where the route enters a field.

Alternatively, drivers who choose to join the walk at its southernmost extremity will need the SS 311 that connects Civita Castellana with Nepi and beyond. Some 5km from Civita Castellana are the scattered houses of San Lorenzo. Just after some newish semi-detached houses on the left at a curve, take the unsurfaced road off to the right, marked by a faint sign for the 'Via Amerina'. Keep left at the ensuing fork, continue down to the bridge then park near the second set of notice boards.

as the political, cultural and economic capital of the Faliscan tribe, who even boasted a language of their own, closely related to Latin which later displaced it. Numerous remains of Faliscan times have been unearthed, including tombs, rock channels for drainage purposes and a number of sanctuaries. Their broad territory, including the sites of Corchiano, Narce and Nepi, was bounded by the Tiber, the lakes of Vico and Bracciano, and the Sabatini Mounts in the south. Contemporaries of the neighbouring Etruscans, as from 5th century BC they were close allies in the many battles against Rome. Following the destruction of the town in 241BC after a six-day siege, the survivors were transferred to Falerii Novi a short distance to the west. As the new site totally lacked natural defences, a good 2km worth of high walls were built in large tufa blocks, reinforced with over 50 watch towers. Moreover the Romans carried out extensive road repair and construction work. The Via Amerina, a branch of Via Cassia, was restructured to cut longitudinally through the newly acquired Faliscan territory to ensure control. The route is believed to have extended north as far as Perugia, and the name actually comes from Amelia in Umbria.

The settlement of Falerii Novi developed at length, but was destroyed by the Normans in the 11th century, leaving only the graceful Romanesque church and convent of Santa Maria di Falerii. Excavations, however, have unearthed the original forum, amphitheatre and a paved stretch of the Via Amerina.

The route described here takes in this site in addition to a longer stretch of the Via Amerina which traverses the countryside. The way is lined with all manner of evocative if modest tombs and columbaria, not to mention Roman bridges. The walk itself is both easy and fascinating, and height gain and loss negligible. Helpful information boards along the way provide detailed historical notes in both Italian and English.

THE WALK

Leave the rundown station of **Falerii Novi** (201m) and go left for about 100m, then right along Via Faleri Novi. A couple of minutes away a lane leads off left for the old town, via the Porta di Giove, one of the extant portals. The recently restored church of **Santa Maria** is the first monument to greet visitors, but it is usually locked. Skirt it around left as its massive bulk hides the spacious 3rd century BC forum and other excavations, as well as the paved start of the Via Amerina. North across the wheat fields stands a decent length of the original wall and other long stretches enclose the site. Back out on the road (20min this far) turn left downhill to cross the valley and the watercourse known as the Fosso del Purgatorio. There's a brief climb up through fields and past an intersection, where you keep straight ahead (south) as the road becomes a sort of dual carriageway. This traverses a residential area and ends up on the edge of a field, near a riding school. Ahead looming WSW on the horizon is the bulk of Monte Soratte.

Turn down left (east) between houses and the field, and where the road drops left at a curve, keep straight ahead on a dirt track (35min in all). As the track itself veers left into wood, you must turn right (south) and follow the edge of the field alongside a line of trees. Though not yet recognisable, you are already walking on the **Via Amerina**, and in fact a monument is soon passed in the undergrowth left. A promising wider track soon commences. Both sides are lined with tombs and several well preserved columbaria, vaults with niches of varying sizes for holding funeral urns. At a cleared area of original paving with interlocking stone slabs, take the path down left, in earshot of a stream. More unusual tombs (3rd–2nd century BC) with decorated cornices are passed. The deceased were placed in excavated elongated bunk-like cavities, or wall niches. The most interesting is the large articulated structure known as the Tomba della Regina, 'the Queen's Tomb', where an arched portico gives onto the sepulchral area.

You drop to a wooden footbridge over the Fosso Maggiore below the massive ramparts of a ruined Roman bridge. The path climbs out of the depression to a vast 'wall' cut from a cliff, and an intriguing moss-ridden necropolis where traces of frescoes can be detected. A lot of time can be spent exploring here.

Old paving stones on the Via Amerina at Santa Maria

The lane proceeds south past Roman tombs then besides a field to another watercourse, Rio dei Tre Ponti (197m), crossed by an authentic and intact Roman bridge. To see it properly, however, take the path left after the bridge and drop to stream level.

Back on the lane, resume the southerly direction past a building to an information board dealing with the Via Amerina. Keep right here and you soon reach the tarmac at **San Lorenzo** (219m, 1h15min total). Backtrack the same way to Falerii Novi, meaning a total of 2h15min.

Alternatively, the SS 311 means 6km west to Nepi, or 5km east to **Civita Castellana**, which spells an interesting archaeological museum doubling as the immense octogonal fortress by Renaissance architect Sangallo dominating the town. On the pratical side there are also shops, not to mention transport towards Viterbo or Rome. Hitchhiking this far is not a particularly good bet as the road is narrow and hedged in.

Lago di Vico: see Walk 41

49: Tarquinia's Painted Tombs and Old City

Walking time:	2h + a good hour or so for the painted tombs
Distance:	7.4km/4.6 miles
Map:	on p.291

'The walls of this little tomb are a dance of real delight. The room seems inhabited still by Etruscans of the sixth century before Christ, a vivid, life-accepting people, who must have lived with real fullness. On come the dancers and the music-players, moving in a broad frieze towards the front wall of the tomb, the wall facing us as we enter from the dark stairs, and where the banquet is going on in all its full glory. Above the banquet, in the gable angle, are the two spotted leopards heraldically facing each other across a little tree. And the ceiling of rock has chequered slopes of red and black and yellow and blue squares, with a roof-beam painted with coloured circles, dark red and blue and yellow. So that all is colour, and we do not seem to be underground at all, but in some gay chamber of the past.'
D.H. Lawrence (1932) on the Tomb of the Leopards.

The scores of painted underground tomb chambers are the glory of Tarquinia, alias Tarchna in Etruscan times. A veritable rabbit warren of tombs containing an estimated 2000 burials lies beneath the surface of the ancient Monterozzi necropolis. Archaeologists are still at work probing the terrain, though the overwhelming numbers mean that only chambers that promise painted interiors are actually opened up. The paintings, said to exemplify the evolution of the Etruscan style, depict a wide range of activities and provide an extraordinary insight into daily life. There are enchanting scenes of competitive sports, hunting and fishing, funereal games with music and dancing, banquets, legendary figures doing battle and even eroticism.

Tarchna itself was a mighty city, foremost in the Etruscan league. The Tarquins, its ruling dynasty, are

Access: From the main Tyrrhenian coast road, the SS 1 (Aurelia), Tarquinia is but 2km inland.

Trains on the Rome–Pisa line regularly stop at Tarquinia, and are met by a local bus for the trip up to the Barriera S. Giusto bus terminal, well-positioned just outside the town walls. A multitude of COTRAL coach lines leave from here, meaning links with Blera, Monteromano, Tuscania, Viterbo and Civitavecchia (hence Rome), to name a few.

Buses are used for the initial sections of the walk: for the necropolis take an appropriately signed local bus (except Suns & hols); from there you'll need to catch the daily COTRAL service for Monteromano as far as the turn-off for the 'Acropoli'. Timetables are available at the tourist office close to the bus terminal, and are also posted on the wall outside.

*Etruscan freize in the
Tomb of the Leopards,
Tarquinia*

believed to have founded Rome and then supplied it with
several influential kings. Tarquinius Priscus, from 7th–6th
century BC, was attributed with the introduction to Rome
of Etruscan customs such as games, triumph celebrations
and the 'fascies', together with grandiose public works,
notably the Cloaca Maxima sewer which still drains the
Forum. In contrast, the seventh and last king of Rome,
Tarquinius Superbus, was a tyrant in addition to being a
constructor. This immense cultural wealth and the information supplied by the tomb paintings lead to fascinating
speculations about the extraordinary richness of the life in
the metropolis of Tarchna. A further intriguing and intense
sector involved divination and the figure of the haruspex
or soothsayer. Legend has it that the practice originated
here, following instruction from a popular hero, Tagete,
grandson of Jupiter, who sprang from the earth beneath a
plough share.

Unfortunately, of the actual city itself little more than
the odd stone remains, with the exception of the impressive ruins of a temple, discovered in the 1930s. Having
begun life at the necropolis area close to the present town,
in the shape of conical Villanovan era (8th century BC) huts,
Tarchna moved across the deep valley to spread over the
Pian di Civita plateau. Nowadays nothing more than
scraggly sheep and giant fennel survive the onslaught of
the chilling winds and scorching sun that beat down
relentlessly on the bare rugged terrain. It is quite frankly
amazing to think that a 135-hectare city once existed here

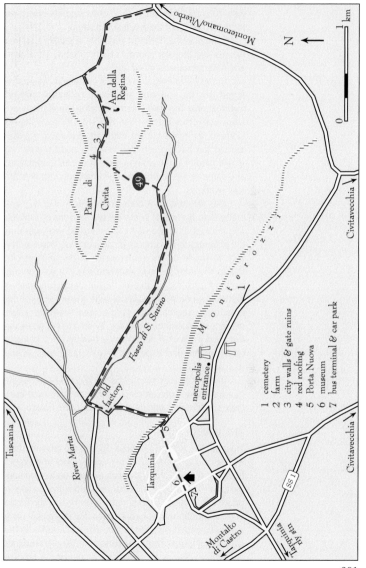

1 cemetery
2 farm
3 city walls & gate ruins
4 red roofing
5 Porta Nuova
6 museum
7 bus terminal & car park

with 100,000 inhabitants, while water supplies now have to be trucked in for the few resident sheep.

Springs to the northeast probably originally supplied the city and the later aqueduct for the Roman settlement, and have presumably dried up.

In the Middle Ages the entire settlement was transferred to the present site, with plentiful natural fortifications. The stones and their Etruscan ghosts were laboriously carted from Pian di Civita for recycling as Corneto, as it was known until this century. A wander around the back streets will reveal a good number of extant medieval towers reminiscent of San Gimignano, and some exquisite Romanesque churches with delicate rose windows.

This varied walk is both worthwhile and easy, especially with the aid of buses for the sections of asphalt. The necropolis at the start can be visited year-round as the underground chambers are always cool, however the lack of shade on the plateau site of the ancient city makes the later section inadvisable in hot weather. Its isolated position, however, means sweeping views across the countryside. Those with a car can skip the conclusive stretch back to the town with its 100m descent and monotonous valley, by driving out along the dirt road to the Ara della Regina temple site. Time can otherwise be spent exploring the panoramic plateau and its scattered ruins.

In terms of accommodation, for those who prefer the coast, starting with Tarquinia Lido (served by local bus), there's a string of camping grounds and other hotels.

THE WALK

From the township of **Tarquinia** (139m), the itinerary starts with a visit to the unrivalled necropolis. (Should no buses be imminent, it's 20 uninteresting minutes on foot through the town via Corso Vittorio Emanuele, following the appropriate yellow signs bearing right – southeast.) The broad ridge of **Monterozzi** was once covered with sizeable earth mounds heaped over the tombs, probably imitating the conical hut forms of the early settlement. Very few mounds are left now, having been flattened by ploughs or levelled

for the horse races once held here. Helpful information boards provide history and explanations in both Italian and English. In addition to the Tomb of the Leopards, try and see Hunting and Fishing, the Painted Vases, the Bulls and the Baron. Tomb visits may be limited in the interests of minimising damage inflicted by the presence of visitors.

Arches of the Roman aqueduct en route to the ancient Etruscan city site, Tarquinia

Do enquire about visiting the Scataglini complex on the other side of the road. This unusual necropolis was dug out of an old 'macco' (marine sedimentary rock) quarry, late 4th–1st century BC. The Aninas family tomb holds both some intriguing paintings as well as a variety of sarcophaguses, including that of a 74-year old family head, an incredibly old age for those times when average life expectancy was 35–40 years.

Back at the road is the painted Tomba dei Demoni Azzurri, recognisable with its long entrance dromos. Excavation and reconstruction work have meant rerouting the road!

Allow a good hour or so for these visits.

Leave the necropolis, heading inland southeast then northwest on the road for Viterbo (COTRAL bus for Monteromano). After the 5th series of arches of the Roman aqueduct that bridges the dips in the land (about 7km), take the dirt road northish signposted for 'Tarquinia resti dell'antica città' and 'Acropoli'.

The rolling hills are covered with vast fields of wheat edged by pretty pink-purple gladiolus in spring, and interspersed with waste ground. Stark and desolate in some seasons, as well as windswept, it has shades of the Sienese 'crete' clay terrain landscapes. This is the domain of the giant fennel, whose towering woody stalks sprout feathery leaves and yellow flowers. Clumps of this gigantic plant are encouraged as it provides the perfect breeding ground for the tasty *ferlenghi* mushrooms, jealously reaped by the locals you'll see combing the area. A little over a quarter of an hour on you turn left for the 'Ara della Regina'. This is the start of the narrow ridge-like plateau of Pian di Civita, erstwhile site of the 5th century BC city. This branch track becomes a little rough, so drivers are advised to park in the vicinity. Ten minutes along is a further signed fork left just before a group of dilapidated farm huts. A few minutes over the rise are the massive ruins of the **Ara della Regina** (Altar of the Queen) sanctuary complex (177m, 30min on foot from the main road). From this dominating position even cone-shaped Monte Amiata can be seen in the distant north while the Monti della Tolfa spread closer over to the southeast. Birds of prey often cruise overhead and sheep wander freely through the fenced-off area, unaware that the light limestone and dark volcanic stones here are steeped in history, not to mention blood from the sacrifices such as that of 307 Roman prisoners in 356BC. The paved roadway below the main wall dates back to Roman times and leads to the forum, which features the base of a sizeable circular fountain in marble (1st century BC). The temple itself, 77 by 35m, dates back to 3rd century BC, and was adorned by terracotta sculptures such as the magnificent pair of winged horses now on display in the museum.

Return to the last fork and turn left through the farm area with its water tanks. Keep westish on the wide track, and a short way downhill is an interesting enclosure around remains of city walls and gate. A slight ascent now leads towards red corrugated iron roofing over more excavations, closed off to visitors (40min).

From this point, by all means continue westwards along the track for a wander along the narrowing plateau which affords a lovely vast outlook.

From the red roofing, leave the wide track and make your way SSW across the plateau, in the direction of the cemetery over the valley, as it were, a useful reference point. Five minutes will see you at the edge of the 'city', where a small but clearly recognisable pass leads down through the modest cliffs. This was in all likelihood an original city exit route, and continued downhill to the valley floor. You reach the edge of vast fields occupied by huge mounds of gathered stones. Keep straight down following what is apparently a ruined wall dividing two fields. The only obstacles are a low wire fence and a ditch, easily detoured. Soon after passing beneath power lines is the track where you turn right to follow the Fosso di San Savino watercourse along the valley floor (50m, 1h this far).

During the ensuing half hour, you stroll northwest below the ridges housing the Etruscan necropolis left and the ancient city right. Soon after being joined by the driveway to a large farm, you pass alongside the unsightly skeleton of an old factory. Turn left at the asphalt past the entrance to a small-scale 'Frantoio' (oil press) within the

The impressive ruins of the Ara della Regina sanctuary, Tarquinia

factory bounds. Keep straight ahead on the unsealed road, ignoring the tarmac that heads diagonally off right. Left again at the corner then first right up the narrow surfaced road that climbs back to Tarquinia. The quiet road makes for a lovely climb between beech and hedgerows to the imposing rocky outcrop, and you enter the township through the 16th-century **Porta Nuova**. Just before the portal is a curious well-shaped hole in the uphill flank – a rubbish disposal point excavated in the 17th century in an attempt at plague prevention (1h50min total).

A scenic terrace with a drinking fountain is the perfect place for a contemplative rest. Over ENE are the Monti Cimini, while in the underlying valley north is the River Marta, an essential waterway for the Etruscan city and link with its port, Gravisca.

To return to the starting point, take the broad avenue Alberata Dante Alighieri down through Piazza Matteotti with its magnificent fountain and palaces. Corso Vittorio Emanuele then leads to Piazza Cavour, close to the bus terminal. On your right is the Renaissance Palazzo Vitelleschi, home to the **Museo Nazionale** with its wealth of Etruscan antiquities, a perfect way to conclude the walk (2h total).

Tourist Office Tarquinia
tel.0766/856384

Accommodation
Tarquinia old town:
Hotel San Marco
tel.0766/842234

The impressive collection includes the winged horses in terracotta from the Ara della Regina sanctuary, sarcophaguses in terracotta, or 'macco' or volcanic 'nenfro', and a multitude of votive objects. There are also a number of reconstructed unusual frescoed tomb chambers, depicting both organised athletics and ships. An English translation of the information boards is available for each room.

50: Cerveteri alias Etruscan Caere

Walking time:	3h30min including necropolis visit
Distance:	6.3km/4 miles
Map:	on p.300

It's a strange experience to wander through the streets and buildings of a city constructed 2600 years ago, especially when it's actually an extraordinary cemetery. Cerveteri's Necropoli della Banditaccia is a full-scale 'city of the dead' in the true sense of the word. The street plan on its own is fascinating, but it is the striking architecture of the monumental tombs that leaves a lasting impression. One after another are huge artificial mounds of earth over a circular base of stone blocks, possibly imitations of ancient dwelling places like huts. Below the surface, partially excavated into the tufa bed rock, is an orderly arrangement of rooms and vestibules, many originally painted with lively scenes in vivid colours and decorated with carved reliefs. Once the deceased had been carried in procession accompanied by relatives and musicians, then laid out surrounded by personal possessions, stone slabs would seal the entrance.

In addition to the archaeological fascination, it is a beautiful peaceful place alive with birdsong. Darting swallows have nests tucked inside the tumuli in the company of sleek lizards. The unusual hoopoe bird has found a haven here, and can be seen flitting through the oak trees on black and white banded wings around pinkish-brown body plumage, and uttering its shrill triple-syllabled cry. Moreover, standing out against the background of the Monti Ceriti is a succession of miniature gardens that have taken root on top of the mounds, in place of the altars for offerings to the gods of the dead. Now there are delicate paper-like rock roses, poppies and the tall white lily-like asphodel.

Access: Cerveteri lies 7km inland off the SS 1 (Aurelia), 45km north of Rome and 30km south from the bustling port of Civitavecchia. It can also be approached from inland, along the minor 16km road from Lago di Bracciano. By public transport from Rome, the most straightforward system is to take the COTRAL bus from the Lepanto stop on the Metro B line, for the 1-hour trip. There are also runs from Civitavecchia. Moreover it's feasible to catch a train to Ladispoli, the nearest stop. As you leave the station, turn right to the nearby cross-roads which leads to an overpass. The COTRAL bus from Rome loops through Ladispoli then picks up passengers here for the final 7km to Cerveteri itself.

The walk can be short-ened briefly at the start by catching the local 'G' bus which connects Cerveteri with the Banditaccia necropolis. However this happens only on Sundays, apart from the midsummer period when it runs on a daily basis.

*Among the monumental
tumuli in Cerveteri's
Banditaccia Necropolis*

The massive swathe of densely packed cemeteries accounts for a surprising 800 hectares. Though separated from it by deep-cut valleys, they formed a ring around the site of the ancient city of Etruscan Caere, later called Caere Vetere (old Caere) hence Cerveteri. Settled since at least 9th century BC, the powerful and wealthy city and foremost member of the Etruscan Confederation, Caere spread over the entire 150-hectare tableland where the present town stands as a mere appendage. Unlike other Etruscan city-states, it was long an ally of Rome, and even provided refuge to the vestal virgins when Rome was invaded by the Gauls in 390BC. Trade flowed through its three nearby ports, dominated by the export of minerals from the neighbouring Monti della Tolfa to Greek destinations. Relationships were intense, and Caere was the sole Etruscan city to have its own building at the Delphi sanctuary. Highly skilled Greek potters fleeing a Persian invasion set up shop there around 6th century BC and developed a distinct style of vases. The city had already made a name for itself in the field of the plastic arts, and in fact the unique black Etruscan 'bucchero' ware was first produced here. Local craftsmen were also responsible for the exquisite sarcophagus known as the 'Sarcofago degli Sposi' (Sarcophagus of the Newly Weds) on display in Rome's Villa Giulia musem, and a similar exemplary in the Louvre in Paris.

This fascinating walk is an easy stroll for everyone, and covers both burial sites and ancient ways, as well as a beautiful wild valley on the final leg. It can be done as a day trip from Rome if an early start is made. The core area, the Banditaccia necropolis, is subject to (extended) opening hours and entrance fee, while the remaining areas are freely accessible at all times, and moreover see very few visitors. A slightly shorter alternative for drivers – though it means missing the wild Fosso Manganello valley – is to proceed by car as far as the entrance to the Banditaccia necropolis. Leave the walk later when it drops to the stream crossing after the Via degli Inferi, then backtrack to the parking area.

As food and drink go, in addition to the bars, shops and the like in the town, there's a *trattoria* on the approach to the necropolis, as well as a kiosk with light refreshments opposite the entrance itself. Picnics are not allowed in the enclosed necropolis site. A torch is handy for the minor tombs, while all the principal ones are lit.

THE WALK

From **Cerveteri's** central open square, Piazza A. Moro and the bus stops, walk downhill on the right side of the public gardens, the site of an ancient city exit. Yellow signposting for the 'Necropoli' indicates the narrow road that curves right around the base of the medieval walls, heading northwards. After crossing the Fosso Manganello watercourse, it climbs to the edge of a plateau and keeps right along a lovely avenue lined with stately pines. The thick unruly wood on the left conceals a multitude of built-up tomb mounds known collectively as the Tombe del Comune. Plenty of pathways lead in and a good number of chambers can be explored with the help of a torch. Watch your step though as the area is particularly overgrown and the ground pitted with half-covered holes. The best tombs of course are locked, and the Banditaccia custodians will sometimes accompany visitors, though the visit to the main area ahead is usually more than sufficient.

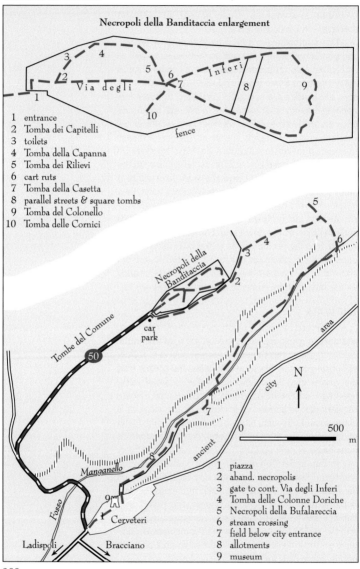

Necropoli della Banditaccia enlargement

1 entrance
2 Tomba dei Capitelli
3 toilets
4 Tomba della Capanna
5 Tomba dei Rilievi
6 cart ruts
7 Tomba della Casetta
8 parallel streets & square tombs
9 Tomba del Colonello
10 Tomba delle Cornici

1 piazza
2 aband. necropolis
3 gate to cont. Via degli Inferi
4 Tomba delle Colonne Doriche
5 Necropoli della Bufalareccia
6 stream crossing
7 field below city entrance
8 allotments
9 museum

Continuing along the avenue, a *trattoria* is passed on the right amongst vineyards, while beyond loom a number of impressive tumuli. Their painted interiors are currently being re-explored and will hopefully be opened up for the public in the not-too-distant future.

Half an hour from Cerveteri will see you at the car park and entrance to the **Necropoli della Banditaccia**. The place name is not a reference to bandits, but comes from 'terra bandita' or forbidden land – it was government property last century and no construction was allowed. For a thorough visit, the best bet is to follow the arrows for the 'Itinerario consigliato' as per the sketch map. The following notes provide a rough guide to a selection of the most noteworthy tumuli.

You bear left at the Tomba dei Capitelli, which features unusual Greek style capitals atop carved columns. Past the toilet block, the next notable is the Tomba della Capanna (hut tomb), one of the largest tumuli, where the excavated interior resembles a hut construction. Next is the spectacular **Tomba dei Rilievi** (bas-reliefs), a hypogeum and one of the few lacking an above-ground structure. Steps descend to the unique chamber where the walls and fluted columns are decorated with an extraordinary series of carved objects that were originally stuccoed then painted in vivid colours. They range from cushions, helmets and a host of household objects such as a coiled rope, a jug and a long knife.

Above ground once more, a little further on is a crossroads where the passage of carts over the ages has left deep ruts in the so-called Via degli Inferi (Way of the Underworld). The interior of the modest tomb in the middle, Tomba della Casetta, entirely dug out of the rock, is an imitation of the layout of an Etruscan house.

Along the left fork, two parallel streets are encountered lined with square tombs. Further on is the massive **Tomba del Colonello**, close to which is an interesting drainage tunnel, part of the complex system fed by individual trenches dug around each mound to draw off rainwater. Along an outer lane parallel to the fencing, walk back towards the crossroads. Here a lane forks diagonally left for the detour to the Tomba delle Cornici,

Cypresses grow freely amidst huge tombs in the Banditaccia Necropolis

which has beautiful moulded decorations over its internal doors and windows.

Back at the intersection, keep left down the 'High Street' once more. In front of a row of square tombs are some curious stone marker slabs with niches holding a house shape to indicate a woman occupant and a cylinder for a man.

(2h has been allowed for the visit, thus a total of 2h30min this far.) Outside again, turn left along the lane through the car park. Many more mysterious tumuli are glimpsed amidst dense wood, then just as the corner of the enclosure is passed, an interesting cleared area is reached on the right (10min from the Banditaccia entrance). Subjected to exploratory work in the 1960s, the bare rock surface hosts a curious underground necropolis, now in a state of total abandon. Rainwater has since filled many of the chambers and niches below the surface, promptly colonised by reeds and frogs whose echoing croaks reverberate almost eerily. Tiny orchids, brambles and even broom grow in others. The parallel grooves on the surface were left by centuries of ploughs as well as bulldozers employed during the excavations! From the highest point are lovely views down into the Fosso Manganello valley and its wild cliffs, as well as over to the plateau opposite, the erstwhile site of the ancient city.

Return to the lane and continue along it for a couple of minutes. As it bears left, turn off right through the gate for the continuation of **Via degli Inferi** (total 2h45min to here). Lined with chamber-type sepulchres now, the delightful mossy lane has sunken into the bed rock through centuries of wear. Just before a deep cutting is entered, a short clamber up right is rewarded by the Tomba delle Colonne Doriche. Proceeding deeper and deeper downhill, you soon reach a T-junction.

It's worth detouring briefly uphill to the area known as the **Necropoli della Bufalareccia**. Some massive tumuli are being freed of the deep deposits of several centuries. Finds have included an elegant sarcophagus lid bearing the figure of a very handsome youth at a banquet, now in the town museum. As the Etruscan drainage systems fell into disuse, the zone reverted to a marshy state and was long employed for grazing buffaloes, hence the name.

Back at the T-junction again, go downhill past more burials, including a square construction from Roman times, in a bay on the right. Flights of steps lead to the upper level of the plateau, but undergrowth usually obstructs passage. In shady holm oak wood now with porcupine quills littering the ground, the Via degli Inferi crosses the trickle of the Fosso Manganello (3h). The way proceeds uphill towards the modern-day cemetery and ancient city, but access to this final stretch is unfortunately closed off by barbed wire.

So, just after the stream crossing take the path that drops to the right to follow the watercourse. After a brief steep stretch you emerge at the bottom of a wild valley enclosed by tall cliffs. With an eye out for insidious marshy patches, take the faint path through the flowered meadows beneath gigantic wild fig trees. Where the valley widens for a short stretch, there are more rock tombs to be explored in the cliffs up right. About a quarter

The exquisite Sarcofago degli Sposi crafted in Cerveteri, now in Rome's Villa Giulia museum

of an hour from where you left the Via degli Inferi, and just before a huge carved boulder in the middle of the field, leave the valley floor on the wide path that crosses the stream bed left. It climbs below cliffs where an ancient Etruscan temple once stood. A gate opens onto a field where horses graze. Ahead, the broad natural opening in the cliffs marks the site of another past city entrance. However instead of continuing uphill, keep right at the gate and stick to the fence, leaving the field quickly through a gap in the enclosure in the corner. A wide lane bordered by elderberry trees then takes you past flourishing allotments on the valley floor where the watercourse has disappeared, hence to the base of the towering dark stone walls of **Cerveteri's** 12th-century castle. Left up Via del Lavatore will bring you out in the main square again (3h30min). A broad flight of steps leads into the castle itself and the **Museo Nazionale Cerite**. Notable exhibits include a pair of hinged wood–iron sandals, Phoenician glass containers and promising painted terracotta fragments from the sanctuaries once dotted around the ancient city. The towering jointed earthenware vases are believed to have served as incense burners or stands for heating purposes.

Other Visits

Below the present town and close to the school (on the road for Bracciano) is the renowned **Tomba Regolini-Galassi**. This resting place of a warrior and a wealthy woman, constructed with unusual vaulting, was opened last century and has since been emptied of its contents – exquisite ivory, gold and ceramics, now in the Vatican's Etruscan collection. Intending visitors to the tomb should enquire at the Banditaccia necropolis, and prepare to be insistent as it is rarely opened.

Furthermore, east of the town is the flat-topped outcrop of Monte Abetone, where the roomy **Tumulo Campana** (always open) can be reached via a path off the road for Ceri.

Some 12km up the coast is **Pyrgi**, alias modern-day S. Severa. Along with Palo Laziale and S. Marinella, it was one of ports of Caere, and linked to it by a long roadway. Visitors can see excavations which have unearthed a 6000sq m sanctuary dedicated to the Phoenician goddess Astarte, warrior and dispensor of love, assimilated to Etruscan Uni. Sizeable fragments of a temple pediment can be seen in Rome's Villa Giulia museum, along with two precious gold foil panels covered with a bilingual text, in Etruscan and Phoenician.

51: Ancient Veio and the Ponte Sodo

Walking time:	3h + more for exploring the ruins
Distance:	9.3km/5.8 miles
Map:	on p.307

Access: By public transport from Rome, two routes are feasible. Either:

a) ATAC bus n.910 from Stazione Termini (Rome's main railway station) to Piazza Mancini, where you change for n.201 to La Storta, hence n.032 for Isola Farnese. Get off at the bus stop at the Veio junction just before the bus climbs to Isola Farnese, or

b) train to La Storta (Rome–Viterbo line), hence ATAC bus n.032 as above. Either way allow about 1h30min for the overall trip.

Drivers, on the other hand, will need the SS 2 (Cassia). Near La Storta are clear signs for the turn-off for the narrow 2km road that leads east to the village of Isola Farnese and the site of Veio.

'He who would make the tour of Veii must not expect to see numerous monuments of the past. Scarcely one Etruscan site has fewer remains, yet few possess greater interest. Veii lives in the page of history rather than in extant monuments... The very skeleton of Veii has crumbled to dust – the city is its own sepulchre...' George Dennis (1848).

A rather gloomy introduction for Veio, once perhaps the greatest of the twelve-member Etruscan Confed-eration of city states. Founded around 9th century BC, it flourished on its high 190-hectare tufa plateau and controlled the upper Tiber River valley with fortified positions. Referred to as the Troy of Italy, it was a mere 17km north of Rome, and attracted the latter's rivalry, leading to a war that dragged on for ten long years. Veio finally fell in 396BC at the hands of Furius Camillus whose men managed to burrow a tunnel to the acropolis. On surfacing in daylight at a temple, the soldiers overheard the haruspex declare that whoever completed the sacrifice under way would become king. Not a moment did they lose in carrying off the entrails in question for Camillus to offer up, before swarming in and burning down the city. After the inevitable Roman centre, ensuing settlements petered out around 5th century.

Things nowadays are much the same as last century when Dennis visited the site. A combination of desolation, peace and quiet reigns on the platform where the bustling city once stood, and in spite of the pollution from nearby Rome, there are stunning views over the countryside of the Tiber valley to the long extension of snowcapped mountains of the Apennines. The area is partially wooded and wild, but there are also cultivated wheat fields, a haven for

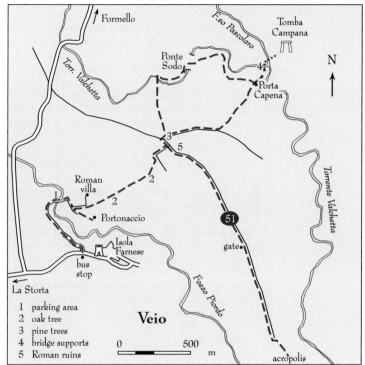

Formello

F.so Pascolaro

Tomba
Campana

Ponte
Sodo

Tor. Valchetta

4

N
↑

Porta
Capena

3
5

Torrente Valchetta

Roman
villa

2

1

2

Portonaccio

51

Isola
Farnese

gate

bus
stop

La Storta

Fosso Piordo

1   parking area
2   oak tree
3   pine trees
4   bridge supports
5   Roman ruins

Veio

0   500
|———————|
            m

acropolis

rabbits, pheasants and larks. Apart from an archaeologist
or two, without forgetting the flocks of sheep, there's little
chance of encountering anyone else up here. The odd
plane heading for Rome is the sole reminder of the proximity of the chaotic capital city.

Of the scarce Etruscan remains, the most extraordinary, and one which alone justifies the walk, is the Ponte
Sodo, a feat of Etruscan hydraulic engineering. It is
believed that this 70m long and 3m wide tunnel was
excavated to divert the flow of the Valchetta, a tributary
of the River Tiber, in order to prevent flooding. A further
tunnel, a good 600m long, is said to run under the entire
site. Other ruins of great interest are the sanctuaries
which have rewarded explorers with huge deposits of

votive objects, not to mention a series of graceful terra-cotta sculptures and roof decorations, now in Rome's Villa Giulia museum. There are also large ritual pools, as well as lengths of roadway paved during the Roman period, including part of the Via Clodia which touched on Veio. Not much in the way of tombs is visitable here, apart from the painted Tomba dell'Anatra with its frieze of ducks (hence the name), and the Tomba Campana (named after its discoverer), whose frescoes of harlequin panthers and horses are fading fast. They are understandably locked, but difficult to visit for reasons ranging from lack of personnel, ongoing excavations and damage due to vandals.

The walk is highly recommended and feasible as a day trip from Rome. However it is emphatically unsuitable in hot weather as there is very little shade on the plateau itself. Hardly any climbing is involved and paths are clear and trouble-free for the most part. Walkers should be equipped with food and drink, as there is nothing on the site itself. Note: only the actual Portonaccio Sanctuary archaeological area is subject to opening times and a modest entrance fee, while the rest of Veio is accessible at all times.

THE WALK

From the bus stop below the castle belonging to the tiny medieval village of **Isola Farnese** (110m), take Via Riserva Campetti, signed for Veio. The narrow sunken road drops quickly into lush wood, heading northwest, and you get a glimpse through the thick vegetation of the ruins of the sanctuary on the opposite side of the stream. The modern cemetery is passed then the road becomes a dirt track to a parking area (10min), littered with all manner of rubbish. Past a derelict mill is a stream crossing (Fosso Piordo), a dramatic waterfall downstream. The path proceeds through one of the city of Veio's ten original gates, the occasional stone block still visible as well as several typically Etruscan drainage channels hewn out of the tufa rock.

Keep straight on for the ticket office at the sanctuary entrance, and ignore the lane up left for the time being.

A stretch of flagged Roman road leads around to the **Portonaccio** Sanctuary, dating back to 6th century BC. It stands outside the actual city area, on a terrace overlooking the stream, and was dedicated to Menerva and other deities such as Apollo. Several buildings have been partially reconstructed to help visitors imagine the original structures. Along the roof of a temple once stood a magnificent statue of Apollo and a series of painted antefixes such as an elegant female figure and ghastly gorgons, now safely conserved in the main Rome museum. There is also a pool for purification rites (15min for the visit – total 30min).

After the visit, return out past the ticket office and take the sunken lane up right. It climbs past remnants of a necropolis through an erstwhile entrance to the plateau thence the Etruscan city. As the lane bears left into an enclosure around a Roman villa (worth a quick look), go straight ahead through a gate. There is a brief dip across a saddle of sorts and a tiny stream, then a path climbs northeast towards a prominent oak tree in the middle of a wheat field. You'll often find sheep huddling in the tree's shade of a hot summer day. With views over right to Isola Farnese and its castle, keep on in the same direction past another oak, then leftish to a barbed wire fence and onto a grassy lane. This point offers the first views of the spread of the far-off Apennines, snowbound well into spring. On especially clear days the pyramidal shape of the Gran Sasso peak, northeast, is also visible.

Follow the lane across a small valley and up to a wider dirt road backed by meagre ruins from the Roman settlement. Turn left here then right at the next junction, to reach two **pine trees** near a concrete shed (45min this far).

Here you'll need to clamber over the green metal gate on the left, then follow the clear path alongside a field. Splashes of red paint guide you gradually downhill through what was yet another entrance to the ancient city. Several excavated tomb cavities are passed before the Torrente Valchetta is reached, all but hidden by a dense band of vegetation. An opportune plank will hopefully be in place to aid the stream crossing, as the rocky banks are smooth and can be slippery. On the other side, head right parallel to the stream, through a pretty open pasture area dotted with wild fruit trees. The sloping flanks on your left were once an extensive necropolis, but very few clues linger on, mostly haphazard holes in the ground, the likely work of tomb robbers. A little way along when you reach a fence, a clear passage presents itself for the short slippery drop right into the trees and the water's edge. Here now before your eyes is an Etruscan marvel, the so-called **Ponte Sodo** (1h total). This name is usually coined for a natural bridge, but this neither a bridge nor natural, but manmade. Apart from the technical aspects, it is an evocative spot, what with festoons of greenery and roots draped down the hillside, moss and ferns adorning the banks, curious layers of light-coloured volcanic tufa alternating with darker friable sediments, then the pleasant gurgling flow of the water through the long tunnel to the arc of green hued light at the other end.

After all that, climb back up the bank and squeeze your way through the fence on your right. A faint path follows the edge of a field and into the trees, directly over the Ponte Sodo tunnel. Keep left at a fork and through light wood, guided by the occasional red mark again. The path soon leads you high above the stream, which reappears down left, then up to a field. Keep left to the nearby fascinating excavations at **Porta Capena**, the northern entrance to Veio (1h15min).

Path to Tomba Campana (20min return)
Should you be granted permission for this visit and be accompanied by a custodian from Portonaccio sanctuary, ford the river at Porta Capena and follow the faint path north and across the minor watercourse (Fosso Pascolaro) to the tomb.

From Porta Capena, by way of the shady sunken lane that follows on from the the paved way, return in a south-westerly direction to the plateau. Turn right onto the unsealed road back to the **pine trees** and turn-off for Ponte Sodo (1h30min).

Keep left at the ensuing intersection and past the Roman ruins once more. The track soon veers left through open rolling fields, past ongoing excavations by the University of Rome where paving from another roadway has been unearthed a good metre below the present surface. While traversing this area make the effort to conjure up the picture of this spread of fields as crammed with dwellings, craft and trade in the busy city it once was. A little further on, where the main track heads down right to a farm presided over by a gaggle of shaggy sheep dogs, keep straight ahead (SSE) through a gate, as per the route of the ancient road. A gradual descent to cross a shallow valley brings you to the natural isthmus, the site of the ancient **acropolis**, referred to as Piazza d'Armi (2h5min this far).

At the entrance is evidence of the typically huge stone blocks the Etruscans used to build their defensive walls. A little further on is an unusual ritual hexagonal pool lined with tufa blocks. A temple dedicated to Juno also stood here, the very spot where Camillus' men emerged during the sacrifice. This fortified acropolis area was never used again after the Roman victory.

Return along the same track to the Roman ruins before the pines, and turn left down the grassy lane followed earlier, hence the wheat field and oak trees, past the villa and down to the car park then **bus stop** once more (3h).

APPENDIX

Some brief notes on important Etruscan sites, monuments and museums not covered by the walking itineraries.

ADRIA

Although it is now 25km inland from the Adriatic coast due to silting from the River Po, Adria was a flourishing port in 6th century BC and even gave its name to the sea. At a strategic crossroads, it witnessed the passage of goods from Greece, northern Europe and of course Etruria. Adria was partially eclipsed by the port of Spina, a little further south, founded soon afterwards as a more suitable site for supplying Etruscan Felsina (Bologna). The museum contains finds from local burials, but the modest collection of ancient pottery and miscellaneous objects is overshadowed by a small but superb display of Etruscan gold jewellery.

Adria can be reached by train from either Rovigo or Venice, and by car via the SS 443 from Rovigo. An English-language guidebook is on loan for visits.

AREZZO

One of the original twelve city states of Etruria, the city now has little for Etruscan enthusiasts, apart from a few fragments of ancient walling. The museum, on the other hand, housed in an ex monastery built into the early Roman amphitheatre, has a reasonable collection of terracotta pieces from the city's sanctuaries together with a series of vases crafted locally by slave labour.

Arezzo is on the Florence–Rome train line, while drivers can reach it via the appropriate exit from the A1 motorway.

BOLOGNA

The powerful city of Felsina (6th–4th century BC), later Bologna, controlled trade at the crossroads between the route from Etruria proper, the Po plain and the Adriatic coast. Today nothing betrays the fact it was once an Etruscan city, as the subsequent series of rulers ensured concentrated stratification. However Bologna does boast a cavernous archaeological museum that houses substantial displays encompassing both historic private collections and material from recent excavation campaigns. A

Unusual tombs at the Marzabotto Necropolis

unique wooden throne and tables hail from Verucchio near Rimini, while La Certosa has yielded astonishing monumental stelae or tombstones. Wooden coffins were used, judging by the huge number of nails found. In addition to hippocampus and other beasts, one frequently depicted scene on the headstones is the passage of the soul the afterworld by chariot. Unusual funerary urns in the shape of bronze pails are on display, one covered with bands of scenes in relief showing processions of warriors, priests and musicians sporting a curious array of headwear, in addition to hunters and ferocious animals.

FLORENCE

The city's massive archaeological museum is one of Italy's most important. On display are finds from Etruscan sites all over Italy, and special pieces such as the superb bronze statue the Orator ('Arringatore'), from near Lake Trasimeno and the Chimera from Arezzo. The latter is a unique hollow cast of a mythical creature with a lion's body, and three heads – lion, goat and serpent. Vast numbers of Greek and Etruscan vases, mirrors, and of course funerary urns and sarcophagi including the painted marble chest known as 'the Amazons'. In the museum courtyard are reconstructed tombs from Orvieto, Populonia, Vetulonia and Volterra, unfortunately closed to visitors at present, as awaiting restoration after the extensive 1966 flood damage. Excellent detailed information sheets are available in English for most rooms.

MARZABOTTO

Exciting surprises await Etruscan enthusiasts at this plateau above the River Reno, 25km south of Bologna. This little known site dates back to 6th century BC, the time of the push northwards. It is perhaps the sole Etruscan city which was abandoned rather than being built over.

Marzabotto lasted a mere century and a half, until invasion by Celts mid 4th century BC. The city plan is clearly visible along with 15m and 5m wide perpendicular streets, each complete with a vehicle lane, footpath and gutters. Foundations of houses, deep wells and workshops for ceramic and metals have been excavated. The picturesque necropolis consists of travertine slab tombs, originally below ground, indicated by a rounded stone marker. On higher ground instead are several temples with monumental altars.

Marzabotto can be reached by train from Bologna on the Porretta branch line, and the site is a short walk uphill from the station. By car, leave the Bologna–Florence motorway at the Sasso Marconi exit, and proceed south on the SS 64.

ROME

A number of important museums for lovers of things Etruscan can be found in Rome. The best is the vast collection of superb objects from major sites crammed into a papal palace known as Villa Giulia. Highlights are the renowned 'Sarcofago degli Sposi' (Sarcophagus of the Newly Weds) from Cerveteri, the Apollo statue and temple decorations from Veio, delightful bronze work from Bisenzio and Vulci, along with surprises in the form of a chariot from Castro, and elaborate gold jewellery from Pelestrina, a little known site south of Rome.

The Vatican museums, on the other hand, boast the ivory, gold and ceramic tomb goods from Cerveteri's renowned 7th century BC Regolini-Galassi Tomb where a warrior and a princess were laid to rest. The riches on display include a wonderful gold breastplate, bronze bed and funeral carriage.

The final museum belongs to the Capitoline complex, its top attraction the 6th century BC Etruscan bronze statue of the she-wolf suckling Romulus and Remus, who are 16th century additions. Imported Greek vases and ceramics from necropolises in southern Etruria are also on display.

ROSELLE

Eight kilometres north of Grosseto, signposted from the SS 223, are the extensive ruins of the 7th century BC Etruscan city, one of the powerful twelve city states. Impressive defensive walls in huge irregular stone blocks stand over 5m high and run for 3km, enclosing a combination of Etruscan and Roman buildings and paved roads. No public transport.

SPINA

One of the northernmost Etruscan outposts, and a main trading centre on the upper Adriatic coast, it flourished 6th–4th century BC. There is very little to see at the actual site, but the finds, some impressive bronzes and painted vases from over 4000 sepulchres, are on display some 60km to the west at Ferrara's Museo Archeologico Nazionale. Ferrara itself lies about halfway between Padua and Bologna on the A 13 motorway and the train line.

VETULONIA

A panoramic hill some 35km northwest from Grosseto, was once the site of powerful 8th century BC Etruscan Vetulonia, one of the ruling twelve city states. It owed its prosperity to the rich mineral resources in the whereabouts, and practised metallurgy as well as extensive trade by way of an ancient lagoon, now drained. Vestiges of the original walls and a tomb or two can be seen in the quiet village, while a couple of larger stone vaulted tombs are signposted a short way outside. These include the Tomba della Pietrera and Tomba del Diavolino, currently being restored. To reach Vetulonia leave the SS 1 (Aurelia) for the signposted turn-off near Giuncarico.

GLOSSARY

abbazia	abbey
acqua (non) potabile	water (not) suitable for drinking
affittacamere	rooms to rent
agriturismo	farm accommodation
albergo	hotel
alimentari	grocery shop
aliscafo	hydrofoil
alto	high, upper
autostazione	bus station
autostrada	motorway subject to toll
azienda faunistica venatoria	private game reserve
badia	abbey
bagno	bathroom, toilet or even a spa resort
basso	low, lower
benzina	petrol
biglietto/biglietteria	ticket/ticket office
bivio	junction
bonifica	reclaimed land
borro	watercourse
bosco	wood
botro	valley
cabinovia	type of cable-car
cala	cove
calanco/calanchi	eroded clayey terrain with dramatic ridges and deep gullies
camera singola/doppia	single/double room
cane mordace	dog that bites
cappella	chapel
castello	castle
chiesa	church
cimitero	cemetery
civita	ancient city
contrada	quarter, district
divieto di accesso/caccia	no entry/hunting
duomo	cathedral
enoteca	wine shop
entrata/uscita	entrance/exit
faro	lighthouse
fattoria	farm, estate
fiume	river
fontana	fountain, usually drinking water

fonte/sorgente	spring
foresteria	guest quarters
fosso	small valley or watercourse
frazione	hamlet
grotta	cave
isola	island
lago	lake
laguna	lagoon
lido/spiaggia	beach
maestà	shrine with religious painting
maneggio	horse-riding school
mare	sea
miniera	mine, quarry
museo	museum
oasi	protected wildlife area, usually run by Italy's World Wildlife Fund for Nature
osteria	tavern
pane/panino	bread/roll
panificio	bakery
percorso pedonale	pedestrian route
pericolo d'incendio	fire danger
pernottamento	overnight stay, accommodation
pieve	parish church
pineta	pine wood
podere	farm, estate
poggio	hillock, knoll
ponte	bridge
porta	door, gate
pozzo	well, pit
rocca	fortress, stronghold
rovine	ruins
scalo	station for a hill town, or port
scavo	excavation
semaforo	traffic lights or signal-station for shipping
senso unico	one-way street
stazione ferroviaria	railway station
strada privata senza uscita	private road, dead end
tagliata	cutting – see 'via cava'
tempio	temple
tomba etrusca	Etruscan tomb
tombolo	sand spit
traghetto	ferry
trattoria	small restaurant
vetta	peak of a mountain
via	road, street, way
via cava/cava buia/cavone	Etruscan roadway sunk into the rock

LISTING OF CICERONE GUIDES

NORTHERN ENGLAND
LONG-DISTANCE TRAILS
The Dales Way
The Reiver's Way
The Alternative Coast to Coast
The Coast to Coast Walk
The Pennine Way
Hadrian's Wall Path
The Teesdale Way

FOR COLLECTORS OF SUMMITS
The Relative Hills of Britain
Mts England & Wales Vol 2 – England
Mts England & Wales Vol 1 – Wales

BRITISH CYCLE GUIDES
The Cumbria Cycle Way
Lands End to John O'Groats – Cycle Guide
On the Ruffstuff: 84 Bike Rides in North England
Rural Rides No.1 – West Surrey
Rural Rides No.2 – East Surrey
South Lakeland Cycle Rides
Border Country Cycle Routes
Lancashire Cycle Way

CANOE GUIDES
Canoeist's Guide to the North-East

LAKE DISTRICT AND MORECAMBE BAY
Coniston Copper Mines
Scrambles in the Lake District
More Scrambles in the Lake District
Walks in Silverdale and Arnside AONB
Short Walks in Lakeland 1 – South
Short Walks in Lakeland 2 – North
Short Walks in Lakeland 3 – West
The Tarns of Lakeland Vol 1 – West
The Tarns of Lakeland Vol 2 – East
The Cumbria Way & Allerdale Ramble
Winter Climbs in the Lake District
Roads and Tracks of the Lake District
The Lake District Angler's Guide
Rain or Shine – Walking in the Lake District
Rocky Rambler's Wild Walks
An Atlas of the English Lakes

NORTH-WEST ENGLAND
Walker's Guide to the Lancaster Canal
Walking in Cheshire
Family Walks in the Forest Of Bowland
Walks in Ribble Country
Historic Walks in Cheshire
Walking in Lancashire
Walks in Lancashire Witch Country
The Ribble Way

THE ISLE OF MAN
Walking on the Isle of Man
The Isle of Man Coastal Path

PENNINES AND NORTH-EAST ENGLAND
Walks in the Yorkshire Dales – Vol 1
Walking in the South Pennines
Walking in the North Pennines
The Yorkshire Dales
Walks in the North York Moors – Vol 1
Walks in the North York Moors – Vol 2
Walking in the Wolds
Waterfall Walks – Teesdale and High Pennines
Walking in County Durham
Yorkshire Dales Angler's Guide
Backpacker's Britain – Northern England
Walks in Dales Country
Historic Walks in North Yorkshire
South Pennine Walks
Walking in Northumberland

DERBYSHIRE, PEAK DISTRICT, EAST MIDLANDS
High Peak Walks
White Peak Walks Northern Dales
White Peak Walks Southern Dales
White Peak Way
The Viking Way
Star Family Walks Peak District & South Yorkshire
Walking In Peakland
Historic Walks in Derbyshire

WALES AND WELSH BORDERS
Ascent of Snowdon
Welsh Winter Climbs
Hillwalking in Wales – Vol 1
Hillwalking in Wales – Vol 2
Scrambles in Snowdonia
Hillwalking in Snowdonia
The Ridges of Snowdonia
Hereford & the Wye Valley
Walking Offa's Dyke Path
The Brecon Beacons
Lleyn Peninsula Coastal Path
Anglesey Coast Walks
The Shropshire Way
Spirit Paths of Wales
Glyndwr's Way
The Pembrokeshire Coastal Path
Walking in Pembrokeshire
The Shropshire Hills – A Walker's Guide
Backpacker's Britain Vol 2 – Wales

MIDLANDS
The Cotswold Way
West Midlands Rock
The Grand Union Canal Walk
Walking in Oxfordshire
Walking in Warwickshire
Walking in Worcestershire
Walking in Staffordshire
Heart of England Walks

SOUTHERN ENGLAND
The Wealdway & the Vanguard Way
Exmoor & the Quantocks
Walking in the Chilterns
Walks in Kent Book 2
Two Moors Way
Walking in Dorset
Walking in Cornwall
A Walker's Guide to the Isle of Wight
Walking in Devon
Walking in Somerset
The Thames Path
Channel Island Walks
Walking in Buckinghamshire
The Isles of Scilly
Walking in Hampshire
Walking in Bedfordshire
The Lea Valley Walk
Walking in Berkshire
The Definitive Guide to Walking in London
The Greater Ridgeway
Walking on Dartmoor
The South West Coast Path
Walking in Sussex
The North Downs Way
The South Downs Way

SCOTLAND
Scottish Glens 1 – Cairngorm Glens
Scottish Glens 2 – Atholl Glens
Scottish Glens 3 – Glens of Rannoch
Scottish Glens 4 – Glens of Trossach
Scottish Glens 5 – Glens of Argyll
Scottish Glens 6 – The Great Glen
Scottish Glens 7 – The Angus Glens
Scottish Glens 8 – Knoydart to Morvern
Scottish Glens 9 – The Glens of Ross-shire
Scrambles in Skye
The Island of Rhum
Torridon – A Walker's Guide
Ski Touring in Scotland
Walking the Galloway Hills
Walks from the West Highland Railway
Border Pubs & Inns – A Walkers' Guide
Walks in the Lammermuirs
Scrambles in Lochaber
Walking in the Hebrides
Central Highlands: 6 Long Distance Walks
Walking in the Isle of Arran
Walking in the Lowther Hills
North to the Cape
The Border Country – A Walker's Guide
Winter Climbs – Cairngorms
The Speyside Way
Winter Climbs – Ben Nevis & Glencoe
The Isle of Skye, A Walker's Guide

The West Highland Way
Scotland's Far North
Walking the Munros Vol 1 –
  Southern, Central
Walking the Munros Vol 2 –
  Northern & Cairngorms
Scotland's Far West
Walking in the Cairngorms

IRELAND
The Mountains of Ireland
Irish Coastal Walks
The Irish Coast to Coast

INTERNATIONAL CYCLE GUIDES
The Way of St James – Le Puy to
  Santiago cyclist's guide
The Danube Cycle Way
Cycle Tours in Spain
Cycling the River Loire – The Way
  of St Martin

WALKING AND TREKKING
IN THE ALPS
Grand Tour of Monte Rosa Vol 1
Grand Tour of Monte Rosa Vol 2
Walking in the Alps (all Alpine areas)
100 Hut Walks in the Alps
Chamonix to Zermatt
Tour of Mont Blanc
Alpine Ski Mountaineering
  Vol 1 Western Alps
Alpine Ski Mountaineering
  Vol 2 Eastern Alps
Snowshoeing: Techniques and Routes
  in the Western Alps
Alpine Points of View

FRANCE, BELGIUM &
LUXEMBOURG
The Tour of the Queyras
Rock Climbs in the Verdon
RLS (Robert Louis Stevenson) Trail
Walks in Volcano Country
French Rock
Walking the French Gorges
Rock Climbs Belgium & Luxembourg
Tour of the Oisans: GR54
Walking in the Tarentaise and
  Beaufortain Alps
The Brittany Coastal Path
Walking in the Haute Savoie
Walking in the Ardennes
Tour of the Vanoise
Walking in the Languedoc
GR20 Corsica – The High Level Route
The Ecrins National Park
Walking the French Alps: GR5
Walking in the Cevennes
Vanoise Ski Touring
Walking in Provence
Walking on Corsica
Mont Blanc Walks
Walking in the Cathar region
  of south west France
Walking in the Dordogne

PYRENEES AND FRANCE / SPAIN
Rock Climbs in the Pyrenees
Walks & Climbs in the Pyrenees

The GR10 Trail: Through the
  French Pyrenees
The Way of St James –
  Le Puy to the Pyrenees
The Way of St James –
  Pyrenees-Santiago-Finisterre
Through the Spanish Pyrenees GR11
The Pyrenees – World's Mountain
  Range Guide
The Pyrenean Haute Route
Walking in Andorra

SPAIN AND PORTUGAL
Picos de Europa – Walks & Climbs
Andalusian Rock Climbs
The Mountains of Central Spain
Costa Blanca Rock
Walking in Mallorca
Rock Climbs in Majorca,
  Ibiza & Tenerife
Costa Blanca Walks Vol 1
Costa Blanca Walks Vol 2
Walking in Madeira
Via de la Plata (Seville To Santiago)
Walking in the Cordillera Cantabrica
Walking in the Canary Islands 1 West
Walking in the Canary Islands 2 East
Walking in the Sierra Nevada

SWITZERLAND
The Jura: Walking the High Route &
  Ski Traverses
Walking in Ticino, Switzerland
Central Switzerland –
  A Walker's Guide
The Bernese Alps
Walking in the Valais
Alpine Pass Route
Walks in the Engadine, Switzerland

GERMANY AND AUSTRIA
Klettersteig Scrambles in
  Northern Limestone Alps
King Ludwig Way
Walking in the Salzkammergut
Walking in the Black Forest
Walking in the Harz Mountains
Walking in the Bavarian Alps
Germany's Romantic Road
Mountain Walking in Austria
Walking the River Rhine Trail
Trekking in the Stubai Alps
Trekking in the Zillertal Alps

SCANDINAVIA
Walking In Norway
The Pilgrim Road to Nidaros
  (St Olav's Way)

EASTERN EUROPE
Trekking in the Caucausus
The High Tatras
The Mountains of Romania
Walking in Hungary

CROATIA AND SLOVENIA
Walks in the Julian Alps
Walking in Croatia

ITALY
Italian Rock
Walking in the Central Italian Alps

Central Apennines of Italy
Walking in Italy's Gran Paradiso
Long Distance Walks in Italy's Gran
  Paradiso
Walking in Sicily
Shorter Walks in the Dolomites
Treks in the Dolomites
Via Ferratas of the Italian
  Dolomites Vol 1
Via Ferratas of the Italian
  Dolomites Vol 2
Walking in the Dolomites
Walking in Tuscany
Trekking in the Apennines

OTHER MEDITERRANEAN
COUNTRIES
The Mountains of Greece
Climbs & Treks in the Ala Dag
  (Turkey)
The Mountains of Turkey
Treks & Climbs Wadi Rum, Jordan
Jordan – Walks, Treks, Caves etc.
Crete – The White Mountains
Walking in Palestine
Walking in Malta

AFRICA
Climbing in the Moroccan Anti-Atlas
Trekking in the Atlas Mountains
Kilimanjaro

NORTH AMERICA
The Grand Canyon &
  American South West
Walking in British Columbia
The John Muir Trail

SOUTH AMERICA
Aconcagua

HIMALAYAS – NEPAL, INDIA
Langtang, Gosainkund &
  Helambu: A Trekkers' Guide
Garhwal & Kumaon –
  A Trekkers' Guide
Kangchenjunga – A Trekkers' Guide
Manaslu – A Trekkers' Guide
Everest – A Trekkers' Guide
Annapurna – A Trekker's Guide
Bhutan – A Trekker's Guide

AUSTRALIA AND NEW ZEALAND
Classic Tramps in New Zealand

TECHNIQUES AND EDUCATION
The Adventure Alternative
Rope Techniques
Snow & Ice Techniques
Mountain Weather
Beyond Adventure
The Hillwalker's Manual
The Book of the Bivvy
Outdoor Photography
The Hillwalker's Guide to
  Mountaineering
Map and Compass

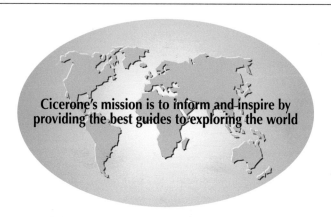

Cicerone's mission is to inform and inspire by
providing the best guides to exploring the world

Since its foundation over 30 years ago, Cicerone has specialised in publishing guidebooks and has built a reputation for quality and reliability. It now publishes nearly 300 guides to the major destinations for outdoor enthusiasts, including Europe, UK and the rest of the world.

Written by leading and committed specialists, Cicerone guides are recognised as the most authoritative. They are full of information, maps and illustrations so that the user can plan and complete a successful and safe trip or expedition – be it a long face climb, a walk over Lakeland fells, an alpine traverse, a Himalayan trek or a ramble in the countryside.

With a thorough introduction to assist planning, clear diagrams, maps and colour photographs to illustrate the terrain and route, and accurate and detailed text, Cicerone guides are designed for ease of use and access to the information.

If the facts on the ground change, or there is any aspect of a guide that you think we can improve, we are always delighted to hear from you.

Cicerone Press
2 Police Square Milnthorpe Cumbria LA7 7PY
Tel:01539 562 069   Fax:01539 563 417
e-mail:info@cicerone.co.uk   web:www.cicerone.co.uk